CREATIVE AND INNOVATIVE MANAGEMENT

SERIES IN ECONOMETRICS AND MANAGEMENT SCIENCES

This is one of a series of books in econometrics and management sciences sponsored by the IC^2 Institute of the University of Texas at Austin, under the general editorship of W. W. Cooper and Henri Theil. In this series, econometrics and management sciences are to be interpreted broadly, providing an opportunity to introduce new topics that can influence future activities in these fields as well as allow for new contributions to established lines of research in both disciplines. The books will be priced to make them available to a wide and diverse audience.

Volumes in the Series:

Volume 1: EXPLOITING CONTINUITY: Maximum Entropy Estimation of Continuous Distributions, by Henri Theil and Denzil G. Fiebig

Volume 2: CREATIVE AND INNOVATIVE MANAGEMENT: Essays in Honor of George Kozmetsky, edited by A. Charnes and W. W. Cooper

Volume 3: TRANSFORMATIONAL MANAGEMENT, by George Kozmetsky

CREATIVE AND INNOVATIVE MANAGEMENT

Essays in Honor of George Kozmetsky

Volume 2 of Series on
Econometrics and Management Sciences

Edited by
A. CHARNES
W. W. COOPER

1984

BALLINGER PUBLISHING COMPANY
Cambridge, Massachusetts
A Subsidiary of Harper & Row, Publishers, Inc.

International Standard Book Number: 0-88410-994-1

Library of Congress Catalog Card Number: 84-2814

Printed in the United States of America

Library of Congress Cataloging in Publication Data

Main entry under title:

Creative and innovative management.

Includes index.
1. Creative ability in business—Addresses, essays, lectures.
2. Management—Addresses, essays, lectures. 3. Kozmetsky, George—Addresses, essays, lectures. I. Charnes, A. (Abraham), 1917-   . II. Cooper, William W. (William Wager), 1914-
III. Kozmetsky, George.
HD53.C74   1984   658.4   84-2814
ISBN 0-88410-994-1

© GITTINGS

CONTENTS

LIST OF FIGURES

LIST OF TABLES AND EXHIBITS

PREFACE

The papers in this volume resulted from a conference on creative and innovative management held on 5-6 October 1982 at the RGK Foundation in Austin, Texas. We are grateful to Ronya and George Kozmetsky not only for making these excellent facilities available but also for participating actively in planning and developing the conference.

The conference was in honor of George Kozmetsky on the occasion of his sixty-fifth birthday. By a fortuitous series of events, the conference dates occurred near the opening of the RGK Foundation's beautiful and innovatively efficient facilities as planned and developed—one might also say dreamed of—by Ronya and George for conferences like this one. Such conferences constitute only one part of the Foundation's efforts at encouraging (and facilitating) creative research that include, inter alia, the research of the IC^2 Institute as conceived and directed by George Kozmetsky when he was Dean of the School of Business at the University of Texas. This conference and the resulting volume could also have been dedicated to Ronya or to Ronya and George Kozmetsky in the husband–wife partnership that is so well described in their recently published book, *Making It Together* (New York: The Free Press, 1981).

This conference, again fortuitously, occurred shortly after George Kozmetsky's resignation after some seventeen years as Dean of the

School of Business and Graduate School of Business of the University of Texas at Austin. Thus the conference might have served equally to honor him for his role in leading these University of Texas schools to their present position of national (and international) eminence.

The conference on creative and innovative management also occurred near the start of the centennial set aside by the University of Texas to mark the one-hundredth year of its founding. Guided by a state constitution that requires the University of Texas to become "of the first rank," what George accomplished in the School and Graduate School of Business forms a very apt part of what the university has accomplished, and will continue to try to accomplish, as announced in its centennial theme.

In discussing the proposed conference with others, namely Professors Timothy Ruefli, Harvey McMains and Dean Seymour Schwartz at the University of Texas, the topic of creative and innovative management quickly came to the fore as a possible organizing theme. A consideration of the needs and challenges of modern management should clarify the importance of this topic—indeed its salient importance—to modern society. The positive responses to our invitations from outstanding, innovative managers and researchers served as further confirmation of its importance. The appropriateness of the topic for this occasion is made clear by George Kozmetsky's own career as a creative and innovative manager, research scholar, and academic administrator. Finally, we can also say that this conference on creative and innovative management is now likely to be only the first in a series. The end result, we believe, will be a new and important academic discipline that presently seems to be missing or at least underemphasized in our schools of management. Hopefully, conferences like this one will begin to provide a background literature that will help these schools to make the contributions that modern society requires for management in this important dynamically expanding area.

The theme of entrepreneurship runs very strongly through George Kozmetsky's career in the form of the founding of new and highly successful corporations—that are themselves creative and innovative—as well as in the form of rejuvenating already existing (but troubled) corporations by turning them in entirely new directions. For purposes of creative and innovative management, we need to begin to drop old distinctions, and the distinction between entrepreneur, manager, and administrator is surely a candidate for elimination. Thus, by creative management, we refer to new conceptions and new ideas, new entities and new methods that can also be used to provide new directions or new modes of operation for already existing organizations and activities. By innovative management we refer to the ability to implement such new ideas and/or to move successfully in such new directions. Making things work successfully is an old and abiding task of management. It is the coupling of this task with new ideas, directions, and the like that makes it innovative and creative. Finally, it is the ability to induce these kinds of activities in others in an organized way that makes it an act of management rather than only the act of an individual.

In conclusion we also want to express our sincere appreciation to Ray Smilor, Assistant Director of the Institute for Constructive Capitalism, for his considerable help and counsel and to Paralee Lukens and Myra Braziel for their help in typing the manuscript. We hope that the papers collected here will contribute to the objectives outlined by George Kozmetsky and help identify some of the new academic frontiers that are outlined in his opening paper to this volume.

A. Charnes
W. W. Cooper

INTRODUCTION
Background, Strategy
and Structure

In the senses outlined in our preface, we need a better foundation than anything now available to secure a basis for continuing, systematic improvements in the present state of creative and innovative management abilities and practices. Nowhere is this more apparent than in the realms of academic transmittal that are represented not only in teaching and research but also in their related publication activities. The basis for commencing to improve this situation is also almost nonexistent, even at very advanced levels of activity at graduate schools of management, and this is apparent in the kinds of related activities and influences that these schools should be effecting beyond their own borders.

As befits the present stage of development in our knowledge of what underlies creative and innovative management, most of the papers in this volume, like the conference that preceded it, are concerned with what we might well refer to as problem identification and structuring—that is, identification and structuring for subsequent research and teaching (or learning) as well as management practice. This is especially true for the first part of the volume where eminent practitioners of management who have themselves effected important innovations attempt to lay out problems and prospects along with their views for the future. Such problem identification and structuring also occurs in the other papers, as in the concluding paper by Allen Newell in which he attempts to lay out what will be involved in needed artificial intelligence research on these topics.

To help in the process of identification and structuring, each paper is accompanied by one or more shorter papers that we refer to as commentaries and counterpoints. We cannot reproduce the effects of the lively exchanges that occurred between conference participants as a result of the paper presentation and discussants' formats that preceded the edited versions that appear here; however, the papers, together with these counterpoints and commentaries, do make a substantial contribution to what is needed to advance the present stage of knowledge. In particular, we believe that these commentaries and counterpoints lend added point to the papers they review and also serve to make rereading the papers a worthwhile undertaking.

CONTENTS AND TOPICS

After the introductory section, a presentation from George Kozmetsky followed by Robert Kuhn's commentary and counterpoint, other papers range over topics in public sector as well as private sector management and extend through issues of public policy to academic research.

Dr. Kozmetsky's paper, which constituted the keynote paper of the conference, points up the need for a new academic discipline directed to research and teaching in creative and innovative management. An important part of the message, emphasized in the commentary by Robert Kuhn (an unusual combination of innovating manager and research academic in his own right), points to the need for eliminating distinctions, or at least blurring them, not only in traditional academic disciplines but also between academia and the world of use and practice. This is already being done in institutions that are attempting to teach (is that the right word?) entrepreneurship, as distinct from, for example, management or administration in the traditional skills-discipline senses.

Along this route of blurring and regrouping of present disciplines also lies the kind of response that we think is needed to deal with the issue noted by Allen Newell near the close of the final paper in this volume—namely, "there is no reason to believe that teaching how to be creative on a small scale will generally prepare one to be creative on a large scale as well."

Finally, there is Dr. Kozmetsky's view of the kind of creative-innovative management that needs to be developed and which, it will be seen, contrasts sharply with presently maintained distinctions between management practice and scientific research and development. Dr. Kozmetsky believes that an obliteration or fuzzing over of these presently maintained distinctions will be needed at all levels from conception through development, testing, and implementation. He means this to occur, moreover, in a greatly magnified version of what is sometimes called the "inventor-manager" or "manager-inventor."

This is a realistic prospect and a needed response, Dr. Kozmetsky believes, to pending developments in information-processing and decisionmaking technologies. He also sees it as a response, and a stimulant, to the kinds of academic research and education programs he is suggesting for the future. Nor is it confined to the future. Thus, for those who would prefer to proceed on a wait-and-see rather than creative-innovative management basis, we might call attention to the fact that this kind of intermeshing between management and science is already present not only in high-technology companies of the "silicon valley" variety but also in experiments being conducted for entrepreneurial encouragement of subordinate managers in well-established companies that feel this is a challenge to which they must now respond.

The scale of creativity and innovativeness needed for present-day society is brought into even larger perspective by considering what is required for public sector management. This is done, well and pointedly, by Dr. Michael J. L. Kirby in the paper that opens the next section of this volume. Using the perspective of his long experience in Canadian Provincial and Federal Government and exploiting his background as a noted academic and researcher, Dr. Kirby also draws upon his experience in helping to bring the new Canadian Constitution into existence (while serving as Secretary for Federal–Provincial Relations in the Canadian Cabinet). The problems to be addressed in being creative and innovative in the governance of a democratic society—a very democratic one in Canada—are of awesome proportions and include the fact that creativity and innovation involve changes that can themselves imperil the sometimes fragile consensus on which such societies rest.

This last point is probably best brought into focus via a comment made at the conference by Professor Otto A. Davis, formerly Dean of Carnegie–Mellon University's School of Urban and Public Affairs, but which is not included in his commentary and counterpoint in this volume. At the conference, Professor Davis took strong exception to Dr. Kirby's comment that "Government should not govern (or be seen to govern) on the basis of giving people what they want." Professor Davis saw the danger of using this as a guiding principle for democratic government while Dr. Kirby responded, equally aptly, by pointing out the danger of following the doctrine of giving people what they want, or seem to want, in pursuit of a consensus—as witness, for example, what has presently occurred in the United States, Canada, and western industrial society generally, from following this route. Together the Davis commentary and the response by Kirby raise an age-old question explored by the nineteenth-century philosopher-economist John Stuart Mill, who, in *Representative Government*, pointed up the need for examining *representative* democracy as a true innovation in government. This innovation, as Mill saw it, made it possible to escape the limitations of *direct* democracy, which Aristotle had characterized as an inherently unstable form of government.

An important feature of the innovation provided by *representative* democracy, we might add, was that it was created and innovated by the British over a long period of time without any especially identifiable part being due to the usual type of management decisionmaking. Is this "nonmanaged" innovative process also a subject for study in the new academic disciplines we are considering? Can it be stimulated to start when needed? Can it be accelerated, guided, controlled—or otherwise improved—or must it be left to its own devices? Is it identifiable at all, or is it only visible after everything has pretty much been done?

Dr. Jack Borsting, in his commentary and counterpoint to Dr. Kirby, points up difficulties in creative and innovative governance in modern large-scale government departments such as, for example, the U.S. Department of Defense. From his vantage point as Assistant Secretary (Comptroller) of the Department of Defense he points out that not only must the management of such a department deal with scenarios involving rapidly changing geopolitical and technological considerations but it must also do so while operating in a "goldfish bowl." A manager in such a department must expect that exposures of his proposals will come into play—via the media and other forms of third party scrutiny—even before proposed innovations get off the ground. This problem, Dr. Borsting believes, is especially severe in the United States with its division of governmental powers, in contrast to, say, the more unified governmental forms of parliamentary democracy such as those to be found in Canada.

One need not argue whether a dose of the experience that Dr. Kirby has had in dealing with Federal–Provincial relations might have altered parts of Dr. Borsting's point of view. One of the authors of this preface served as a consultant to the Auditor General of Canada as well as the Comproller General of the United States and can testify that the U.S. government's separation-of-powers organization[1] is greatly admired by staff of the Auditor General since it provided possibilities for governance—for example, in performing audits and reviews of executive agencies—that are not present (or at least are more difficult to come by) in a parliamentary form of government.

On the other hand, some of the limits that Canadians believe they encounter in implementing their concept of comprehensive audit[2] may come from the fact that this new and innovative approach to auditing was borrowed from the U.S. model as pioneered by Dr. Elmer Staats. In his role as Comptroller General of the United States, Dr. Staats was responsible to Congress and not to the executive branch of the U.S. government, a fact that he extensively exploited. Indeed, it is not too much to say that, under Elmer Staats, the U.S. General Accounting Office became the main professional arm of Congress. In any case, the U.S. Congress has now come to rely on the GAO for these functions, although it has yet to reach the limits of what this agency can do for the oversight duties of Congress. Sensitive activities of the government such as its intelligence-gathering activities, for example, are an area where such oversight aids are badly needed, after suitable innovation, as is observed in the counterpoint by Professor N.C. Churchill.

We noted earlier the function of the commentary and counterpoint papers included in this volume. Assigning them this function does not preclude additional possibilities, however, such as using one or more of the papers as counterpoints to the others. Thus, we might draw attention to the possible use of improved accountability along the lines discussed by Dr. Staats and suggest that it may open a route for dealing with some of the issues addressed by Dr. Kirby. What role can an improved comprehensive audit play in producing a more informed consensus on important issues, assuming that this kind of audit competently performed and objectively reported and disclosed to the relevant publics? Even those who believe that a return to direct democracy via protest and demonstration may find that they stand to benefit by such comprehensive audits and disclosures. Some such basis for "intelligent action" is surely required at least on complex issues such as biogenetic engineering, atomic power—or some of the far reaches of foreign policy—that are really beyond the ken of those who are not experts in these topics. In any case, improvements in accountability are candidates for innovative management research even from the standpoint of inside executives and specialists; indeed, one such topic for innovative development might well be directed to improving the goldfish bowl atmosphere referred to by Dr. Borsting.

In his commentary and counterpoint, Neil Churchill notes that improved accountability may itself provide a new alternative to the "regulate versus don't regulate" controversies that seem to be sole occupants of the stage in modern public policy discussions. The idea is to allow managers a great deal of freedom in their choices while holding them strictly accountable in all pertinent dimensions. There is also an "anticipatory effect" of such accountability audits that can induce salutory behavior, as Churchill notes, even on prospective management performance. Needless to say such anticipatory effects, which may also be less than salutory, should form a part of the research on improved accountability as an alternative to goldfish bowl performance at all stages of a developing innovation.

Professor David F. Linowes of the University of Illinois joins Professor Churchill in an interesting way in his counterpoint and commentary on Dr. Staats' paper. Both he and Churchill actually exhibit examples showing that part of what Dr. Staats is forecasting for the future is already occurring in some of the more innovative (private sector) companies. Whether these innovations in accountability will spread to other private sector firms and how to insure that this spreading will occur, as conditions warrant, are inadequately researched at present; this, too, is an area that offers inviting prospects for those with a taste and a talent for doing or managing such research.

Turning to private sector management and related issues of public policy, one might expect the discussion in this sector to center on high-technology firms with well-recognized reputations for creativity and innovation. That, however, is a well-traveled route—or at least a route that has been much traveled—in recent years. Hence we turned in a different direction for the papers and counterpoints in this section.

In "Creative Management in Mature Capital Intensive Industries— The Case of Cement," B. Collomb, executive vice-president of the French firm Lafarge Coppée, and J. P. Ponssard, professor of management at l'École Polytechnique in Paris, provide interesting insights into what creative and innovative management can do for a mature capital-intensive industry even in the face of what appears to be a declining demand for its products. Partly, they argue, there should be no undue reliance on analytical tools such as are provided in so-called portfolio-modeling approaches to strategic management planning. They also argue that there should also be innovation in the social institutions used to guide and control (i.e., regulate) industry. In particular, they single out the U.S. antitrust laws as administered by the Federal Trade Commission as a candidate for revision. Drs. Collomb and Ponssard proceed to document this by reference to the vigorous progress in products and the resulting expansion of this industry in France (e.g., at Lafarge Coppée) in contrast to the declining and almost moribund nature of the U.S. cement industry.

Dr. Maurice Saias, Professor of Business Administration at the Université d'Aix Marseilles, Aix-en-Provence, supplies further detail on the portfolio approach to strategic planning which was critically reviewed by Drs. Collomb and Ponssard. Expressing agreement that mechanical applications of the tools associated with these approaches would have led Lafarge Coppée away from the opportunities it has now been able to exploit (in both France and the United States), Dr. Saias goes further than Drs. Collomb and Ponssard in calling for new tools and concepts for strategic planning. Looming large in Saias' discussion is the fact that much of French industry is of a variety that would call for divestment under these portfolio approaches. This leads Professor Saias to observe that business itself may not survive with the divestments called for in these approaches. Society now demands that the "production of jobs" and a large variety of constituencies must be serviced. From this he concludes that many of our regulatory agencies and programs are in need of review and possible redesign as, for instance, in the case of the U.S. Federal Trade Commission and the antitrust laws it regulates.

The latter approaches assume that many relatively small competing enterprises each following its own economic self-interests will produce what is wanted by society. This, however, is not the way to deal with modern international competition—for example, competition from Japan—when much of it is beyond the purview of the FTC. In general, creative and innovative approaches to the design of social as well as business institutions is required, which leads Dr. Saias to suggest that parts of our present approaches to management education are less than adequate.

In his commentary and counterpoint, Claude le Bon, Dean of Laval University in Canada, expresses an economist's skepticism with respect to the proposed institutional revision. If concentration is so good, he asks, why not the other way around? Why not, for instance, have a concentration of the consumers of cement? In either case, what is to protect those who are "concentrated against" and what is to ensure that expansion or liquidation will be made at the right time, and in the right amount and places? The latter is a forbidding topic in its complexity, since it carries with it the problem of whether it might be a good thing to liquidate even more of the cement industry in favor of, say, freeing resources for movement into other industries such as electronics and information processing.

By considerable analysis, and with an almost equal amount of belief, the economics profession has persuaded itself (and others) that free competition, especially between relatively small private firms, is always the best of all regulators and that concentration is to be discouraged, much in the manner that the U.S. antitrust laws say it should. They worry that other things also, including those of non-economic variety, may be influenced by allowing government-industry collaboration and concentration, and this includes possible dangers to political freedom and democratic processes. This, we might say, is a very good worry!

The success of the Japanese in government-industry collaboration, however, seems to have been accomplished without these accompanying consequences. Of course, one cannot say for sure that the resource allocations resulting from these government-industry decisions in Japan have been "correct." The same is true, however, for the supposed applications of the canons of perfect competition as interpreted by the Federal Trade Commission. In any event we think that it is worth looking at other possibilities in addition to the extensively tried "U.S. approaches." Among the alternatives worthy of study, we think, are possible arrangements for government-industry-academic collaborations accompanied by expansions of the accountability functions that we mentioned earlier.

At this juncture we might find it useful to distinguish between "research for discovery" and "research for invention." The intended distinction can perhaps be illustrated by the research of a physicist to discover how friction behaves and the research of an engineer to discover how to get rid of it—for example, by inventing a self-lubricating ball bearing for this purpose. The two types of research are intimately related, of course, and so we might be criticized for overemphasizing the distinction. On the other hand, we also think that others have underemphasized it, especially in the social sciences where the orientation has been toward discovery research with much too little attention paid to research for invention.

This is illustrated, perhaps inadvertently, in the paper on "Risk Management" by Karl Olof Faxén, Chief Economist of the Swedish Employers Confederation, in his discussion of work by Milton Friedman, E. S. Phelps, and other economists whose work is cited in this paper. Almost all of this work is discovery research. One perhaps needs to qualify this last sentence since, as Faxén notes, Friedman and Phelps had formulated the "Expectations-Augmented Phillips Curve" some "ten years or more before the phenomenon existed." Nevertheless, the nature of this discovery research is well indicated by its terminology such as, for example, the existence of a "natural level" of inflation and employment that is represented in this curve. The best thing that can then be done by government is to adjust to the situation that has thus been discovered. Contrast this, however, with what we said about the engineering approach to invention research where the objective was to get rid of the friction that is, indeed, very much present in the natural state.

As we already noted, it is possible to make too much of this distinction. Discovery research is needed as a guide for intelligent invention, and some of this is indicated by Dr. Faxén in his discussion of gain sharing and new versions of contingency contracts as possibly improved ways for sharing uncertainty by labor as well as management.

Other and even more innovative approaches to risk and uncertainty sharing are suggested in the commentary and counterpoint offered by Professor Bertil Naslund of the Stockholm School of Economics and New York University. For instance, as he notes, there is an urgent need for new planning models and approaches that should include, we think, more emphasis on flexibility in contrast to presently proposed emphases on productivity and efficiency.[3] The very basic level of research needed for this invention is deep, however, since Naslund sees a great need to go beyond what classical statistics and probability theory can reasonably be expected to deal with. This is needed, Professor Naslund believes, because probability theory is really not up to being able to deal with a world where major disruptions are an almost regular occurrence.

An example of this kind of disruption—in fact, a regularly occurring if somewhat minor one—is the regulation risk (i.e., risk of new regulations) that is identified in the counterpoint and commentary offered by Dr. Sten Thore of the Institute for Constructive Capitalism at the University of Texas at Austin. Other examples of such descriptions have been regularly provided by OPEC (and its members) and by the activities of governmental agencies, including monetary policies of the U.S. government, represented in abrupt changes in taxing and spending programs. Even in a situation of labor-management bargaining on a national level, as Dr. Faxén notes, such changes in behavior are really quite beyond control, or even prediction, and hence are best characterized as "exogeneous." More particularly they represent "changes in market regimes. At least to some extent, however, as Dr. Thore notes, the market system can be expected to respond by replacing managers who were very good at anticipating the future under one set of regimes or exogeneous shocks with a new breed. The new breed of managers will then be better than the old ones, he believes, at dealing with these discontinuities, and they will continue to prevail as the best available resource managers until, at last, the world situation changes again. The important thing, according to Dr. Thore, is to make sure that creative and innovative management is rewarded in the marketplace.

Even if this is the case, however, there still remains the task of seeing whether the innovation of new planning tools called for by Naslund can help in the allocation process, and we would extend this to whether new and improved methods of identifying and developing new breeds of managers can be devised when needed.

Professor Wayne Holtzman of the University of Texas Psychology Department, and President of the Hogg Foundation, reviews what light research in psychology might throw on the latter topic in his paper "Psychology and Managerial Creativity." This, however, is only one of many subjects covered by Professor Holtzman as he provides us with a survey and evaluation of past and present psychological research on this topic.

Lester Fettig in his commentary and counterpoint believes that creativity is not enough. The important topic is innovation and, as

Fettig rightly notes, not enough research attention is being devoted
to it. His repeated references to President Lyndon B. Johnson as one
of the really great innovators of our time is probably correct, we
think. But what about the pace of innovation? Senator Patrick
Moynihan once pointed up the pace of innovation under Johnson by
estimating that some 500–600 pieces of major new social legislation
were enacted under the regimes of Kennedy and Johnson compared
to less than 50 in the entire preceding history of the United States.[4]
Was this pace too fast? There are those who think it was, but, of
course, there are also those who think that this too can be addressed
by improved methods of administering innovation along the lines of
the kind of psychology (and organization theory) research described
and evaluated by Professor Holtzman.

Allen Newell, Professor of Computer Science at Carnegie–Mellon
University, presented the banquet address at the conference, entitled
"On Computers, Creativity and Management." It addresses the topic
of "artificial intelligence" and outlines how this relatively new academic discipline might contribute to the conference topic by reference to present and future research. As was the case with Professor
Holtzman, we also arranged the references so they may all be conve-
niently found at the back of Dr. Newell's paper. Thus, those who
want to continue on the research paths outlined by Dr. Newell will
have easy access to these sources.

The paper by Allen Newell offers much more than a survey of the
topic of artificial intelligence research. It represents a contribution in
its own right to the direction that such research might take. What is
perhaps of special interest here, however, is Dr. Newell's failure
to distinguish between managerial creativity and innovation (Vide
the comments and counterpoints of Lester Fettig which we just discussed). Indeed, a point of special interest in Newell's paper is his
description of the computer system ZOG that he and his associates
devised at Carnegie–Mellon University to guide the new aircraft carrier, USS *Carl Vinson*, through its test trials.

Is this an example of the blurring of the distinctions between management and science and between creativity and innovation that
Dr. Kozmetsky said would occur? We think it is and to document it
we suggest reading Newell's description of the role of the ship's
captain in these developments and the kinds of judgments he was
called upon to render.

From our standpoint, we find it equally interesting to compare
this artificial intelligence research approach with the more classical

experimental and observational approaches in psychology described by Dr. Holtzman. Important changes in methodology almost always involve changes and the blurring of boundaries in the sciences. They also provide new approaches to old topics as well as opening new topics to approach. Witness, for example, the use of computers to provide simulation models as alternatives to previously experimental (only) modes of approach in what is now called computational physics, and witness also the role of computers in new approaches to psychological research in the area of cognitive information processing (where Dr. Newell himself has figured prominently). Hopefully these artificial intelligence, computerized approaches to research will be able to help in doing something more than has been done to date in improving managerial creativity and assisting in managerial innovation.

Because Professor Newell served as the banquet speaker, no counterpoint and commentary was provided for his talk. However, we pressed the commentary and counterpoint of Dr. Jared Hazelton, Director of the Texas Research League, into this capacity because we thought his counterpoint and commentary on Wayne Holtzman could also serve for Dr. Newell's paper.

Dr. Hazelton notes that "There is a Janus-like character to organizations. On one hand they encourage individual autonomy by inculcating skills and values for self-realization but, on the other hand, they demand conformity with the organization's needs and the means used to achieve these needs." In this way Dr. Hazelton highlights what he refers to as the "darker side" of the humanistic psychology approaches surveyed (in an approving manner) by Professor Holtzman that, Dr. Hazelton fears, may be used more to achieve the organization's needs than to foster individual development.

What about creativity and innovation, and what does all this have to do with artificial intelligence and the other kinds of developments we have been discussing? We can hardly do better than conclude our own commentaries and counterpoints by referring to the concluding paragraph in Dr. Hazelton's paper as follows:

> We might take some hope from the fact that organizations may also be changing. As the nature of work has changed, as the nature of the economy has changed, as more and more of our economy has gotten into services and away from basic manufacturing, as the work force has changed, and as the development of professionals in organizations has emerged, we may begin to have a "professional" organization as an alternative to the traditional model of

bureaucracy. In such organizations pluralistic and collegial kinds of relations may replace the strictures of monocratic and hierarchical organizations. We may have specialization of people rather than tasks. We may also have a situation in which workers, as professionals, will assume responsibility for defining the problem as well as for solving it. This may also produce greater creativity. But if it is going to produce greater creativity, it seems to me we are going to have to face up to the fact that, in the end, managerial creativity is also going to have to evolve. As George Kozmetsky observed, this will involve much broader concepts of decision theory and decision making, and it is going to involve a much more direct approach to the handling of values within organizations and to the distribution of power. If we can come to grips with these kinds of challenges, we might be able to promote managerial creativity and also point it in correct directions.

A. Charnes
W. W. Cooper

NOTES

1. This division-of-powers form of government, provided via a written constitution, is itself an important innovation in government which, unlike the evolution of representative government in England, came out of a period of explicit managerial-political deliberations preceded by a period of rational discussion and research. See, for example, Hannah Arendt, *On Revolution* (New York: Viking Press, 1963), especially pp. 151 and 221.

2. Cf., J. J. MacDonell, Auditor General of Canada and Chairman, Canadian Comprehensive Auditing Foundation, "Comprehensive Auditing—A New Approach to Public Sector Accountability in Canada" (Ottawa: Canadian Comprehensive Auditing Foundation, 1980).

3. Flexibility refers to the ability to change from one level or direction of operations to another without great changes in cost or other disruptions. Efficiency refers to the level of costs attained. We believe a category called adaptability should also be added, to identify the speed or rate with which management can reach the lowest possible levels of cost performance, after the direction and scale of operations has been set. See, for example, A. Charnes and W. W. Cooper, "Silhouette Functions of Short-Run Cost Behavior," *Quarterly Journal of Economics* LXVIII (1954): 131–150.

4. Senator (then Professor) Moynihan suggested that it might be helpful to think of each such piece of legislation as involving the creation of a new federal agency, such as the Internal Revenue Service (for administering the income tax) and the Social Security Administration that were innovated under preceding presidents.

CREATIVITY AND ITS PLACE IN EDUCATION AND MANAGEMENT

1 CREATIVE AND INNOVATIVE MANAGEMENT
A New Academic Frontier

George Kozmetsky

Educating and developing creative and innovative individuals is not a new academic frontier. Educational systems have always had the goal of producing scholars and graduates who will extend the frontiers of knowledge and benefit society. The primary focus of education, especially at the graduate level, has been vertical within the depth of each specific discipline rather than horizontal with the integration of other academic disciplines for the solution of important societal issues. Academic institutions have concentrated on scholars to extend specific fields of study. They have produced creative and innovative individuals who have made or are making major contributions to our society in the public and private sectors.

Only a few of our creative and innovative scholars in and out of academia have been willing to forsake their specializations to concentrate on management in the broader sense. Of those who have become creative professional managers, few have returned to academia to educate the future teachers, researchers, and management leaders that our complex and constantly changing society requires. The various presenters and discussants of papers during this conference have much to say on these requirements.

The thesis of this paper is that the university of tomorrow must get prepared to research and teach creative and innovative management as a new discipline that requires understanding and implementation of solutions to generalized as well as specific problems of society. The solutions will require knowledge of the fundamentals of the

3

best practices of both the physical and the social sciences. Tomorrow's managers of our key institutions must understand that resources include science, technology, and information, and that these are also assets for the solution of the nation's problems. Managers need to understand that information, science, and technology are not free economic goods but are assets to be used, planned, earned on, and replenished.

There is a current requirement for a new breed of managers to operate under new principles of governance. The simpler distinction between owner or entrepreneur and professional manager has to a large extent disappeared in the past decade. The functions of professional managers have been extended by newer and more complex organizational structures, newer governmental regulations and relations, and changes in generally accepted ethics and morals. In other words, our society has changed dramatically. This change has been characterized by a widening gap in the management knowledge base. Society has impacted directly on the management of various institutions while these institutions have in turn forced society to reexamine basic values and responsibilities.[1] What do these changes in basic values and responsibilities mean for the new frontier for creative and innovative management?

Clark Kerr, former Chancellor of the University of California, made the following observation:

> I think that we shall have increasing demands for communicative links across ... intellectual interstices, as well as demands for the generalist who can view problems as a whole and can foresee the new problems that grow out of answers to current questions. We must find a way to restore a sense of unity to the intellectual world.[2]

In my definition, creative management involves abilities to take a problem or crisis and develop its issues, generate alternative solutions, and select feasible initiatives from among the alternatives. Furthermore, creative and innovative management includes the ability to use initiatives as a first step to solutions. These initiatives need to be monitored to determine that the actions are indeed solving the problem and not creating new ones.

Issues are problems that are defined well enough for beginning the solution process. Thus, the creative aspects of management center on turning crises or ill-defined, fuzzy, and sometimes messy problems into viable issues. Creativity is the input to innovation; innovation is actualization of solutions to problems and crises. Creative and innovative management is concerned with understanding the state of the institution and that of society in order to improve each in terms of the general welfare.

Traditionally, managers have been concerned only with their institutional well-being; their focus has been on the status quo and the shorter-run. However, the environment in which all managers operate today is no longer traditional. This is particularly so in the case of managers of our large and dynamic-growth institutions. Therefore, I believe now is the time to begin the process of creating an academic field for creative and innovative management. We need to find examples and role models for our students that they can study and relate to. Fortunately, we have many techniques, methodologies, and tools to offer to the discipline. There are numerous managerial problems and crises that need to be organized and solved. We do not at this time, however, need to decide which current academic discipline should be assigned the leadership and coordinating role in this new frontier.

Creative and innovative management will not be confined to business graduates. In fact, it never has been. Creative and innovative management graduates will be cross-disciplinary—or, in Kerr's terms, "generalists." As a field of study, creative and innovative management needs a home where the appropriate set of disciplines can form a consortium and work together in the development of a distinct body of knowledge that can be taught and used.

I would like to examine the evolution of this new frontier from three key perspectives that are both personal and professional: (1) the role of the University of Texas at Austin in the evolution of creative and innovative management as an academic discipline, (2) first initiatives for the creation of a journal for the identification and extension of creative and innovative management, and (3) structuring areas for creative and innovative management research and experimentation.

ROLE OF THE UNIVERSITY OF TEXAS AT AUSTIN IN THE EVOLUTION OF CREATIVE AND INNOVATIVE MANAGEMENT AS AN ACADEMIC DISCIPLINE

The University of Texas at Austin's centennial celebration period is an ideal time to explore the feasibility of academic pacesetting in creative and innovative management. The University has the potential to become one of the world's leading universities in the development of this new discipline. The University of Texas at Austin has in place some of the required policies and practices for cross-disciplinary education and research as well as a sufficiency of all resources. The more important of these are the following:

1. There are university-wide policies for interdisciplinary faculty appointments that have been successfully implemented for more than twenty years.
2. It has outstanding research and teaching scholars in many nationally and internationally recognized academic disciplines. There are over seventy-eight academic departments and over 300 Professorships and Chairs currently.
3. There are already a large number of joint degree programs in place among the fourteen colleges. These programs integrate a number of academic disciplines that are important in the solution of societal problems and issues.
4. Facilities for teaching, research, and learning are among the most modern in the United States.
5. The University is not solely dependent on state funds. It receives a large share of the return on the Permanent University Fund and has substantial gift and endowment funds.
6. The University of Texas System, of which the University of Texas at Austin is a part, allows access to additional faculty and disciplines in health science, nursing, and dental and medical care — including research.

As early as 1966, the Regents, the University of Texas System, and the University of Texas at Austin administration took the lead for business education to be extended into the management of technical and intellectual resources. By September 1966, the College and Graduate School of Business faculties accepted the following challenge:

> To train the managers of the second half of the twentieth century. More specifically, the College must educate future managers of the technical and intellectual resources of our nation. In this respect, our curriculum must be cross-disciplinary as well as embracing new methods and techniques.
>
> It is our firm belief that the managers for the second half of this century must deal with emotional as well as technical changes . . . must learn to converse in the appropriate language of mathematics . . . communicate with and manage scientists, engineers, accountants and artists . . . use new tools for

effective planning and control, strategic and tactical decision making . . . understand and implement the social value system of our nation. To the best of our knowledge, no other school of business has set forth such objectives.

It was recognized that the implementation of these objectives would require the establishment of a vigorous research program; a review of the establishment of our undergraduate, master's, and Ph.D. programs in consonance with the objectives; and the establishment of a required executive development program.

The research programs directed toward management initiated in 1966–67 were international resource management; management of research; biomedical research and transfers of technology from aerospace; economic development, health maintenance, and transference of technology; information processing; cognitive machine processors; and marine science and related business potentials.

The key requirement was the establishment of management curricula with a system and structure for those who would manage our technical and intellectual resources. There is a distinction between educating managers of technical and intellectual resources and the creation of a discipline for creative and innovative management. The former provides for the effective development of middle managers of the nation's high-technology sector as well as updating the traditional business functions. The latter is more concerned with the creative and innovative management of all resources and their applications in meeting societal and general welfare needs. In its broadest context, the focus is on a private enterprise system and its interface with the public sector.

The creative process used at the University of Texas at Austin to develop the curricula for management of technical and intellectual resources is now in place. The current curricula accommodate the notion of system and structure. The notion of system is that our graduates will have more than one career. The structure is based, first, on a core area divided into required knowledge modules and, second, on elective courses to support future career choices that can be taken in any of the fourteen colleges and seventy-eight academic departments.

At this point, it is appropriate to enumerate briefly some of the problems that led to a need for a review of management curricula in 1966:

1. Developments in management in the United States since World War II had closely paralleled the growth of our nation's technol-

ogy. Advances in the developments of both management and technology are inextricably interwoven.

2. There was increasing recognition for the need of management in fields other than business; for example, government, biomedical research, health and welfare, urban planning, and international trade.

3. Important academic curricula revisions and discussions on inter-disciplinary approaches were taking place on most of our campuses.

4. Many professions had recognized that they must be able to keep pace with the growth of new knowledge. Equally important, there was increasing recognition for continued professional education to reduce the obsolescence rate or, conversely, to maintain the degree of knowledge required for competency.

5. National policies were being established in social areas.

6. Attitudes of management toward the utilization of scientific research as a basis for managerial decision making were changing.

The routine requirements of the past two-thirds of this century are rapidly being replaced by machines and complicated by overseas competition. To date, much of our business education system has been geared to educate and develop people for an industrial need that can be generalized as "routinized" or mass production and distribution.

The task that the latter part of the twentieth-century industrial state imposes on our education system is the increasing development of people for nonroutine tasks. These problems can be characterized as follows:

1. The end products are few in number and often one of a kind in contrast to mass-production products.

2. They are large in scope and often require interrelated government, university, and industry efforts to help solve the problems.

3. The problems are complex and require integrative systems for their adequate solution.

4. The problems are often messy and fuzzy with no clear-cut, acceptable solution to them. Current methods, techniques, and tools must often be supplemented with individual ingenuity, creativity and judgment.

5. The problems are one of a kind, and the solution to each is often inapplicable to any other problem.

There are two underlying needs to all these "nonroutine" pursuits. They demand large quanta of technical and intellectual resources such as individual scientists—social and physical, engineers and other professionals, with service personnel and technicians as aides to these professionals. They require also information necessary for the solution of nonroutine problems, and this may extend to generating new information from additional research in one or more of these disciplines. The key requirement, however, is managers with the ability to identify and formulate problems and to manage the technical, intellectual, and information resources.

Any approach we may make for meeting the supply of talent for the nonrepetitive tasks will bring changes in the way we manage these resources. There are good reasons for this: intellectual resources are scarce, and their supply is relatively inelastic at any moment of time.

In short, the change has set up a self-amplifying system in the demands for intellectual resources. Technology generates new advancements which, in turn, generate a still greater need for sophisticated intelligence. The task for management education is not merely to select the gifted or excellent student for training but to develop on a broad front the levels of skills—new and existing—to meet the requirements for this change. People must be developed for all the new roles in a society that are essential to produce the number of individuals needed with the required talents and abilities.

The history of the development of curricula for management shows that it proceeded very slowly from zero courses to the series of specialized professional and academic fields that we have today. Highlights of these developments are shown in Figure 1-1.

For many years, business management was made up of gifted, non-business-trained, creative, and innovative individuals.

Our perceptions of the importance of science, inventions, and innovators for creative and innovative management were honed by the seminal work of my Texas colleague, Professor Walt W. Rostow, in his book, *How It All Began.* To quote Walt:

Scientists, Inventors and Innovators. Stemming from the Faustian outlook, the pursuit of principles of maximum generality by the experimental method was understood, from an early stage, to open the way to practical and profitable inventions and innovations. This was, of course, a central theme of Francis Bacon before Newton emerged on the scene, and, from Galileo's interest in shipbuilding, mine pumps and artillery to Newton's fruitless alchemy, some

Figure 1-1. Significant Developments in Management Education.

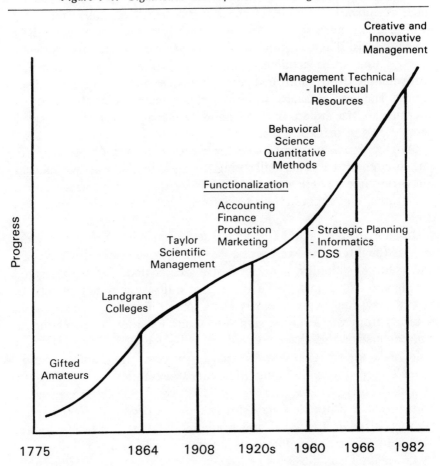

Adam Smith—Theory;   James Watt—Engineer;   Charles Babbage—Scientist.

of the scientists interested themselves directly in practical matters. The Baconian linkage of science to material progress was greatly strengthened by the web of osmotic ties that grew up between scientists, inventors and entrepreneurs. . . .

The three indirect linkages set out here between the world of science and those of invention and innovation were powerful. They withdrew, as it were, the graphite rods from the atomic pile and permitted an ultimately explosive set of interactions to occur.[3]

Formal business training started in the United States about the time of the land-grant colleges. Its need was first recognized in the agricultural sector. Taylor produced the methodology for scientific management about 1908, and his methodology is still taught in industrial engineering courses. By the 1920s, we saw the functionalization of business become important in the educational process. The 1950s saw the rise of the behavioral sciences and management sciences and the development and use of new kinds of quantitative methods. These were all important steps in the progression of management education and theory.

The explosion of information and the management of technical and intellectual resources required that management curricula take another quantum jump at this time for the development of our new class of managers, management faculties, and university administrators. Now there is a foundation in place at the Graduate School of Business that has been extended to and coupled with the Lyndon B. Johnson School of Public Affairs, the College of Engineering, the College of Communications, and the School of Law. There is an environment in which the new discipline of creative and innovative management can be developed. While there is much to be done, we have already pioneered in directions that can open up this new frontier.

A JOURNAL FOR CREATIVE AND INNOVATIVE MANAGEMENT

There is a need and the time is right for establishing a multidisciplinary journal that will be eclectic in its choices of articles on creative and innovative management. Creative and innovative management articles are not being published in the literature. I can personally attest that, in the past sixteen years, there has been a paucity of journals that would even accept academic articles for publication in this field. There are still fewer professional journals that would accept how-to-do-it articles if we could get the creative and innovative managers to write them. There are new theories, methods, principles, and selected programs that are used in creative and innovative ways that should be published in academic journals. It is a thesis of this conference that there is a need for the critical exploration of this new academic discipline.

There are several initiatives that are necessary to extend this new discipline:

1. Identify the large amount of specialized academic work that lends itself to broadening for this discipline
2. Recognize innovative and creative managers and firms
3. Understand social innovations and large-scale programs and projects
4. Commission surveys and syntheses

I believe we will find there are a significant number of successful creative and innovative managers who have established and developed creative and dynamic organizations and who have successfully pioneered and implemented many scientific, technological, and social innovations. Their experiences need to be gathered, analyzed, and evaluated to provide us with the rich history I know is there. These analyses go beyond case studies, institutional histories, history of technological innovations, or archival accumulations.

I would like to refer to selected works of those that immediately come to mind and who have had an impact on my own thinking and practice in the area of creative and innovative management. Of the several that come to mind, Abe Charnes, Bill Cooper, Herb Simon, and Walt W. Rostow are four outstanding representative examples.

The cochairmen of this conference—Abe Charnes and Bill Cooper—have been my colleagues for more than thirty years. They have extended my abilities beyond mathematical modeling. While at Hughes Aircraft, Litton, and Teledyne, I learned from them how to formulate managerial problems for modelers so that problems can be subjected to modeling and subsequent managerial implementation and independent assessment. Their encouragement over the years, and especially in the past three years that we have been together at the University of Texas at Austin, has made it clear that it is appropriate to publish and to encourage what we, our students, industrial and government colleagues, and others have learned in terms of creative and innovative management for the benefit of the emerging future managers.

Herb Simon, Nobel Laureate in Economics, continues to have an impact on scholarship for the creative and innovative management discipline. In many respects this has been done through his books, *Models of Man, Models of Bounded Rationality: Economic Analysis and Public Policy, Models of Discovery, New Sciences of Manage-*

ment Decisions, The Sciences of the Artificial, Representation and Meaning, Human Problem Solving, and *Models of Thought.*

These eclectic writings reflect a wide ranging interest in research in a variety of topics from which a scientific foundation for the emerging area of creative and innovative management and its subsequent epistemology can be formed. It was to my benefit to have worked with Herb during my stay at Carnegie–Mellon. We had many discussions during the 1950s and early 1960s on computers, technology, and the process of learning through experience how to become a manager. A journal will be filled with many articles extending and deepening the theories, methodologies, and principles developed by Professor Simon that will further creative and innovative management as an academic discipline. We need a journal where future Simons can publish.

Professor Walt Rostow, a colleague at the University of Texas at Austin, has broadened my horizons in the field of creative and innovative management from the scholarly perspectives of the economic historian. Our relationship started with my reading of his book *The Stages of Economic Growth* while I was executive vice-president of Teledyne. We have since collaborated as faculty members investigating proposed national energy policy implications for the economy. He has broadened my understanding of the need for an evolution of economic theory and the role of history in the field of creative and innovative management.

These eminent scholars and others like them are truly today's role models for our future scholars and creative managers. Each of these scholars has been involved in successful and innovative solutions to national policies and state and local government problems as well as business decision problems. Each has reached the apex of success in his respective academic discipline. Each has crossed other academic specialties and has made lasting contributions.

To date, it has been troublesome to find a place to publish creative and innovative management contributions. Creative and innovative practitioners often find it difficult to determine whether their contributions are to management or to a specialization. At times, they have found that issue and initiative formulation is not deemed academically respectable or as important as a specific technique or methodology. Consequently, there needs to be a place where creative and innovative constructs and their usage can be published and deemed important. Constructs, when properly done, can provide creative solutions without being subjected to the normal standards of scientific approach; for example, cause and effect. A lack of acceptable places to publish diminishes the interest of academicians to invest their time in this important pioneering field of current and future needs.

Let me review one critical area that is essential to the process of creative and innovative management and that could form a multi-disciplinary basis for journal articles. In the 1970s, Dr. Tim Ruefli and I referred to this area as "information technology"; Professor Ed Summers, the Arthur Young Professor of Accounting at the University of Texas at Austin, has recently called it "decision technology."

There is a dichotomy in the evolution of developments in and applications of decision technology. Too often, problem formulators are working on predicting problems of the future without reference to present realities or available resources to actualize their predictions. Too often, managers are working on current problems without adequately considering the consequences of their actions on the future. This, perhaps, is the major point: important choices lie before us, but they cannot be made in any monolithic way. Decision technologists, managers, users and assessors are in an era of critical experimentation.

Decision technology itself is in the same situation. All researchers and practitioners involved in decision making activities are trying to find their own best way. There is probably no best way at all, only better ways for a while, for different groups, in different areas. But we are well advised to observe closely what we are about and what results from what we do. I would point out that it has been shown that creative people have a need to rebel against the past. The rebellion is often more impersonal than personal. That is, it is against ideas, techniques, and points of view rather than against people. Creative people learn to substitute the impersonal for the personal in order to avoid becoming enmeshed in the latter.

The management of change becomes the management of the creation and application of knowledge. The problem for managers of all policy making centers becomes the problem of assessing and selecting or altering the elements of information technology or decision technology. Managers as well as scholars need access to appropriate internal and external data bases that will enable individual institutions to achieve their goals within an institutional setting as well as a wider context of social objectives. Policy making centers are innovative concepts in developing the context or environment for the management of change.

If one regards policy as an intention to affect or direct the future in a specified manner, and if one identifies policy making centers as those institutions or organizations that have the ability to affect the future, then developments in decision and information technology become the results of policy setting and subsequent action on the part of the policy making institutions. It should be noted that in concentrating on *policy* centers, the focus is on the *context* for decision making rather than on the *operations* associated with the production of goods and services. That is, the emphasis is on the expanding roles of the office of the Chief Executive Officer, Board of Directors, and corporate staff specialists rather than on the traditional activities of owners, top management, and lower-level managers.

Most people have an image of business as being a set of specific clusters of corporations, people, buildings, and the like, identified with and identifiable by the goods and services they produce as well as their geographical location. Those outside the clusters often perceive them as monolithic interest groups. In some cases, it has become convenient for those within the clusters to adopt a similar perception, while in other cases those who formed a cluster found the need to adopt an identification as an interest group to promote their image or to enhance the adoption of their policies.

One can clearly see that businesses and businesspeople today are associated with or are members of varying organizations such as trade associations, chambers of commerce, other business/social clubs and professional societies. In no formal way are such associations policy making centers in the sense that they set policy for the nation. Yet in many respects they are viable and influential organizations within our current theory of political democracy.

Policymaking clusters within business can, therefore, provide an image generated for convenience of communication, make a point, or serve as actual makers of policy. For example, the need for private personal transportation led to the development of the automobile. The development of a personalized vehicle has created an automotive cluster that employs one out of six Americans. Within the cluster are automobile and parts supplier corporations; service and maintenance entities; the oil industry; steel, glass, paint, textiles, rubber and insurance companies; and other important private suppliers of goods and services. Other classes of business clusters, such as highway construction, hotels and motels, recreational areas and centers (private and public) have also appended themselves to the growth of the automotive clusters. At the same time, these clusters affect other policy making centers within the governmental and educational policy centers.

In many respects it is possible to view clusters as following a mitotic natural process, much along the line of cells splitting into other cells. However, by their association with different industries and services as well as governmental entities, we can see a shift of policy making from one type of cluster (e.g., auto production) to another cluster even outside of business (e.g., the federal government). In this respect, policymaking centers are not static but dynamic. One needs to be able to assemble information that both identifies the policymaking locus over time and shows relationships. Information technology may serve to identify these series of centers that somehow combine to make policy decisions that affect society.

Decision Technology Process

It is important to analyze the formulation, use, and assessment of the decision process. Only by understanding this currently loose process can we adequately assess the impact of present and future information technologies on decision making. Too often the issues and problems that need solutions are not communicated to the theoretical management scholar. Consequently, intellectual power is not focused on the more critical areas of institutional concern.

Table 1-1 identifies the activities in decision technologies, their output, and their skilled human resources. Following are several points that also need to be considered when interpreting this table:

1. The activities have produced important outputs including new theories and techniques that have led to real improvements in decision making.
2. The advances to date have been unlinked. By that I mean each group, be they the theoretical builders (problem formulators and modelers), the users (decision makers), or auditors (assessors) have not really been coordinated with the decision making process. It is my estimate that less than 5 percent of all the new

Table 1-1. Decision Technologies: Activities, Outputs and
Human Resources.

Activity	Output	Human Resources
Theoretical Problem Formulation	Scientific formulation, New Knowledge and Theory	Theoretical Management Scholars
Modeling	Testing and extending the formulation of new knowledge and theory	Applied Management Scholars
Decisionmaking	Decisions based on new knowledge and theory	CEO's and other managers
Assessment	Evaluation for effectiveness and efficiency of the outputs	Auditors for legal, engineering, managerial and financial decision functions (internal and external)

ideas in the composite activities expressed or published are used
or even understood by managers who could benefit from them.
3. The need for such linkage in the decision technology has never
   been a primary concern of management schools, managers, or
   auditors.
4. Issues which are fundamental to national welfare, as well as
   emerging information technology, make it virtually certain that
   the issue of establishing linkages will be the next major frontier
   for all involved in decision technology activities.

Impacts of Decision Technology

The first issue that confronts today's would-be creative and innovative managers is whether they are to approach the future on the basis of choice or on the basis of prediction. If the issue is resolved in favor of prediction, we have left the future in the hands of the problem formulators without providing any assurance that the insights they may develop will ever be acted upon. On the other hand, if the issue is resolved in favor of choice, we have left the future in the hands of the managers without any guarantee that their solutions will be directed toward the anticipated problems of their institutions or society.

The point is that this issue and all of the issues that follow are not "either/or" decisions; they can be "both/and" decisions. Rather than choose either prediction or choice, we can select a system in which both choice and prediction play a role.

Management scholars in a large number of academic institutions, professional groups, and corporate laboratories are currently engaged in developing new operations research techniques, new computer algorithms, and new models directed toward solving important classes of problems for the development of a creative and innovative management discipline.

New classes of management planning and control decision problems to be investigated by management scholars and scientists have the following characteristics:

1. They involve more than one level of management.
2. They involve highly complex and diversified activities.
3. They deal with service processes.
4. They involve interrelationships between economic, social, and cultural objectives of individuals and institutions.
5. They require the handling of great volumes of data.
6. The time frame for the solution of these classes of problems is compressed.
7. The effects of possible alternative solutions are far-reaching in terms of both timing of impact and number of individuals affected.

Any attempt to address these new classes of problems must go beyond merely developing new techniques, algorithms, models, and searching for new applications of existing tools. These new problems require that we develop new conceptual constructs that will extend the capabilities of our discipline across a broad front and along many dimensions or new expertise. It will require an even higher order of information technology than is now on the drawing board.

Conceptual constructs for the application of management decision models have not, as a rule, been in the forefront of management scholar considerations. They rarely appear in the current literature in explicit fashion—if they are present at all. Yet, such constructs are implicit in the presentations of both theory and application.

There is a need to delineate the more applicable management principles, theories, practices, and logic found through a select survey of broad managerial literature areas; for example, a management epistemology. This is necessary in order to identify critical and applicable management principles and practices to link the decision technology processes.

Decision formulating and modeling for management has yet to have its own well-defined epistemology. It is still fragmented; its techniques are piecemeal. Many of the techniques that exist are found outside the study of business; for example, economics, psychology, sociology, mathematics, computer sciences, control and feedback engineering, and production control.

Impacts of Future Information Technology Developments on Decisionmaking

Thus far, I have reviewed current decision technology processes, literature, and education. It is now important to look into future advances in the technologies of computers and communications linked to knowledge processing and decision support systems. The computer complex for the 1990s hopefully will overcome many of the problems in today's decision systems. Some of these problems are:

1. Computers were designed primarily for numerical computation and not for business decision processing.
2. The cost of hardware required performance ratios that put emphasis on speed of central processing and larger memories.
3. The volume of software has increased to where it is almost ineffective to organize and maintain.
4. Communications has not been effectively integrated with computers.

Today's managerial decision processes are limited. To deal with more complex problems, future managerial decision processes will require more knowledge about what is available and feasible; conversation in natural language as contrasted with current software language; the ability to retrieve and use decision models with associative knowledge, data and information bases including error analysis as well as the ability to retrieve and use pictorial and image data; and the ability to compress data for decisionmaking in order to generate better alternative choices.

As we move toward the 1990s, we will need to become a knowledge/information-processing society rather than a data/information-processing society. In our highly developed technological culture, there are no longer any simple problems or issues. Even the design, manufacture, marketing, and sale of a toy to bring joy to a child produces a series of management decisions requiring the most sophisticated knowledge data bases and analysis techniques in order to assess the risk and rewards associated with this task.

It is my opinion that the new academic discipline of creative and innovative management that will evolve during the 1980s and 1990s will play the central and most important role in the decisionmaking process. This kind of management and hence this new academic discipline will comprehend organization and use of basic software systems, knowledge data base managerial systems, basic knowledge data bases, an intelligent interface system, and a problem-solving interface system, all working in harmony with the hardware system and in support of the decision function and our economic growth. What will it do for us? Among many things, it will allow us to ask questions and get answers; help us organize our knowledge for the decisions we want to make; provide office automation, computer-aided design, engineering, and instruction; use applied speech understanding; and use applied problem solving.

The impacts of educating creative and innovative managers coupled with the effective use of future technology could be the step ahead that the nation must have to maintain the economic growth that is required to meet already forecasted demands of society. In addition, creative and innovative management must be concerned with distributed national and global networks with access to knowledge bases worldwide, and intelligent, friendly interfaces with increased function and scope; measures of efficiency and flexibility for our institutions; decision support sciences and laboratories; new expertise, relationships, and training; measures of the efficiency and effectiveness of management beyond return on investment, liquidity, work unit efficiency, earnings per share, and so forth; and measures of effectiveness of current operations in meeting goals, technology transfer, development and delivery of new products, goods and services. It will be quickly recognized that these impacts affect many of our current concerns and issues, but it also needs to be recognized that their realization depends on how we link our human and technological resources through creative and innovative managers.

AREAS FOR CREATIVE AND INNOVATIVE MANAGEMENT RESEARCH AND EXPERIMENTATION

It is difficult to launch a new discipline if one cannot delineate areas for research and experimentation. This section sets forth some of the more significant areas for creative and innovative management research and experimentation. A core of research can be started by working on selected current national problems. These problems are almost always broad and complex, require solutions within a reasonable period of time, demand cross-disciplinary talent and allocation of considerable resources. Their solutions often involve cooperation between government, business, labor, and educational institutions. The areas for effort include national security, the behavior of the economy, environmental protection, education, use and reserving of natural resources, international trade, technology transfer, and a host of other matters.

What we call decision technology is in Herb Simon's terminology "innovative research in nonprogrammed decisions." To quote Simon:

> Decision processes with these characteristics would be "unreasonable" under the conditions usually assumed in formal theories for rational choice. They become "reasonable" when we consider situations where the alternatives of choice are not given in advance, but must be discovered; where the means-ends connections between choices and consequences are imperfectly known, and must be explored; and finally, where a simplified and approximating frame of reference must be chosen before the choice can be brought within the limits of human computation.[4]

The problems that will form the basis of creative and innovative management as a new academic frontier will need to be drawn from one or more of the following:

1. In giant and dynamic-growth companies, corporate governance and their processes are radically changing from traditional decision making and formal behavioral-organization theory to prob-

lems, issues, and initiative generation; for example, nonprogrammed and technology decision making with creativity and innovation.

2. An abundance, if not an overload, of creative technical and social inventions are available.

3. Occasions for innovations will occur under adverse conditions at the firm or national level because of international and domestic competition. The competition will be more than economic; it will include scientific advances, national security—defense and economic—and implementation of new technology into end products and services.

4. Choice criteria will involve more than optimization or satisficing of economic magnitudes; these criteria will need to allow for the use of power in many different dimensions.

Specific matters for research are:

- Wants versus Needs—An Economic Analysis
- Public versus Private Communication Systems
- Centralization versus Decentralization in Corporate, Social, and Political Governance
- Organization and Distribution of Information and Technology
- Individual Privacy versus the Public's Right to Know
- "Real" versus "Informational" Environments—Fact versus Perceptions
- Managerial Technology—Application versus Theory
- Newer Organizational Forms—Governance and Management Styles

Academic Experimentation

If my assessments are correct, now is the time to experiment in developing a new frontier of creative and innovative management. There are two stages to these experiments: (1) establish the goals, and (2) initiate interdisciplinary programs that are in consonance with the goals.

One set of goals could be as follows:

1. To become a pacesetter in education for creative and innovative management as a catalyst for a renewed American society.
2. To train managers in the total environment of managing people, technology, and natural or replenishable resources on a state, national, and global basis.
3. To develop innovative leadership on the part of academic faculties and business administrations so as to delineate linkages between business on the one hand and the modern American capitalistic society on the other.
4. To train managers to deal with global, political, and social changes.
5. To see that managers learn to converse in appropriate foreign languages as well as the language of mathematics, statistics, and computer linguistics, and to become more sensitive to cultural differences and how they can be accommodated.
6. To train managers to manage and use remote data bases.
7. To understand and communicate with diverse and shifting constituencies.
8. To set forth a modern and appropriate contextual economic role for private enterprise that removes the cultural contradictions of capitalism.
9. To provide a renewed foundation of individual and institutional social values that are not based on hypocrisy and divergent standards for an institution and the individual.
10. To establish basic areas for creative and innovative management that can coordinate faculty research, the university research centers, the academic curricula, teaching laboratories, and the recruitment of a high quality, diversified, and representative student body dedicated to leadership responsibilities.
11. To develop and make available unique and useful knowledge data bases that do not now exist.
12. To develop analytical techniques and relates models and data that will provide a competitive capability for doing business in the arena of world markets.

How should we measure success in meeting these goals? The clearest indications of an institution's value to society and the general welfare revolve around seeing who asks for its expertise, who wants the services of its students and faculty, and how often its contributions are locally, nationally, and internationally recognized.

Measuring the State of a Society

One area of personal interest that I would like to see included in this new discipline of creative and innovative management is the development of a way of identifying and, if possible, measuring the state of society—and at the moment I am focusing on American society. The past two decades have seen the rise of research on a series of indicators attempting to measure some of the aspects of our society in a piecemeal way. We have microeconomic indicators, social indicators, science indicators; the Department of Commerce has established annual industry outlooks; there are countless polls of opinion, attitude, and concerns; and the Bureau of Census demographics are a source of information on the "people state" of our society. Even with all this, however, it has not been possible to establish a benchmark on the current state of our society. Many have already told me that the measurement of the state of American society is an impossible task; they end their remarks by saying, "Good luck!" But that, after all, is the beginning state for all significant innovations. To see its significance we only need to observe that it is necessary to know where we are if we want to plan rationally and set goals to advance the state of our society. It is a good challenge for our new discipline.

In concluding this paper, I would like to share what I believe are the two most critical issues that will need to be solved by the future leadership of business, government, educational institutions, and society as a whole: (1) managing the future in terms of declines in sales and employment in our basic industries such as steel and automobiles, loss of overseas and domestic markets for low and high technology, goods and services, and changes in natural resource mix; and (2) development of shared and desired goals for the management of resources, for the growth of wealth, and for income distribution.

Let me end with a brief comment as to why I believe that creative and innovative management will be an ever-expanding, exciting, and rewarding academic field. An awareness of the interactions of science, technology, social, economic, political and cultural factors on the constituencies of a society is evolving. The past two decades have seen a rapid transformation of American society in a way that challenges us to unify and disseminate ideals, values, and dreams and to use power in a constructive manner in the solution of societal problems.

If we extract its lessons, the past can help us establish an understanding of what we need for a better future. Our combined intellectual capacities and individual experiences and capabilities will then allow us to build a better society. These are times for bold pioneering—pioneering based on optimism but grounded in reality and with determination to improve what exists and what can be. We must do better in this period of rapid transition. It will be marked by national and international economic interdependencies. We can create this new discipline and the tools that are required to implement it. This is the time to dream of what can be if we are truly to manage into being the kinds of futures that are now beginning to be possible.

NOTES TO CHAPTER 1

1. George Kozmetsky, "Society's Responsibility to Business as an Institution" (Presentation to the Southwest Division Board of Advisers Conference, U.S. Chamber of Commerce, Dallas, Texas, May 1975).
2. Clark Kerr, *Excellence in Education: An Opportunity and a Challenge* (Berkeley: University of California, 1963), p. 7.
3. Walt W. Rostow, *How It All Began: Origins for the Modern Economy* (New York: McGraw-Hill Book Company, 1975), pp. 154–156.
4. Herbert A. Simon, *Models of Bounded Rationality: Behavioral Economics and Business Organizations*, vol. 2 (Cambridge, Mass.: The MIT Press, 1982), p. 393.

CREATIVE AND INNOVATIVE MANAGEMENT—A CHALLENGE TO ACADEMIA

Robert Lawrence Kuhn

The emergence of a new academic discipline in business, like the eruption of a supernova in astronomy, is an event of remarkable impact, bold and beautiful in form, stark and stunning in content. In the 1950s it was management science, the application of quantitative methods to solve business problems. In the 1960s it was behavioral science, the employment of psychological theory for organizational understanding. In the 1970s it was strategic planning, the use of formal methods for mapping corporate strengths and weaknesses onto opportunities and threats. In the 1980s it will be creative and innovative management, the generation of novel and unique responses to internal stimuli and external shocks.

Human civilization is founded on social groupings, the gatherings of individuals in organizations and institutions of all kinds. The running of these transpersonal amalgams, the capacity to maintain and develop cohesive order, is what management is all about. From despots to deputies, managers have always made groups go. Good management was defined operationally by success, in whatever form success was meant to each particular group. Managers were chosen by instinct and survival, and information was transferred by observation and osmosis. The system worked for generations, for millennia (though even Moses was advised to "delegate" by his father-in-law).

27

The world today is very different. As much as we have gained in technology and sophistication we have lost in robustness and stability. While we have progressed in collective power, we have retrogressed in individual control. A manager just cannot assimilate the incessant barrages of high-density data that are the nervous impulses of modern organizations. Frameworks are needed to simplify and reduce, trading off precision for accessibility and accuracy for comprehension.

Management concepts and administrative systems have historically developed more by necessity than by design. Always, it seems, what comes about is what is already essential; there is no time to savor the developing process. The history of management in this century—from Taylor's scientific management to functionalization to operations research to organizational structure and strategy—is the story of theory striving to keep pace with practice, of academics trying to formalize for all executives what the best executives were casually doing by the feel of their gut.

Once more we are at an impasse. Strategic planning, having promised to forecast and guide, has too often extrapolated the past and missed the future. What will happen is no longer governed by what *has* happened. Problems exist today that are difficult to factor into component parts, much less solve. Decision support systems and the like notwithstanding, what we need now is more than a new form of management; we need a new form of thinking!

Creative and innovative management, in George Kozmetsky's vision, must become the focal point of nonroutine pursuits and nonprogrammable administration. The coordination of myriad quantas of information is beyond any person's capacity, but decisions can be made with confidence and commitment when appropriate data reduction is combined with directed insight. Creative management, almost by definition, defies upfront quantification and early verification. Creative solutions are often suboptimal when measured by conventional yardsticks. Yet such suboptimal initiatives can often overwhelm reason and blow out logic. These startling mental processes, performed constantly without awareness by corporate executives, must be subjected to study and analysis. This, then, is the new academic frontier.

Interdisciplinary coordination, we have said, is necessary for the flowering of creative management as a formal academic discipline.

Yet interdisciplinary cooperation, we all know, is more easily promulgated than implemented. Academic departments, like corporate divisions (or wild animals), maintain conflicting spheres of interest, innate imperatives to secure boundaries and defend territories. Interdisciplinary pronouncements, though given superficial support by all academics, are sometimes sources of suspicion and doubt, a feared Trojan Horse of imperialistic conquest and subjugation. Academic business leaders must come to recognize that the true interdisciplinary process enhances rather than attenuates the power of the component disciplines.

The same uncertain banner of interdisciplinary cooperation hangs over the academic-business-government interface. Here the problem is attitudinal rather than competitive. Academicians and businessmen have different objectives, different value structures, different ways of evaluating importance. How can we transform the impenetrable wall separating academic departments and business divisions into a semipermeable membrane allowing the controlled flow of information to pass between them? A key mechanism, I believe, is to attack microproblems at the level of the company rather than macroproblems at the level of the economy. Let us deal deductively with the particular, and only then inductively with the general.

Beyond the academic-business connection, in ever-widening concentric circles, it is important to involve government in the multisector mix. As Michael Kirby notes in the paper that follows, which deals with creative and innovative management in the public sphere, nowhere is the need greater and nowhere is the task harder. The media, as well, should not be ignored. Often felt to be the antagonist of large institutions—government, business, and academic—the media should become a potent force for relevance and impact. Its independent investigative role, while occasionally abused, must be protected in a free society. (For the media to remain truly independent from the much larger institutions of our society, it probably has to skew slightly away from those socioeconomic megaliths and position itself just marginally on the other side of "fair.")

Creativity, Kozmetzky says, is the input to innovation, the raw material of which revolution is built. At this time in human history, we need such a revolution; not a political one, of course (we've had enough of those), but an administrative one. The issue before us, therefore, becomes one of leveraging creativity, of maximizing its appearances and applications. We need means of generating families of fresh ideas, clusters of original alternatives, so that in the analytical/evaluation phase best choices can be made.

Creativity in the context of management elicits, at least heretofore, images and patterns of activities and organizations that have a common sense of style and a rigid connotation of meaning. Such creativity, paradoxically, becomes structured and unidimensional, wooden and confined rather than fluid and free. In order to enable creative and innovative management to break the traditional mold and attain full potential as both an academic discipline and a business technique, it is vital to explore its broad sweep and wide scope. We should view creative management in multimodes, walk around it, visualize it in three dimensions, see it nonlinearly, dissect it in diverse ways.

An epistemology of creative management might begin with a conceptual taxonomy, a classification system cut from different angles:

CONTEXTUAL

Transactional Creativity: Firm-specific activities such as mergers and acquisitions, financial and tax maneuvers, corporate reorganizations, and the like. Examples: Penn-Central's growth by acquisitions into a huge tax loss; debt-equity swaps; matrix organizations.

Competitive Creativity: Interfirm rivalries in the marketplace. Examples: Miller and Budweiser in beer; Jordache and Levi in jeans; Colgate and Crest in toothpaste.

Productive Creativity: Efficiency enhancements in the plant, the office, and the executive suite. Examples: robotics; office automation; personal computers.

CONTENT

Product itself
Producing the product
Marketing/distributing the product
Financing
Human management and control systems

PROCESS

Encourage creativity: Stimulation of fresh ideas
Formulate creativity: Generation of novel approaches
Assess creativity: Analyze and evaluate alternatives
Implement creativity: Choice and action
Leverage creativity: Maximizing benefits and minimizing
 disruptions

Figures 1-2 and 1-3 portray simple paradigms by way of two-by-two contingency tables. Figure 1-2 graphs "creativity" and "innovation" against "macrolevel of the economy" and "microlevel of the firm," and Figure 1-3 identifies "business" and "academic" versions of "theory" and "practice"—all, of course, within the overall context of creative and innovative management. Such models, though simplistic, dissect out, differentiate, and highlight essential elements among the component categories.

Decision making has essentially two modes, two approaches to the process: the incremental and the strategic. Operating in the incre-

Figure 1-2. Macro and Micro Levels of Creativity and Innovation.

	Creativity	Innovation
Macrolevel: Economy	Directional Philosophy	New Programs and Projects
Microlevel: Firm	New Business or Product Ideas	Technological or Managerial Development

Figure 1-3. Business and Academic Versions of Theory and Practice.

	Business	Academics
Theory	Strategic Formulation	Model Building
Practice	Strategic Implementation	Empirical Observations and Analysis

mental mode, the manager begins reactively by recognizing a problem, some unexpected shock, whether internal or external, large or
small, opportunity or threat. He then searches heuristically through
a restrictive variety of potential solutions, making marginal deviations from the status quo, analyzing and evaluating each possibility
in sequence. Deviations from the current policy are widened progres-
sively until the first satisfactory solution is found. It is accepted immediately and all other alternatives, even if potentially better, are
ignored. Simon and March's "bounded rationality" is the keystone
here. The executive cannot know everything, and so if he wants to
do anything, he must replace optimizing with "satisficing"—the
realization that problems need only be solved satisfactorily, not
perfectly.

Operating in the strategic mode, the manager begins proactively by
defining general goals and setting specific objectives. He scans the
external economic environment seeking opportunities and threats,
and analyzes the internal company milieu discerning strengths and
weaknesses. He then maps the latter onto the former and generates
a comprehensive, even exhaustive, list of alternative policies. Each is

assessed for probable consequences and internal consistency. Implementation, feedback, and control systems complete the process.

It is common to judge incremental decision making bad and strategic decision making good. Each is good, but in its own arena. One would not resolve an urgent inventory crisis in the strategic mode, just as one would not formulate a five-year plan in the incremental mode. Creative management, however, can function in both modes. While the strategic process lends itself to original thinking in devising alternative choices, the incremental mode can be fertile soil for the spontaneous sprouting of "Ah-Hah" insights.

Though attention in recent years has focused on the new tools of decision technology—data processing, statistical analysis, modeling, forecasting—the real story is what happens next. How can enormously complex problems, involving competing and interwoven social, cultural, ethical, and personal issues as well as economic ones, be integrated and synthesized into coherent wholes? Considering the large numbers of people often involved and the compressed periods of time in which solutions must be found, the situation becomes baffling.

Computers are a powerful tool for data collection and analysis. Our most critical need, however, is not more information but less. We need data reduction techniques, systems of selection and discernment, intelligent search for meaning. We need mechanisms that work like brains, probabilistically not deterministically.

Brains generally cannot attend to more than one conscious thing at a time but can shift rapidly from one to another, like time-sharing in a computer. This neural apparatus, called the reticular activating system, highlights and habituates information, directing our attention. Furthermore, patterns of sensation can be traced throughout the brain, appearing not only in the highly specific conscious areas of the cerebral cortex but also in the unspecific (or association) areas of the cortex and in the lower subconscious centers of the brain. Among these areas, data pass back and forth, being synthesized and transformed in the process. Waiting some time before making a crucial decision could give these subtle systems a chance to work their creative magic.

Rational inquiry and nonrational insight should be complements, not opposites, in seeking solutions to complex problems. Modern brain research has shown that one side of the cerebral hemisphere, usually the left, is logical and cognitive while the other side, usually the right, is holistic and affective. The left brain, the one that speaks, dissects the pieces; the right brain, the one that visualizes, synthesizes wholes; the left operates deductively and rigorously, the right by patterns and images.

Ideal decision making involves an exquisite interweaving of programmable logic and nonprogrammable impression. An executive requires both hemispheres to be active; he must see both the forest and the trees. Personal opinion and values used to be deemed irrelevant. Of course, they could never be avoided. Now, however, we take a different tack; we consider individual desire and intent perfectly respectable inputs for the decision maker. Intuition has come out of the closet.

There is new appreciation for the art of conceptualizing decisions amidst the science of analyzing them. A manager's subjective feelings should not be intimidated by so-called objective tests. An executive should not be afraid to contradict the computer, but neither should he leap to arbitrary conclusions without concern. I usually advise a decision maker to assess a problem intuitively at first. This allows the psyche minimum creative interference and coercion, mitigating the imposition of predetermined boundaries and long-standing lines of logic. On the other hand, wholly intuitive decisions can be dangerous if quantitative input is ignored. Executives should make a nonrational decision—a "creative" one—only after they clearly understand the rational alternatives and the logical implications of the innovative choice. Intuition and analysis must be tested against each other constantly in a recursive process, with each iteration producing greater confidence.

Creative management should encompass more than external analysis and internal intuition. Psychological motivation and political positioning should also be considered. "Stakeholder analysis" is a qualitative methodology that segregates out the relevant parties and projects the personal attitudes of each. What are everyone's driving mechanisms, their "stake" in the matter? Crucial here is an assessment of individual feelings and hidden agendas. Potential political standing and perceived career paths are often lurking just beneath the surface and must be involved in all creative management decisions.

Are most executive decisions made rationally? If the answer is yes, that is not necessarily good; if the answer is no, that is not necessarily bad. Decisions are made by people, and people are constrained by organizational traditions and manipulated by political bargaining. The inertia of functional departments to do things according to standard operating procedures is a potent regulating mechanism, just as the influence of powerful personalities is a reality of the corporate hierarchy. The pervasive strength and profound pressure of established bureaucracies—corporate staffs, assistant-to's, budget directors—is now recognized more as a focus of serious study than as the butt of ridiculing humor. "Networking" a company— discovering the channels in which decision-controlling influence flows—is often a shock to top management. How real power patterns are structured can differ markedly from the official organization chart.

Creative decision making must take into account the nature of the organization. How to cut a company is essential for making the innovation ring right. Numerous dimensions are involved. Decision making is a function of the sociological structure of the ambient environment. Is the sector profit making or not-for-profit? The organization large or small? The product original or repetitive? The level of managerial decision top or middle? The personalities assertive or passive? The procedure individual or collective?

For example, in a high-technology company, how should the chief operating officer direct the key research scientist? In a charitable foundation, what dollar value should be placed on subsidized concerts for poor children? In a manufacturing firm, what level of losses can be sustained before a division is dispatched? In the media, should a magazine's publisher stop its editor from printing a story critical of a top advertiser? Each decision, while similar in superficial form, differs in fundamental substance. The scientist is a creative sort, perhaps not taken to close supervision. The artistic enrichment of the children defies quantification. The manufacturing division may become a vital resource in future years. The magazine may not exist without editorial freedom.

Creative management decisions begin novel in character, vague in structure, open ended in process, and ambiguous in content. Complex decisions in unfamiliar areas must be factored into simpler subdivisions in familiar areas. Then common routines and procedures can be applied in recurrent fashion: problem recognition, diagnosis, solution search, alternative generation, alternative analysis, preliminary screening, serious evaluation, final choice, authorization, feedback, and review.

Figure 1-4. Dimensions of Thinking.

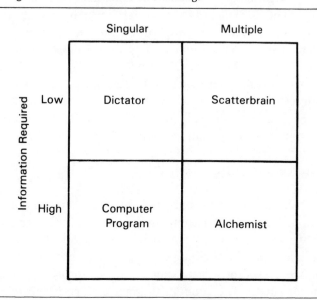

Models can be used as classification frameworks, as long as one does not take them too seriously. For example, consider "Information Required" and "Dimensions of Thinking" (see Figure 1-4). If the decision maker uses low information and thinks in only one dimension, he's decisive and independent, a Dictator. If he uses high information and thinks in one dimension, he's analytic and rigorous, a Computer Program. If he uses low information and thinks in many dimensions, he's flexible and fleeting, a Scatterbrain. If he uses high information and thinks in many dimensions, he's transformational and synthetic, an Alchemist. (The integrated attitudes of the last fellow would seem to make the most effective executive under normal circumstances—although a company nearing bankruptcy might need a Dictator, a mutual fund might want a Computer Program, and an advertising agency might like a Scatterbrain.)

One often associates creativity with the arts and innovation with technological inventions. While wholly appropriate in these contexts, creative and innovative management attains its potential as a policy making mechanism even more than a decision making one. Thus a difference emerges between policy making and decision making, the former subsuming much larger scope and complexity. More than the traditional tradeoffs between optimizing and satisficing reside here. Power and global impact are the chips being bet. Creative and innovative management, desirable for decision making, becomes essential for policy making. If the game we play is management, the stakes we gamble are everything.

INNOVATION IN PUBLIC SECTOR MANAGEMENT AND ACCOUNTABILITY

2 INNOVATION IN GOVERNMENT
Problems and Possibilities

Michael J. L. Kirby

I very much welcome this opportunity to contribute to the symposium on creative and innovative management because this symposium performs the vital function of bringing together both management theorists and practitioners. The benefits to be gained from enhancing the relationship between theory and practice are obvious: for theory to be of utility it must reflect the way the "real world" operates, and for practice to maintain its effectiveness while keeping up with the changing needs of society, it must learn and profit from new developments in theory.

I suspect that for some years in Canada, and perhaps in the United States, the management theorist and the practitioner have been getting out of touch with one another. One of the principal reasons for this lies in the increasingly turbulent political, economic, and social environments in which managers attempt to manage. The average practitioner has not had time to investigate theory, and the theorist has not had the appropriate insights to help him even when guidance was sought. Hence both have drifted apart, the practitioner to become more and more ad hoc and the theorist to become less and less relevant. This has been unfortunate, because it has occurred at a time when there has been a growing need for modern organizations, particularly large organizations like governments, to increase their capacity to innovate.

Innovation is needed in the private sector in order to keep a firm competitive. Innovation is needed in the public sector in order to ensure that public services are delivered as effectively and efficiently as possible—a factor of particular importance in the current period of restraint in government. But innovation in government is also needed for another, more important reason: innovation is one way governments can show leadership and thus help to restore public confidence in government—a confidence that has declined dramatically in recent years.

I must confess that I have become increasingly concerned about this decline and the charges that are being leveled against public services and public servants. In part, this antigovernment attitude reflects a general revolt against large bureaucracy and the impersonal character it brings with it, and in part the fact that leadership is very different in a period of declining economic growth and in which special interest or single issue groups play such a major role.

This decline also reflects the fact that citizens have now become deeply doubtful about the will, the capacity, and the potential of government to perform creatively, to develop innovative policies, and to put them into effect efficiently. This has created a crisis of confidence in government leaders that, in turn, makes the development of a national consensus on difficult issues almost impossible. Yet given the very difficult problems all industrialized nations face, a national consensus is a virtual prerequisite to their successful resolution.

Therefore, I believe that the organizers of this symposium have chosen a very important topic: creative and innovative management. The need for such management in government has never been greater than it is today, and yet for reasons that I shall outline below, the environment for innovation has never been more hostile and the probability of success never less certain.

It is interesting to note, at the outset, that private sector management in North America is also "under the gun." The rate of productivity growth is at an abysmally low level, and, despite the fact that North America pioneered organizational techniques for improving productivity, it seems to have lost its leadership to other nations, particularly Japan. In fact, after eyeing the success of their Japanese competitors, many North American companies are currently attempting a managerial revolution based on practices that are commonplace in Japan. For example, Intel Corp., a technological leader in the microelectronic field, has fostered a collective work ethic by dividing employees into project teams. At Hewlett–Packard, worker turnover has been kept to a minimum during economic slumps by reducing the work hours for all employees rather than laying off some while employing others full time. In many of its plants, consumer-products giant Proctor and Gamble uses semiautonomous worker groups that allow employees to govern their own jobs and achieve gains in productivity. The Buick assembly plant in Flint, Michigan, which once had very low-quality workmanship, used Japanese management techniques in 1978 to gain the cooperation of workers and their union. Within two years, the plant had become the most efficient General Motors facility.

In fact, due to international crises and both foreign and domestic competition, North American companies have been spurred to increase their rate of innovation. A recent survey of 101 companies in the United States showed that 5 out of 6 American companies see technological innovation as the main engine to growth. Similarly, in a survey of sixty-one firms conducted by the *Financial Post* of Canada, twenty-two said that they plan to increase their research and development spending substantially during the next five years, and thirty-one expect to increase research and development somewhat above the inflation rate.

With this increased willingness of the private sector to develop a greater innovative capability, there is a natural assumption that some of this interest in innovation will rub off on the public sector. The question is, Will it? And, if it does, can management in the public sector borrow some of the managerial innovations that have worked in the private sector, just as the private sector has borrowed them from other nations like Japan?

In other words, can innovative business techniques be applied in government to improve both the political process and the efficiency of governing? The answer is probably not, or, at best, maybe. The question, then, is why?

I shall try to address the question in three parts. First, I will assess the obstacles and limitations inherent in trying to transfer private sector managerial innovations to the management apparatus of the public sector. Second, I will comment on the extraordinarily complex nature of the environment in which public sector managers work and in which they must make decisions. Finally, I should like to leave you with some suggestions of different ways that are available to encourage innovation in government.

Alfred North Whitehead once said: "It requires an unusual mind to make an analysis of the obvious." The obvious in this case is that the use of management science methods in the public sector, particularly those borrowed from the private sector, has severe limitations. These limitations exist due to fundamental differences between the public and private sectors. Such differences can be seen more specifically in what I call the four O's: the different types of objectives, output, orientation and operation that characterize the two sectors.

In terms of "objectives," the corporate purpose is clear: to continue to exist by making marketable goods and services. Thus, activities aimed at strategic planning in the private sector are "internally directed" toward improving products, sales techniques, and investment practices. In striking contrast, the objectives of government are not easily defined, often taking the form of vague goals to "reduce poverty," "improve the quality of life," or "strengthen national unity." Public sector influence is "externally oriented," extending its sway over the entire society, with power to redistribute resources of that society through taxation, regulation, and subsidization.

It has been said that the key to good planning rests on the ability of a planner to define with sufficient precision the objective that is to be achieved. While a business firm sets goals for itself, government must identify goals for society as a whole. Thus, whereas private sector managers are able to set clearly defined, measurable objectives, consider the problems of the government planner who must try to integrate the goals of over 200 million Americans with diverse interests and backgrounds or 24 million people in a country such as Canada where agreement on even something as fundamental as a "Charter of Rights" within the constitution has proven to be more difficult than almost anyone imagined. In this government setting, what is creative or innovative to one segment of the population will be regressive to another group of citizens, thus creating great pressure to stick with the status quo rather than innovate.

A second key distinction between business and government organizations is "output." Business has the task of producing goods and services that will generate a profit and will fill real or perceived needs and wants of individuals and groups in the marketplace. The production of goods and services, therefore, is the essential part of a business firm's activity.

Governments, on the other hand, have the task of maintaining particular situations in society that would not otherwise be maintained (e.g., provision of national defense forces, or management of fish resources inside the 200-mile economic zone). In most western countries, the public sector also has assumed a responsibility for providing a variety of products in terms of education, health, and welfare services (although these could be converted into production-type operations through techniques such as revenue dependency).

But while some outputs, such as consumer goods, are easily produced, others, such as safe streets at night, are not. It is a much more difficult problem for governments to produce situations than it is for the private sector to produce objects, and hence innovation is more difficult because of the output that governments is trying to achieve.

The third critical difference between the private and public sectors can be seen in terms of "orientation." It is normal for a successful executive to spend a decade or more gaining high-level management experience. The fact that most senior business managers have had extensive experience in a business environment allows a continuity of ideas and management experience to be built into the decision making structure of the business enterprise, at the top. In the past, this has permitted strategic planning in the private sector to be effective for periods of well beyond a decade. For example, some firms have developed strategic plans for a single project which will take ten to fifteen years or longer to complete (e.g., tar sands plants, new aircraft designs, and the development of new mining or forestry complexes).

In contrast, the nature of the political system in a democracy tends to foster a shorter term orientation. The overriding objective of most politicians is to retain elected office. It is argued that the pressures of the electoral cycle cause governments to sacrifice long-range plans for the short-term necessity of not alienating or antagonizing an important constituency. Thus, innovation in the public sector, which must include an element of long-range planning, becomes more difficult because the vision of the political leader is always obstructed by the life of his political mandate (i.e., four to five years).

It is interesting to note, however, that this focus on the short term may now be affecting the business environment as well. In April 1980, at a Harvard conference on competitiveness, U.S. Senator Lloyd Bentsen, a former corporate chief executive, told participating businessmen that "part of our problem with competitiveness and productivity resides . . . in the corporate boardroom, in the way . . . business is managing its affairs." For managers, Bentsen said, "the measure of achievement and the goals to be reached are as short term as a politician at the next election. Bonuses, salaries and promotions are too often dependent on this year's increase of profits over last year."

Business Week magazine highlighted this matter further by accusing today's private sector managers of being "business mercenaries who ply their skills for salary and bonus but rarely for vision."

The last characteristic that differentiates government from business can be seen in the final O: "operation." The corporate organization is characterized by distinct, direct, and effective lines of authority. Policy decisions are developed by management and are carried out swiftly through vertical lines of responsibility that follow the corporate hierarchy.

In contrast, the operation of government decision making is much slower and is of a different order of complexity. An array of players, often competing and antagonistic, including public servants, special interest groups, provincial governments and opposition parties, impact directly on the decision making process. The problem is compounded when one considers the slow, laborious legislative process. This system has been instituted in order to prevent an abuse of power while attempting to maintain some basis of accountability.

Because the power of government is potentially so great, in a democratic society it must be constrained by institutional decision making processes. For example, it is possible for government, through an incorrect decision, to imperil our whole economy. Power of this magnitude is outside the grasp of a single business (although, as the automobile industry has shown, it may be within the grasp of a few industry sectors when they collectively make wrong decisions). But it is the decision making processes—both legislative and internal to the government itself—that make the implementation of innovative managerial approaches in government more difficult than in the private sector.

In addition, in a corporate environment, where the operation of the firm is clearly defined, plans concentrate in detail on individual sectors of the economy and on factors likely to affect that particular industry. Moreover, in general, corporate managers have access to most of the information required to quantify the major variables that affect a firm's activity.

In contrast, the environment in which government operates is enormously complex, affected by such extraneous and unpredictable factors as unrealistic expectations on the part of the general public, societal interdependence among individuals and nations, and system-wide externalities. Trying to function in such an enormously complex environment, where even output is not clearly defined, causes great difficulty for government managers because, in most cases, sufficient information or even good yardsticks are not available to enable them to make good decisions.

It is, for example, difficult to design a national economic plan when the economic factors of national life—inflation, balance of payments, monetary issues and so on—are factors affected just as much by the actions of other countries as by one's own govenment. If OPEC nations raise the price of oil, the Canadian and American economies suffer. A poor coffee crop in Brazil results in increased prices in North America. Loss of confidence in the Canadian dollar by foreigners affects the price of much of what Canadians buy. It is far more difficult to plan and innovate in an interdependent environment where, as Prime Minister Trudeau said in referring to the United States, "the elephant sneezes and we get pneumonia," than in a more defined environment where one owns the elephant and takes precautions against its catching a cold.

It is clear from reviewing the characteristics of the four O's—objectives, output, orientation, and operation—that the contexts in which the private and public sectors operate are quite different. This can be put another way. It has been said that in a business organization the basic rule for decisions is to optimize—to find the most favorable ratio between effort and risk on the one hand and results and opportunities on the other.

But in a government organization there are far too many constituencies to optimize. Optimization can be the rule of an organization that has one clear goal but, as we have noted, a government tends to have many, vague goals. As a result a government attempts to satisfice—to find the solution that will provide minimum acceptable results rather than the optimal results. In government, one tries to find a solution to which enough constituencies can acquiesce. Satisficing is what politicians mean when they talk of an acceptable compromise. Not for nothing is politics known as the art of the possible rather than the art of the desirable.

But now even the art of the possible is getting more and more difficult to achieve. Government is facing a new type of environment in which there is increasing evidence that solutions to many of the problems facing it are verging on the art of the impossible. How prescient the words of John F. Kennedy (1962) sound: "The central . . . problems of our time . . . do not relate to basic clashes of philosophy or ideology, but to ways and means . . . sophisticated solutions to complex and obstinate problems . . . [we] deal with questions which are beyond the comprehension of most men."

Let me briefly describe some of the characteristics of this new environment in which government finds itself operating. They include unrealistic expectations by citizens, a decline in the authority of governments, the fragility of many of our institutions, the counterintuitive nature of solutions to complex problems, and the "global village" problem.

Since World War I, governments have grown primarily because politicians have offered the public major new programs, particularly social programs, that are essentially redistributive in nature. These programs (including unemployment insurance, medicare, welfare) first gained acceptance from citizens as a desirable method for the equitable sharing of the country's wealth and in response to their desire for a better life. Unfortunately, as the economy has soured, citizens have not lowered their expectations or demanded an end, or even a reduction, to current levels of service. They have instead blamed government for mismanagement. After all, no one, least of all governments, anticipated that programs would become as expensive as they are now. Consequently, even when program costs are now shown to be prohibitive, levels of expectation are not changed because the public believes that governments, if they were properly managed, could provide the current level of service at a much reduced cost.

The dilemma for government is that, in the face of these unrealistic expectations, it not only has to provide services that meet the public's needs in a conventional sense, but it has become, in Daniel Bell's terms, "the arena for the fulfillment of private and group wants" as well. Political scientist Richard Rose describes this situation as an overload in which expectations are far greater than the system can meet. When government is not satisfying the rising levels of citizen's perceived entitlements, the result is frustration, apathy, and cynicism. These constitute the most difficult elements of the environment in which government managers operate today. They make creative management extremely difficult because of the cynicism with which any innovative proposal is greeted by a sizable portion of the general public.

This difficulty is compounded by the general decline in respect for authority that exists throughout our society. It is axiomatic that governments operate most effectively when mutual trust and respect are present between those governing and the governed. Yet this mutual trust and respect does not exist anywhere in the world today. Indeed, during the last decade, government has undergone a dramatic decline in the public's trust. The individual no longer feels that he counts for much or that political leaders care about the same issues as the people. During the past ten years the percentage of individuals feeling this way has more than doubled and now composes a clear majority of the population.

This fundamental change in the public's attitude toward government is not unique to Canada. There is ample evidence that a similar change in attitude has taken place in most western democratic countries. For example, two decades of research by the Center for Political Studies of the Institute for Social Research at the University of Michigan show that, during this period, the percentage of people who trust government has plummeted by more than 50 percent.

Equally important, the public's evaluation of those in power has deteriorated with even greater speed. Over a five-year period in the 1970s, the Harris survey registered a jump from 36 percent to 60 percent in the number of people who agreed with the statement that "Most people with power try to take advantage of people like yourself." And the Gallup poll revealed an astounding 84 percent expressing dissatisfaction with the way government was running things in the United States at that time. Similar results have been obtained in Canada.

This exceedingly negative view of government is not simply a matter to note and then ignore. To the extent that the average citizen no longer sees government as acting in ways that appear rational and beneficial, attitudes of cooperation with government will be replaced by more obstructive behavior that often seems to offer greater rewards. Consider, for example, the extensive increase in public demonstrations of all kinds in recent years.

Worse still, this change in public attitude toward government takes on added significance when we realize that governments represent large, growing, and complex social systems that, evidence suggests, decline in performance as they become larger and more complex. Moreover, large, complex systems are less amenable to control than small, simple systems and are more vulnerable to disruption at key points. This observation has not gone unnoticed as witness, for example, airline hijackers, air traffic controllers, antinuclear demonstrators. These examples illustrate the fragility or the lack of resilience of many of our modern institutions. This fragility is made worse by the fact that we have a wealth of examples demonstrating that the seemingly best or most obvious solutions to problems caused by large, complex systems are often counterproductive.

This phenomenon, which is referred to in the business management literature as the counter-intuitive nature of the solution to social system problems, stems from the fact that the best ways of attacking many public sector problems are often neither obviously apparent in principle nor straightforward in practice. In an interesting illustration of the counter-intuitive effects of some public policies, Jay Forrester cites the results of his research into the dynamics of urban systems. He studied four common programs for improving the depressed nature of a city's inner core. The first was the creation of jobs by busing the unemployed to the suburbs or by government's acting as the employer of last resort. The second was a training program to increase the skills of the lowest income group. The third was financial aid to the depressed city. The fourth was the construction of low-cost housing.

Forrester's conclusion, irrespective of the criteria used for evaluating the four programs, was that all four failed. They ranged from ineffective to harmful, judged either by their effect on the economic health of the city or by their long-range effect on the low-income population of the city. In every case, the reason the program failed was that it led to an unanticipated behavioral response on the part of those affected by the program.

Finally, public sector managers now operate in an environment where even the theoretical assumption of the competence of governments to deal with problems independently is untenable. Hitherto, we in Canada have tended to regard the rest of the world as an aspect of foreign relations, in terms of foreign trade and military and political alliances. The unspoken assumption was that we could have as much or as little of this as we chose. This is no longer so. It has become clear that our future, good or bad, is inextricably linked to our willingness to work to develop an international system based on consultation and shared responsibility.

Economic factors of national life—inflation, balance of payments, monetary issues, unemployment and so on—are factors affected just as much (if not more) by actions of other countries as by our own government. Nor is our interdependence with the rest of the world limited to economic matters. Consider environmental concerns like acid rain, terrorism, and third world issues, for example.

Contemporary public policy problems exist, therefore, as an untidy tangle of intertwining difficulties that give government incentive to develop more evolutionary rather than revolutionary solutions— solutions that are more incremental than innovative in nature. Public sector managers are facing not a series of discrete difficulties that are clearly delineated and can be tackled successfully one by one, but a cluster of intertwined problems so tangled that it is increasingly difficult to formulate discrete problems and apply discrete solutions without disturbing other, often remote, areas of the tangle. In this environment, survival rather than innovation becomes the order of the day.

This brings us to the key question: Is there a way out of this "bottomless pit" for government? The optimist in me says yes, particularly since there does not seem to be any constructive alternative to government. It is, therefore, imperative that government achieve both greater efficiency in the way it delivers services and greater support as an institution from the governed. To do this it must be willing to innovate despite all the pressures not to do so. Let me outline a number of proposals that I believe could encourage and enhance greater innovation in government.

First, it is evident that reform of government institutions is necessary if they are to have the structural capacity to be innovative. For two weeks this past March, the Parliament of Canada was stalemated due to a procedural battle within the House of Commons. The paralysis began over the legislative form and procedure of a proposed energy bill. The crisis disrupted weeks of regular House of Commons business as both sides armed for a protracted war over their respective principles. Responsible government in Canada is largely based on a common "understanding" between the major parties in Parliament, but the energy bill showdown indicates that the basis of this understanding is eroding.

As one parliamentarian remarked: "Everyone talks about parliamentary reform, but the only reform that's needed is reform between the ears of the Members." I will not comment on the need for change "between the ears," but what is clear—and both the government and opposition agree—is that other institutional reforms are needed if Parliament is to achieve a renewed effectiveness.

Such reforms, if they are to be of substance, must include issues such as the role of the Speaker, the use of closure, the use of omnibus legislation, the rules on voting, on written questions, on length of speeches and parliamentary sessions, and on the effectiveness of committees. More than a patchwork job is required if the reforms are going to have an impact in making Parliament more streamlined, efficient, and effective—and, most importantly, if they are to restore the credibility of Parliament in the eyes of Canadians.

Other types of institutional changes are needed to reduce the sense of alienation and frustration in outlying regions of the country toward the federal government. In this regard, it has been suggested that hostility in the Canadian West toward Ottawa might diminish if we could abolish our Senate as it now is and substitute an elected one. Every other federation has a second chamber where voices of the states or regions are heard with clarity. Those voices in our Senate tend to be muffled because the Senators are all appointed by the federal government. Some have suggested that a Senate with an equal number of Senators from each province, elected by proportional representation, would give new strength to the Canadian Parliament as an institution to represent the regional differences of Canada.

Similarly, a vast array of proposals for institutional reform have been suggested for the American system. For example, in a 1980 article in *Foreign Affairs*, Lloyd Cutler, a former Councillor to President Carter, argues that amendments to the existing constitutional framework are needed to assist Americans in adjusting to the changes in the world in which the Constitution must function. Cutler believes that the division of powers between the legislative and executive branches, whatever their merits in 1793, has become a division that almost guarantees stalemate today. He says that because the United States does not "form a government," it has not been possible for the government to propose, legislate, and administer a balanced program for governing. This view has also been espoused for years in the *New Republic*.

Among the ideas for reform Cutler puts forth are requiring the President to select half of his cabinet from among the members of his party in the Senate and the House, who would retain their seats while serving in Cabinet. He also proposes to provide the President with the power, to be exercised not more than once in his term, to dissolve Congress and call for new Congressional elections. Overall, Cutler argues for a set of changes to the Constitution that would make the American structure work more in the manner of a parliamentary system, with less separation between the executive and legislature than now exists.

A second structural innovation that may be able to inspire greater innovation can be found in the increased use of temporary institutions. Temporary institutions take the form of ad hoc structures set up to cope expeditiously with specific issues of multidepartmental or priority concern of government. They have a defined existence, usually short term, and are set up under a chairman, with independent status, who has the responsibility of selecting staff. The great potential of temporary institutions such as Royal Commissions and Task Forces can be found in the fact that as they carry out their work, increased public attention will be focused on the issues under investigation. (This, of course, does not prevent their reports from simply ending up on the shelf, as many of them do, because their recommendations are not pragmatic or politically feasible.)

For example, the Federal government of Canada has recently set up a Task Force, under my chairmanship, to investigate the problems of the nearly bankrupt fisheries industry in the Atlantic provinces. The Fisheries Task Force has a lifetime of only nine months. It consists of twelve members, drawn from the Federal government, the fishing industry, and fishermen unions. In carrying out its work, the Task Force has consulted widely, partly to gain information and partly to lay the groundwork for public acceptance of the policy changes which will inevitably have to be made. If the Fisheries Task Force can generate sufficient public awareness of the key issues, it may be able to mobilize enough support within relevant constituencies to make significant change possible.

The strength of temporary institutions can be found in their ability to generate public support for their recommendations, thus having an impact in the political marketplace by applying pressure on the government to make innovative policy changes. This is a particularly useful device now that we live in the era of more issue-based, rather than party-based, politics. In this new kind of environment, any device that might help to form a positive political consensus is useful.

A third way innovation can be encouraged in government involves improving the training of civil servants either through internships at schools of public administration, sabbaticals, or on-the-job training programs. In the United States many civil servants have little government management experience before assuming high-level responsibility in government. In Canada this is not the case because we have a permanent public service. However, because continuous experience in one management system has the potential to be very stultifying, Canadian public servants, too, could benefit from special programs of advanced management designed for the public sector executive who needs training in the complex problems of organization, program evaluation, and the potential of the latest technological developments.

Canada could also learn much from the U.S. practice of bringing in members of the business and academic communities for short-term assignments in government. We do not do nearly enough of this kind of cross-fertilization.

Canada could also profit from the U.S. experience in relation to its use of "think tanks" (e.g., the Brookings Institution, the American Enterprise Institute) as a vehicle for providing experience for those who have served, or who someday might serve, in government. We need to encourage more movement between such institutions and government, something I tried to do when I was President of the Institute for Research on Public Policy (Canada's largest nongovernmental public policy research organization).

In addition, less job hopping and more planned job rotations within government ought to be encouraged so that managers get experience in several departments within the government structure. In this regard, Canada seems to be substantially ahead of the United States. The Canadian civil service has been implementing interdepartmental transfers as a key element of career development plans for the last decade with good results.

Although nothing replaces good experience, new types of educational seminars may also be useful. We have a plethora of technique-oriented seminars; maybe the time has arrived to teach ethics and global thinking, perhaps even philosophy and English literature, if for no other reason than to teach managers to think and to ask questions. The training programs that I have suggested would attempt to develop a new type of public sector manager, with greater emphasis on cultivating a public philosophy.

A fourth option to encourage innovation in government can be obtained through the introduction of an incentive compensation program that rewards achievement. We will not recruit the best and the brightest until we do. At the present time, a small element of public sector management pay schemes offers executive incentives for efficiency and creativity. But more in the way of such bonus schemes are needed if public sector management is to link performance with reward.

One suggestion is to "leverage" bonuses. In such a scheme, a public servant would receive, in addition to salary, a series of bonuses when specific targets based on departmental objectives have been met. This is now, in part, the case in the Canadian public service, where senior members of the bureaucracy have a bonus plan, although the bonuses are admittedly modest when compared to those in the private sector.

In another proposal, my fifth, government departments would be allowed to retain, for use in policy improvements, 50 percent of any economies they realize through greater efficiency. Traditionally, any such savings revert to the treasury, a situation which, it has been argued, removes much of the incentive for innovation.

A sixth element that may enhance government's innovative capability is the use of new information technology in improving the governing process. For example, interactive television could soon play a part in increasing public understanding of social issues and government policies. It has been argued that interactive broadcasting, which pemits TV viewers to communicate instantly and directly with the broadcasting source, could function as an electronic polling feedback mechanism. If citizens are asked to voice their opinion on political issues or social problems, it is technologically possible to get first-hand reactions literally within seconds. Combined with other sources of information, such feedback can provide an insight into what viewers think about proposed policies.

Make no mistake, though. Government should not govern (or be seen to govern) on the basis of giving people what they want. As I have explained earlier, we have already found ourselves in troubled waters as a result of this approach to governing. Leadership means providing for needs, not wants, no matter how politically difficult it may be to resist the latter.

The new communications technology will also permit government affairs to enter a new era. With new information systems and improved dissemination tools, government executives will be able to call up historical data, evaluate the results of previous programs, and develop systematic public affairs impact statements for all major projects.

The prospects are almost infinite as to how new communications technology can be used in government to develop good policy and to put it into effect creatively. At the very least, communications technology could help to lessen the adversarial atmosphere that now exists between government and its citizens, and it could help loosen the grip of centralization in large, geographically dispersed countries like Canada and the United States. It might even remove some of the mystery from government.

My seventh option for achieving a more innovative approach to management in government lies in the encouragement of volunteerism in North American society. The voluntary sector has been subject to serious problems and challenges in the last decade. The general economic climate, with rising costs due to inflation—together with the failure of contributions to keep pace with the funding requirements of voluntary organizations—have posed severe threats to their ability to function effectively. In addition, the growth of government and its assumption of responsibility over wide areas of economic and social life has diminished the public's belief in the need for volunteerism and in the importance of individual action. But with the current retrenchment of government services, volunteerism has once again become vital to North American society.

More importantly, however, to the extent that it offers a mechanism for active involvement in society, volunteerism can offer a remedy to the sense of alienation arising from disillusionment with government. Thus what is needed is a rehabilitation of the traditional values of volunteerism together with concrete government policies to encourage the growth of voluntary action.

Eighth, and finally, innovation is also required in the way governments deliver services. I addressed this issue in considerable detail in the A.B. Plaunt Lectures that I gave at Carleton University in Ottawa two years ago.[1] It is nonetheless worth summarizing part of the list of possibilities I discussed there.

The range of service delivery options includes the following:

- government employees delivering a service directly to citizens

- government contracting-out a service so that it is provided by another level of government or a private sector firm

- government providing a private sector firm with a monopoly to provide a service that the firm then sells to the public, usually at regulated rates

- government providing a subsidy to the producer of a service, thereby enabling the producer to sell the service to the public at a lower cost than would otherwise be the case

- government giving users of a service vouchers that enable them to purchase the service in the marketplace at a cheaper rate than they would otherwise have to pay

Each of these delivery mechanisms is different. They differ in the role they assign to government; they differ in the role that is played by the private sector; they differ in the role that the consumer of the service plays; they differ in the degree of consumer choice; they differ in the degree of competition that is possible (and indeed that can be encouraged) in the delivery of the service; and they are also subject to different economies of scale, since the unit cost of delivering the goods or service will vary with the delivery mechanism that is used.

Of equal and perhaps even greater importance, these various methods of delivering public services differ in their political characteristics. In some of them, government pays the full cost of providing the service, thus increasing government expenditures and the public attack on the size of government. In others, the service is paid for directly by its users and the role of government is a regulatory one, designed to ensure that users are charged a "fair" price. In still other cases, the service is delivered on a universal basis rather than on the basis of being delivered only to those who need it. In particular, each delivery system results in different winners and losers, a key factor from a political point of view.

Moreover, these delivery mechanisms (and others given in the Plaunt Lectures) are not mutually exclusive; they all, either individually or when considered in combination with one another, offer the possibility for considerable innovation in the management of government. In fact, because service delivery is the problem government managers face that is most similar to the problems faced by private sector managers, it is probably in this area that governments can learn most from innovative management techniques in business.

The eight suggestions that I have put forth for helping government deal with the complex tangle of problems it faces are not derived directly from the ways management science has been applied in the private sector for, as we have noted, quite often these principles are not applicable to the public sector. Indeed, as Wallace S. Sayre has somewhere observed: "Business and government are alike in all unimportant respects."

But if the institutional and personnel policy changes I have suggested—institutional reform, temporary institutions, improved training programs, incentive compensation policies, budgetary reforms, improved uses of communications technology, better utilization of volunteerism, and new methods for delivering public services—are put in place, it seems to me that government will be in a better position to adopt appropriate creative and innovative management practices.

Innovation is an attitude and a process. It is considered a prized quality in individuals, systems, and organizations. It is a function of pride, energy, and creativity. It should, and can, permeate the individual and collective response of Canadians and Americans to the economic, political and technological challenges of the decade.

In most societies and nations, new ways of doing things evolve naturally, in response to fundamental changes in their environment. However, as the rate of change and the level of complexity of society and government increases, institutional innovation needs to be approached in a much more orderly manner than in the past. Governments can no longer be simply an expression of the will or the wants of the people; nor are they a divine creation or a creature to resolve class conflict. They are enterprises providing services that must be made to function efficiently within a framework that reflects the best in human values.

Our challenge as management scientists and public servants is clear. We must both create and innovate. We must help design and implement new tools that consist of the best quantitative and qualitative techniques available in our society blended together in a way that enables them to be usefully applied to the problems that all governments face. We are on the edge of a frontier, one akin to the space frontier we faced in 1960. To quote John F. Kennedy again: "The new frontier is not a set of promises, it is a set of challenges. . . . It will not be finished in the first one hundred days. Nor will it be finished in the first one thousand days, nor even perhaps in our lifetime on this planet."

The challenge of designing new techniques for the effective management of a democratic government is at least as difficult as that faced by those who developed the space program. It will not be met easily or quickly. But meet it we must. To quote from Jerome Deshusses in his much acclaimed critique of contemporary society, the Eighth Night of Creation:[2] "We cannot do otherwise . . . for at the bottom of the nameless gulf into which everything is hurling itself is inscribed a motto that is easier and easier to read: Death or Transfiguration."

NOTES TO CHAPTER 2

1. M. J. L. Kirby, *Reflections on the Management of Government in the 1980s* (Ottawa: Plaunt Lectures at Carleton University, 1980).
2. From p. 405 of Jerome Deshusses, *The Eighth Night of Creation*, Life on the Edge of Human History, translated by A. D. Martin Sperry (New York: The Dial Press, 1982).

SIMILARITIES AND DIFFERENCES IN INNOVATION FOR GOVERNMENTAL AND PRIVATE ENTERPRISE MANAGEMENT

Otto A. Davis

INTRODUCTION

It is a pleasure and an honor to be able to comment upon a paper by the Honorable Michael J. L. Kirby. Dr. Kirby has been able to fashion a career that has combined the best of the academic and the world of practice in government. He has made important and lasting contributions in the intellectual arena that range from abstract developments in mathematical programming to practical applications that represent impressive contributions to modeling. Similarly, his career in public service in Canada, where he has been an active leader in Liberal politics, is so successful that it is the envy of those of us who harbor well-hidden but deep-seated desires to make real contributions to government. Only rarely does one find a person with the ability, the intellect, the drive, and the personality to be so successful in two worlds that meet all too seldom. It is appropriate to add that it is especially fitting for Dr. Kirby to be giving a paper on a program honoring Dean George Kozmetsky, whose own career has spanned the worlds of academia and practice in a manner somewhat different, with an emphasis upon private rather than public management, but with great distinction and with impressive contributions in both worlds.

In this comment I will briefly review some of the contributions of the Kirby paper, argue with some of his remarks and suggestions, and conclude by stating my own perspective upon the notion—which is one of the underlying themes of the paper—that the worlds of the theorist and the practitioner need to be drawn closer together.

GENERAL PREMISES

It is extremely popular in some intellectual circles to make a great distinction between the management practices of the public and private sectors. Practice in the public sector is characterized as being backward and generally poor. The private sector is viewed as the source of innovation in management. The solution is seen as the importation of the innovative practices from the private sector into the public arena.

There may be some merit to this position. Certainly, one can find instances in which practice in the public sector is so backward as to be depressing, and in some portion of these dominated by examples of better performance in business management. Kirby does not buy this obvious solution for improvement in the public sector. Perhaps because I have some sympathy for his view—and can thus let his considerable experience reinforce my own prejudices—I find it appropriate to review the basic components of his argument.

Although he did not begin by pointing out that the private sector in North America has management problems of its own in the area of international competition, he did refer to certain management practices that are being borrowed from the Japanese. Hence, it might be appropriate to begin this review and interpretation of his basic argument by pointing out the obvious: management, both public and private, faces a challenge today that will fundamentally determine whether we remain the dominant force in the free world. Further, it is not obvious to me that the flow of innovations in management is always from the private to the public sectors. I believe that we have witnessed important instances of a reverse flow. As a consequence, I shall take the liberty afforded a discussant to broaden and reinterpret Kirby's argument to an examination of the difficulty of having managerial innovations move from either sector to the other.

Kirby's argument really boils down to the fact that public and private operations are different in some important dimensions. He argues that the public manager operates in a much more complex environment. He differentiates these by what he classifies as the four Os—the differing objectives, output, orientation and operation that characterize the two sectors.

Private objectives are characterized as being simpler than public ones. In fact, Kirby argues that public objectives are difficult even to specify, while business can simply attempt to make profits.

Similarly, private outputs are characterized as being more obvious. Businesses produce goods and services while governments often have to generate an environment or situation.

The orientation of democratic governments is characterized as being so interested in the short run as to be almost shortsighted. On this point, however, Kirby draws less distinction by claiming that one of the difficulties with private management, at least in North America, is that businessmen are paying too much attention to the short term at the expense of longer term objectives.

Finally, the mode of operation is supposed to be different in the two sectors. The corporate organization is supposed to have clear lines of responsibility and effective authority so that decisions made with sufficient information can be swiftly implemented. Government organizations, on the other hand, are plagued by overlapping jurisdictions, inadequate information and poor yardsticks, and too many constituencies.

A MATTER OF DEGREE

It is difficult to argue with distinctions that are so clear, well drawn, and obviously based upon experience. Government, especially at the top, is extremely difficult. Further, there is obvious truth in parts of these distinctions. I shall argue, however, that at best they are overdrawn and might even mask a deeper confusion. Although there are differences of principle, which Kirby has pointed out with eloquence, many of the differences are matters of degree only.

It is probably true that an accepted goal of corporations is to stay in business by operating profitably. At about the same level of generality one can argue that an accepted goal of governments is to govern effectively. Neither statement provides very much in terms of guidance for operations. Operating profitably leaves open the issues of which goods and services should be provided and how. Governing effectively does little to inform one as to which laws should be framed, which regulations formulated, or which services provided. It is true that the two problems are not identical, but I hold that the guidance provided by the two goals is not very different.

One could easily pass over this point as being a trivial quarrel, but it may mask a deeper and more fundamental point. The basic issue is more clearly framed when Kirby asserts that businesses are able to "optimize" while governments, operating in a more complex environment, have to settle for "satisficing."

There may be fundamental differences in the ways in which corporate and public officials operate. However, such differences cannot be described or summarized as optimizing versus satisficing. These two terms refer only to the type of model that has been constructed to represent a particular problem, and neither may be an accurate description of a solution process employed by a public or private executive. Further, optimizing models are constructed for both public and private sector problems. Public choice models often employ the methodology of optimization even when modeling legislative or committee processes. Satisficing models can be and are developed to represent problem-solving behavior in both the public and private sectors.

It may be that the popularity of simple economic models of the firm has caused us to confuse models with reality. However, I know no corporate consultants, especially those specializing in fundamental problems of strategy, who make their living applying the economic theory of the firm. The basic point, however, is that optimizing or satisficing are properties of models rather than descriptions of real behavior. Depending upon the purpose of the modeler, the same real behavior might be modeled with either a satisficing or an optimizing methodology. Both methodologies are available for application to problems of either sector.

Kirby may have had something else in mind, but I do not believe that either goal—maximize profits or govern effectively—provides very much direction. Both beg the fundamental questions. Now it may be true that profits are more easily measurable than public sector effectiveness. In fact, even though profits are less clearly defined than is often thought to be the case, measuring effectiveness in government is a difficult task indeed. However, the problem of measurement does not seem to me to be the distinction that Kirby was trying to make.

One can also argue that the distinction between the outputs of the two sectors is overdrawn. Many "outputs" of businesses can be characterized as services. Legal services, for example, are traditionally provided by partnerships that can be thought of as firms operating in the private sector. Some services are even provided by both sectors—education is a good example. However, whether one agrees with the distinction or not, it is difficult to see how the difference makes it more difficult to innovate in the public sector. Kirby states: "It is a much more difficult problem for governments to produce situations than it is for the private sector to produce objects, and hence innovation is more difficult because of the output which governments are trying to achieve." Innovation may well be more difficult in the public sector for a variety of reasons, but I am not convinced that a distinction between the nature of the outputs of the two sectors is a primary reason for the greater difficulty.

I tend to agree that on the average democratic governments have a notoriously short-term orientation and that the private sector has a somewhat longer time horizon. I even share Kirby's view that innovation is made more difficult in the public sector because the vision of the political leader can be obstructed by the limited term of his political mandate. Yet I must admit that my agreement may be more a matter of shared prejudice rather than objective facts. After all, any experienced benefit-cost analyst can cite numerous examples (water resource examples tend to come to mind) where no matter how great the strain or even the allowed cheating by double counting, the present values of benefits cannot be made to equal or surpass costs without the aid of unreasonably low rates of discount. I hardly need to remind the reader that the lower the discount rate the greater the importance assigned to events far into the future. If one dwells upon such objective examples, it is easy to find evidence pointing to opposing points of view in regard to the time preference of governments. I suspect that a careful search in the private sector can also unearth conflicting evidence. I may feel more comfortable on this point by sticking with my prejudice and relying upon Kirby's experience rather than searching for, and trying to draw inferences from, the facts!

Finally, there is the matter of differing styles of operation. Kirby makes a distinction between the "distinct, direct, and effective lines of authority" where policy decisions made by private sector managers can be carried out and implemented "swiftly through vertical lines of responsibility that follow the corporate hierarchy" and the complexity of the public sector where an "array of players, often competing and antagonistic, including public servants, special interest groups, provincial governments and opposition parties, impact directly on the decision making process."

How can one disagree with such eloquence? Especially, how can one disagree when there is so much truth in the distinction? Yet it is a matter of degree. Many private organizations, even relatively small ones, operate on the basis of committee decisions. In fact, I am not aware of a single corporate board of directors that consists of less than three people. When one considers corporate giants such as General Motors, the private bureaucracy can become rather complex. The city council in a small town may be much more simple politically than the committees that make decisions in these large organizations.

Further, parts of the argument associated with the distinction may be fundamentally incorrect. Take almost any manager struggling with the decision to introduce a new product and try to tell him that "corporate managers have access to most of the information required to quantify the major variables that affect the firm's activity," and despite all surveys and market analyses that he might have, you are likely to be laughed out of the room.

In summary, I argue that at best Kirby's fundamental differences between public and private management boil down to matters of degree. Differences of degree may, of course, be important. Yet, these distinctions—or differences of degree—do not seem to me to be important or obvious reasons why managerial innovations produced in one sector do not have an immediate and easy transition to the other. Since I do agree with his position that at best such innovations are transferred with great difficulty from one sector to the other, I am left with the uneasy feeling that although we share an intellectual position, the only basis that the two of us have been able to find for it is my own casual observation and his own extensive experience. Somehow, we ought to be able to provide better intellectual support for a position that seems to me to be so clearly true even if it is so seldom acknowledged.

ADMIRATION

There is much that I like in the Kirby paper. I find his insights into and descriptions of the problems of government to be intellectually stimulating and even profound. Governments have grown in this century because politicians competed for power by offering the public major new programs, particularly social programs that are redistributive in nature. As programs proved to be less effective than claimed, as the ability to produce the good life turned out to be more difficult than originally thought, as the goal of eliminating poverty turned out to be illusion, and as economic growth became less rapid, it has become increasingly apparent that our political institutions do not have smoothly functioning mechanisms to match expectations with reality. In the political competition for power, there seems to be an advantage in claiming despair over a half empty glass rather than happiness over one half full.

Kirby points out that in trying to satisfy these unrealistic expectations, the dilemma of modern government is that it can produce little more than frustration, apathy, and cynicism. This dilemma is one of the prime reasons why we are witnessing a general decline in respect for authority throughout our society. It is an important reason why government has undergone a dramatic decline in the public's trust.

Kirby also observes that the dilemma is made more difficult by the fact that in our complex world the best ways of attacking many of our public sector problems are "neither obviously apparent in principle nor straightforward in practice." Further, solutions that seem obvious sometimes make the situation worse when applied or implemented.

Despite the situation—what he calls the bottomless pit for government"—Kirby is optimistic. One has to admire his ability to be optimistic in view of his perspective upon the nature of the dilemma of government.

CONCLUDING OBSERVATIONS

I shall not dwell upon Kirby's suggestions for innovation in government. Let me simply say that they are interesting and merit consideration. Given his argument, I think that it is only fair to infer that Kirby's position must be that no suggestion—even those that seem to have obvious merit—should be adopted without careful study and examination.

What is clear is the urgent need for innovation in the public sector. Kirby's basic position, at least as I have chosen to interpret it, holds that one cannot expect a great flow of managerial innovations from one sector to the other. Although I have argued with some of the reasons that he gave to support this view, I do share his view and support the basic thrust of his argument that there are important differences—sometimes only of degree—in problems and especially processes that characterize the two sectors.

If our shared views are at all accurate, then the task of producing an increased flow of managerial innovations in the public sector is more basic than the somewhat simplistic notion cited at the beginning of this essay. Public sector managers cannot expect that a panacea for their problems is to be found in private sector practices. This does not mean that the flow of innovations between the two sectors will be zero, for historically there have been developments in each sector that have found application in the other. This view does imply a strong disagreement with the notion that significant innovative ideas and practices are abundant in the private sector and that governmental administrators only need to copy to produce improvement. My own view, which I think Kirby shares, is that both sectors have urgent needs for help in producing creative managerial ideas. We are in difficult times all around.

Kirby begins his essay with the argument that the worlds of the theorist and the practitioner need to be drawn closer together. This thought is a basis for much of what he has to say, although he does not always bring it to the forefront as much as I might have liked. However, I agree with him that the intellectual flow between those two worlds can be a source of great creativity. It is, I believe, the cross-pollination that brings the greatest hope. I can even argue—although I will not make the attempt here—that those who have learned to bridge the two worlds in an intellectual sense have been a very important source of the basic progress that we have witnessed over the past few decades. This is a bridge that needs to be expanded. How best to accomplish this is a topic that has seldom received systematic attention.

PERSPECTIVES FROM THE U.S. DEPARTMENT OF DEFENSE ON REQUIREMENTS AND OPPORTUNITIES FOR INNOVATION IN GOVERNMENT

Jack R. Borsting

Kirby's stimulating paper is divided into three parts, as was Gaul. The first, in which he outlines the divisions between the private and public sector, I generally agree with and find to be the best of the three parts. Kirby initially points out that the practitioner and the theorist have drifted apart. This conclusion is not too surprising since practitioners take the structure and the process as usually fixed, but the researcher has great flexibility in changing both structure and process. He also points out that citizens have become deeply concerned about the will, the capacity, and the potential of government to be innovative, creative, and effective.

Kirby provides an insightful discussion of the differences between the public and private sector using four categories: objectives, output, orientation, and operations. Objectives and output of the public sector are substantially different than those of the private sector. Let me list briefly the various objectives of the Defense Department as follows:

1. The Armed Forces need to deter armed conflict and if necessary to fight. They need to be organized. That organization includes formulating doctrine, creating strategy and the supporting war plans, recruiting people and training them, and deploying and sustaining forces.

2. The Defense Department needs variously to procure, maintain, and often develop and repair material ranging from aircraft carriers to lifeboats.
3. An important responsibility of the Secretary of Defense, working both with his subordinates and his colleagues elsewhere in the National Security Council, Departments of State, Treasury, and Commerce, is to see that defense policy and the actions of the Defense Department support the foreign policy of the United States.
4. The Defense Department needs to deal with constituents—including the public, Congress, the media, associations of retired military personnel, and the various national security-related associations. The acceptance of defense budgets, programs, and other defense activities all depend critically on the attitude of some or all of these constituents. These views therefore have to be taken into account. A great deal of consultation, explanation, and persuasion must be undertaken. For example, Elmer Staats, as the Director of the General Accounting Office, sent Secretary Weinberger a long letter on January 20, 1981, outlining his view of savings of $4 billion by 1985 and an additional list of $10 billion in annual savings that DoD should implement. These lists are two of many examples of constituency interface with DoD. A few specific comments on each of the four O's are given below.

Objectives. In the first section, Kirby advocates a rational system of government: "Government must identify goals for society as a whole." This is only one view as others might criticize the process as "sweaty" and disorganized.

Output. Government does provide goods and services but, in many cases, they are collective versus private goods. Also the private sector services (and goods) contain a subjective evaluation by the consumer.

Orientation. We should not overdraw the difference. By that I mean that the time horizon in government is not as short as the length of time of the political appointment. The permanent civil servant provides substantial continuity to government management. In fact, this has been a complaint of political administrations. They have often complained that it is difficult to move government management in new directions. Business has rotating managers but has a corporate structure that has sustaining mechanisms. The governmental sector has a process of insuring continuity by its "voluminous" rules and regulations.

Operations. Kirby implies that decision making in the private sector is more direct than in the public sector, but this observation, in my view, is not always correct. In many major corporations the management decision process is substantially convoluted, complex, and lengthy. Executive decisions at various levels are part of the political process. Corporations do not always have access to information to quantify major variables. A good example of this would be the recent financial crises and the information that some of the central banks had about the financial condition of different countries.

Next Kirby outlines the environmental characteristics in which government operates: the current lack of mutual trust, cynicism growing out of failed expectations, the complexities and size of government that suggest a decline in performance, unanticipated behavioral responses from attempted solutions that in turn lead to failure of the solution, and, finally, the complexity and general intertwining of problems that encourage incremental versus innovative approaches to solutions. Dr. Kirby quotes some polls in his talk. While most general polls about public sector government are negative, most pollsters find out that the voters support their own congressman—it is only those other 534 congressmen who are spending too much money.

In addition to some of the environmental characteristics that Dr. Kirby discusses, I would like to add two additional ones. First, a manager in the Pentagon has to operate in a goldfish bowl. If any of your memos are of interest to the press, they will be quoted in the national media, possibly the next day—including even, to some degree, classified information. This makes it extremely difficult to have a free flow of information within government. It is a function of the media to point out to the public any incompetence or mismanagement. Therefore, when a weapons system has cost overruns, the media, quite properly, report those overruns to the public. On the other hand, when the weapons system comes in under schedule and under cost, this achievement is not reported. I can understand why, if a weapons system comes in on schedule and on cost, this would not be reported, but it seems to me we should have symmetry. This lack of balance makes the job of management in the public sector more difficult. Second, external forces like Congress and the White House are more important than a rational systems analysis, because what may be a rational approach for the Department is not a rational approach for a Congressman. A Congressman may prefer a certain weapon system since the plant that produces that system is in his district.

One misconception that many people have is that all civil servants are lazy, worthless, and bureaucratic in the worst sense. My experience with government employees over two decades has been the opposite. Most of them are very dedicated and hard working. Recent attacks by all administrations on the public sector members do not contribute to innovative work.

Government must operate with efficiency and must get greater support from the public. Kirby says that government must be able to innovate, although this is against all the institutional pressures. In the third section of his paper, Kirby then proposes eight possibilities or proposals to foster innovation. Most of these proposals have been tried before in some form.

The first two—reform of the government structure and temporary institutional processes—have been tried by every new administration in this country and do not in general produce the desired results. As an interesting aside, Michael Kirby's government has a unique way of keeping itself going when Parliament cannot appropriate money. The Governor General is appointed by the Queen and has the authority to issue warrants to continue government. Our government does not have an equivalent process, as I am sure you are aware. Various parts of the federal bureaucracy have been shut down for periods of time due to the lack of an appropriations bill and a continuing resolution. One way to reform our government structure would be, of course, to have a Queen so that we could appoint a Governor General. On the serious side, a bill in Congress, the Budget Reform Act of 1982, proposes that we establish a two-year budget process, conferring congressional control over the budget, streamlining parts of the budget process, improving the legislative and budgetary process by providing additional time for oversight and other legislative activities, and providing stability and coherence for replenishing federal funds. Based on my experience in Washington, I believe that a bill of this type would significantly improve the overall financial structure of the government. It would allow more time for our governmental leaders to be innovative.

The initial impetus of ad hoc organizations is good, but many times they lose their effectiveness by lasting too long. Recently, an ad hoc group was created by the federal government. This ad hoc group, under the chairmanship of Ed Meese, is titled REFORM 88. It has an ambitious set of goals and objectives. The main goal would create a federal governmental management system based on a "holding company" approach with centralized policy and coordination, but with decentralized responsibility of agency heads for carrying out the programs. In recent years, differing reforms of the governmental management structure have been tried. They have all had varying degrees of success but were not continued as permanent government-wide initiatives.

Kirby's proposal on training is a good idea, but again it has been attempted with varying degrees of success. Unfortunately, in the civilian sector of the U.S. Government, we do not train our civilians as well as we do our military. The military has had what Clark Kerr has called the sandwich principle—that is, education, experience, education, experience, and so forth. Due to various pressures in the system, many of the best civilian people are not allowed, for various reasons, to pursue further education. A typical reason is that their military boss does not want to let them go because he is only there for three or so years and wants their output to make his performance better in that short period of time. Also there is a tendency of "out of sight, out of mind." People have gone on educational leaves and have arrived back on the job to find that they have been replaced with no equivalent or better position available. The military services have improved in this area in recent times. The Air Force has a Comptroller Cadre Program that identifies, trains, and tracks careers of selected civilians. The payoff is downstream but it looks promising. Finally, Kirby proposes training programs with greater emphasis on cultivating a public philosophy. I am confused on whether he is separating policy setting from policy administration.

The next proposal is an innovative compensation program. The bonus system was put into effect by the U.S. Congress. I do believe it is a definite improvement over the previous system. Unfortunately, the bonuses are small and limited. This system, combined with the low government pay cap, does not produce the motivation intended. We must get competitive wage scales in government.

Kirby's next idea, a retention of savings, is a good one, and the Defense Department has been trying this during the last two years. We have been frustrated by other government organizations such as the Office of Management and Budget, who say that savings of surplus lands must go to the Treasury. It is, therefore, no incentive for the base commander to dispose of the surplus government land. The Department has also tried to pass savings to a field commander if he is successful in various economies and efficiencies programs. So far, this has met with only limited success.

The next suggestion, information technology, is a very promising one for the future. The fifth generation computers and the application of new artificial intelligence (smart systems) techniques to various management processes can, in my view, encourage both innovativeness and creativity by managers.

I am a bit confused by his proposals on volunteerism. In the past, volunteerism was the primary mode for delivering any social goods, but it could not cope with the demands. This was why society turned to government to provide such services.

His eighth proposal is more a statement that innovation is needed in how government services are delivered, and Kirby outlines five options, each of which has been used by government. I certainly agree that government delivery of services is most like the private sector, in that it would be in this area that government can learn from business. However, the differences that he outlined earlier in his paper seemed to me to argue that the process of private sector experience will have to be tempered by these differences.

The lack of success of innovation in government has not been the absence of creative macro ideas by high-level management, but in being innovative about their implementation. In the last two years, we have redefined the Defense Department's Planning, Programming, and Budgeting System and also outlined thirty-two acquisition initiatives to improve defense purchases. Most everyone I have talked with agrees that these innovations are good and well thought-out. The main problem is to make sure that we implement them properly at all levels. Putting out a directive from the Secretary of Defense does not necessarily accomplish this. For example, one of the acquisition initiatives is to increase competition. Most everyone would agree with this, but I have already received several complaints that people in the field were making competitive awards for a one-person yearly contract every year, rather than, say, every third or fourth year. Also, many times political leaders make changes for symbolic reasons. They will not be around to be held accountable for the results, and the career bureaucracy understands this well.

One recent innovation in the financial management area was timely payment of military salaries. Our Congress approved an increase in military and civilian salaries when they passed the 1982 budget but did not appropriate funds until near the end of the fiscal year. This delay created definite problems in management. We could not meet the military federal payroll on 30 August. Congress had not yet passed the pay supplemental bill. In the last few days before the payroll date, we worked with the Adjutant General, Office of Management and Budget, and the Treasury to work out a legal way for us to meet this military payroll. The key innovative point was an idea to delay payments to the Treasury of income tax and social security payments made by the military.

Later in the paper Kirby indicates that innovation is an attitude and a process—a function of pride, energy, and creativity—and that it should and can permeate the individual in collective processes. He also indicates that new ways to do things evolve naturally. If so, how do we get innovative if that innovation flies in the face of the environment? In general, organizations do not foster innovation but are more likely to hamper it. Organizations can nurture innovation and creativity in the following well-known ways:

1. An organization will be creative to the extent that creativity exists in the top management group itself. The old adage about "doing what you say to do" is still true.
2. Management groups will be creative to the extent that top management cultivates an attitude of democracy toward the creative attitudes or ideas of its people. Respect and support are key prerequisites for a healthy environment that promotes responses from employees. Ideas must be listened to and not squelched. Research should be presented at a high level.
3. An organization will be creative if management provides it with the necessary tools of the trade: privacy, proper laboratory facilities, and many more.
4. Creativity in the organization will prevail to the extent that the administrative structure is flexible and opportunity oriented. The organization must abolish bottlenecks and eliminate wasted motion.
5. An organization should encourage managers to use outside sources of stimulus and inspiration. When I became Comptroller of the Department of Defense, I created a small Special Projects

Group that was outside the normal line organization. They have worked well with the line organization, and I believe they have contributed to innovation in the organization.

6. The stated organization goals should include innovation and creativity.

Innovation in government is a difficult subject, not because no one wants or can do it but rather because of the complexity of the environmental objectives. We must be able to teach ways of implementing innovative ideas in our management schools. Organization development has focused on micro problems to a large degree. What is needed is future research on the macro problems of implementation.

3 CHANGING APPROACHES TO ACCOUNTABILITY IN AN INCREASINGLY COMPLEX SOCIETY

Elmer B. Staats

I was pleased to accept the invitation to participate in this conference honoring Dean George Kozmetsky, who for the past 16 years has provided the University of Texas, College of Business Administration and Graduate School of Business, with outstanding and creative leadership. His contributions to higher education and to management fit well with the theme of this conference on creative and innovative management. Today's problems will increasingly challenge the best thinking which the nation can marshal if we are to achieve the goals that we all aspire to. Accountability is certainly one of these objectives.

I need not dwell at length on the severity of the problems that we face in both the public and private sectors. Our problems of high unemployment, high interest rates, and a depressed economy are well known. With reductions in taxes at the federal level—reductions that were designed to stimulate the economy and offset the tax cuts with increased revenues—we face massive deficits in the years ahead, and the depressed economy has continued. These deficits in turn have placed great pressure on interest rates, rates that have been major factors in the depressed conditions of the housing industry, the construction industry, and the automobile industry. Thus, we seem to have created a vicious cycle of uncertainties, the results of which cannot yet be foreseen.

Cutbacks in federal programs have placed additional burdens on state and local governments at a time when they too are faced with growing financial problems. Proposition 13 in California was one response to this problem. Similar actions have been taken or contemplated in many other states. Now there is talk of a constitutional amendment further restricting the role of the federal government and placing even greater burdens on the states.

In the private sector, nearly every company is going through a major belt-tightening, cost-cutting period. Bankruptcies have tripled in three years. The unemployment rate is approaching the level of the early 1930s, and the end is not yet in sight.

The nation's financial and economic problems have given new impetus to the major points that I would like to deal with today in my remarks. I would especially like to address myself today to the changing role of the accounting and auditing profession in this environment. I refer to the role that it is playing in assuring that our institutions—public and private—are accountable. It also faces new problems that will call for creative and innovative approaches in the years ahead.

Standard dictionaries provide several definitions of the terms "accounting" and "accountability"[1] but perhaps the most widely recognized is "to furnish a reckoning to someone of money received and paid out." This is the definition associated most directly with the traditional role of the accounting and auditing professions, but there is another that I believe more encompassing in today's complex society: "to give satisfactory reasons or an explanation for 'one's actions'" and to give "a good account of one's self." To be accountable is an obligation to account for one's acts in a responsible manner. Accountability, therefore, becomes the basis for the rule of law, the constitutional framework of our system of government, the rights of our citizenry, and assurance that government and nongovernment organizations discharge their obligations in a responsible manner.

Thus, we need to think of accountability in a broad framework. Let me illustrate this broader concept by citing several recent events.

Item: In a letter dated 10 August from the steel industry to the Secretary of Commerce, rejecting the latter's request that the industry accept the latest European Economic Community proposal to limit steel imports into the United States, it was stated that "we believe that the Europeans must in some way be held accountable for their violations of U.S. trade law . . . which have produced serious injury to the domestic steel industry." Failing agreement, the industry will take its case to the Court of International Trade.

Item: Eighteen members of the House of Representatives have filed suit in the U.S. District Court, arguing that the recently enacted tax law is unconstitutional on the grounds that the measure did not technically originate in the House of Representatives as required in the Constitution. The *Wall Street Journal* editorialized that the issue is not one of a technicality but "reflects the Founders' deep conviction that the raising of taxes should begin in the Chamber whose members are most accountable to the people."

Item: In Montreal, Canada, today the Third Annual Conference of the Canadian Comprehensive Auditing Foundation will conclude its session. The subject of the Conference: "Strengthening Public Sector Accountability."

Item: Next week, the International Federation of Accountants will hold its Twelfth International Congress of Accountants in Mexico City. More than 3,000 accountants and auditors will be convened to discuss their responsibilities under the general theme, "The Accounting Profession: Leadership Opportunities in a Changing World." One topic is "What Can The Accounting Profession Do for Government?" This is of particular interest to me in that it will involve Value-for-Money auditing of public expenditures.

Item: An article in the *Wall Street Journal* of 10 August entitled "SEC Goes Easier on Accountants, Relying More on Self-regulation" notes particularly that the SEC had dropped a rule that had discouraged auditors from expanding into fields such as management consulting. This is perhaps not of major importance in and of itself, but it is symbolic of the changing regulatory role of the SEC, affected in major part by the self-regulatory measures that have been adopted by the accounting profession in recent years. The *Wall Street Journal* in another article of 9 July, entitled "Accounting Scams Are on the Rise, Putting More Pressure on Auditors," points out that the accounting profession is still highly vulnerable when irregularities take place which the public believes that the auditor should have been responsible for preventing.

Item: The Audit Act under which the Malaysian Auditor General carries out his responsibilities was recently amended to require the Auditor General to ascertain whether monies spent had been applied for the purposes for which they were appropriated or authorized and carried out or managed efficiently "with due regard for economy or the avoidance of waste and extravagance." It was pointed out that prior audits which focused only on financial accountability were too narrow, and that the auditor in the future must address himself to the question of the efficiency and effectiveness of programs in achieving established objectives.

Item: How does accountability fit with the increased emphasis currently being given to programs of participative management and quality of working life? Is there a conflict between the philosophy of participative management and the more traditional methods of supervision and measuring employee performance—as individuals or groups—and rewarding them for outstanding work? Is there a conflict with respect to accountability, and, if so, how do we resolve the conflict?

As the above well illustrate the problems of accountability in American society are multifaceted and complex. An agenda for challenging the talents of all of us who are concerned with improving the processes by which accountability is rendered would be a long one indeed. But let me suggest a few which seem to me to be central to the broad issue.

A BROADER CHARTER FOR THE AUDITOR

In spite of the changes that have taken place in recent years, the conventional definition of the role of the accountant and auditor still tends to be one which is confined only to technical accounting and auditing for the accuracy of funds received and expended. Having said that, I should stress that there has been a tremendous change in the last ten years in the role of the auditor. The Auditing Standards promulgated by the General Accounting Office in 1972, with the help of the accounting profession and auditors at all levels of government, have now been widely accepted, not only in the United States but in other countries. The terms "operational," "performance," and "economy and efficiency" auditing are now synonomous with the extension of the auditor's role to include the manner in which programs are carried out and whether the programs are achieving the results intended. At the central auditing level in the Federal Government today, 90 percent of U.S. General Accounting Office work is now concerned with matters relating to economy, efficiency, and effectiveness of programs administered. To a lesser extent, this trend is noted in the work of the internal auditors in the agencies of the Federal Government and in many of our state and local governments as well. In Canada, Sweden, Australia, and many other countries, "value-for-money" and "managerial" and "program effectiveness" auditing are now well recognized and supported.

For those of us who are concerned with behavioral sciences, the extension of the work of the auditor is an interesting case study. The recipients of the audits—the legislator, the agency head, and the corporate official—would have found the extension of the concept to embrace program and efficiency audits either unclear or unwanted just a few years ago. The fact that the auditor has demonstrated that he can produce a product of value has done much to dissipate this fear and it has also dissipated the concern of members in the accounting profession that the auditor might be moving into troubled water and stormy weather. The legislation that has been enacted in many countries broadening the scope of the audit supports this.

Broadening the scope of the audit has brought with it a change in the makeup of the audit staff to include individuals with a wide variety of disciplines—engineering, operations analysis, economics, international relations, public health, and many others. Teaming individuals with widely varying disciplines improves the product and provides for innovation in the way that auditing is carried out. With it has come a new and satisfying challenge to the individual trained in accounting—namely, that his or her skills can be brought to bear upon problems of current and long-term concern, suggesting solutions to decision makers. The auditor increasingly is cast in a problem-solving mode.

In the public accounting profession, we have seen this development take a somewhat different form, with the expansion of the management consulting services offered by most if not all of the major accounting firms. The best result is one in which the financial audit function and the management consulting function interact with each other, each retaining its independence but recognizing that the financial audit may serve as one of its most important purposes the identification of problems that challenge the skills of the management consultant.

The internal auditor, certainly in the major commercial corporations, has shown a similar disposition to expand the scope of his product for management. I recently inquired of an outstanding internal auditor as to how much of his operational audit work was self-initiated and how much of it was requested by management. His reply was that in the beginning virtually all of it was self-initiated; now he finds the reverse to be true. I believe we could recite a similar experience within the Federal Government. The challenge to the internal auditor is to assure that his product is one that is relevant, objective, and sets forth options that are useful to management. One of the areas in which the internal auditor can play a particular role involves the adequacy of internal control systems. In part, responding to the enactment of the Foreign Corrupt Practices Act of 1977 and the extended use of computers in all phases of corporate work, the internal auditor is called upon to assure management that internal control systems are in place and adequate to prevent loss of financial control. Audit Committees of Boards of Directors now routinely probe the internal auditor as to the care that he has exercised in assuring that these controls are in place.

One of the more intriguing possibilities for the internal auditor is to include information in public financial statements to describe the operating results of the agency or corporation. For example, if a unit within a government agency has a mission to plant a certain number of trees in a fiscal year and does it for a specified number of dollars, it would be possible for the agency's financial statements to note that the trees were planted at that cost or less or that fewer trees were planted or that it cost more than planned. This type of supporting data in government financial statements could prove useful to management, to the Congress, and to the taxpayer. We may be seeing this type of data in government—and perhaps in corporate—financial statements within this decade.

INNOVATIVE AUDITING APPROACHES REQUIRED

One of the more interesting changes that we may see in the future is using auditors—particularly government auditors—to audit models of programs before these programs are undertaken and to render opinions on the reliability of factors used in estimating the cost of these programs before they are started. This has already proven to be a useful concept in the Federal Government and should be equally useful in corporate auditing. As you know, some of the largest of our Federal programs, such as Model Cities and the Food Stamp Programs, started at modest levels and grew to gigantic proportions, often to the surprise of those who initially approved them. In the future, this kind of unwelcome surprise may be eliminated if program models are competently and objectively audited and assessments of potential cost factors made known before development is undertaken.

I would like to take a moment to elaborate on this thought. As you know, a model is a simplified representation of the interrelationships among elements of some portion or aspect of reality. This definition can be applied to many different things, from a toy car to a full-scale prototype of a supersonic aircraft, from the game of Monopoly to a set of mathematical equations that represents the behavior of the national economy.

When it is impractical to manipulate a completed system itself, a model generally can be used to capture the system's key features. A model is thus an abstraction of reality that preserves only those features that are most relevant to its basic purpose.

Models, of course, must be used judiciously. However, because Congress is becoming increasingly interested in the use of models and because the number of more complex audits is growing, I predict that the General Accounting Office, in the future, will be doing more reviews using models.

GAO was able to develop models to evaluate how the Navy's spare engine support system for the F-14 engine would function using GAO's stock level proposal. This was done in conjunction with a report entitled "Alternatives Available For Reducing Requirements For Spare Aircraft Engines."

GAO also developed a model during its review of the Defense Department's plans for a new Naval hospital in San Diego. That model proved to be a better method than ones previously used to measure the need for acute care beds. The Defense Department now uses the model for determining the size of its new and replacement hospitals, and the Veterans Administration is expected to adapt the model to its hospital construction projects.

Another model was developed at GAO to evaluate the effect that the antirecession assistance of Title II of the Public Works Employment Act of 1976 has had on stimulating the economy during a downturn.

In addition to developing its own models, GAO has often used models developed by others in making its reviews. For example, it used models to determine the potential impact on trade of increased taxation of U.S. citizens employed overseas and to predict the probability that individuals will or will not file income tax returns.

From this, I think you can see that the role of models is growing in government and in all probability will continue to do so. Eventually, auditors in government as well as in private industry will have to become familiar with modeling concepts—including how to develop them and how to evaluate those developed by others.

Modeling, of course, places the auditor in the public sector in a role that is not usually found in the private sector. I think a useful point for discussion, however, would be the extent to which the reports of the external auditor and the corporate financial statements should include more future-oriented information in annual reports or otherwise. We are all familiar with the difficulties involved—the danger of misleading forecasts, possible adverse affects on the external auditor in the event that expectations are not realized, and the possibility that information would be used by competitors to their advantage. This function has, therefore, been largely left to the financial analyst.

However, as suggested in an article by John Burton and Patricia Fairfield,[2] this attitude may be changing. There are undoubtedly benefits that could accrue to management by reducing uncertainty among investors with respect to future prospects and plans for the corporation. With such a change in viewpoint, the accounting profession could substantially add to the capability of corporation management to provide such information. Future-oriented information for investors is being recognized increasingly by the standard-setting bodies. The SEC has lifted its prohibition on forecasts; the Financial Accounting Standards Board has identified the objective of financial statements as providing information that will allow investors to predict the amount, timing, and amount of uncertainty in cash flows; the American Institute of CPAs (AICPA) has also proposed such a role for accountants in reviewing financial forecasts.

I hesitate to use the phrase "social accounting" because it means different things to different people; however, I believe that increasingly in the future auditors will be doing work that could clearly be categorized under this term. For instance, I believe that we will find better ways to measure the costs and benefits of many things that today are imprecise and subject to much controversy, such as: whether the energy spent in certain pursuits is worth its cost to society; whether the quality of life of the community and workers is enhanced by certain pursuits; and whether the benefits of certain industries, including the products or services they produce and the profits and salaries generated, are worth the costs to society in terms of pollution and consumption of scarce resources.

I believe that we are in a society that will become increasingly concerned about these issues and will, in the future, insist that auditors and program analysts be called upon to help evaluate the costs and benefits involved in issues of social accounting.

Complicating the work of the auditor has been the sharply increased use of instrumentalities not directly administered by government employees to carry out government programs—the private corporation, the quasi-governmental organization, nonprofit groups, and international organizations. These take the form of subsidies, contracts, grants, cooperative agreements, and other arrangements. But they all have a common denominator in that they share accountability to their own management and to government. It is essential that these organizations be held accountable for the use of public monies. The real question is how we can build accountability into these organizations in such a way that government can be assured that funds are used wisely while at the same time avoiding direct governmental intervention and control. This concern about accountability versus independence is a real one for which to date no good answers have been supplied. The acceptance of high professional audit standards by external auditors is, of course, important. Here is an area that challenges the ingenuity and innovativeness of government and nongovernment auditors alike.

As more and more financial transactions are handled by automatic data processing, the first problem the auditor of the future is going to face is the virtual disappearance of paper transactions. Already such innovations as electronic funds transfer are becoming commonplace in the banking industry. What will auditors do when this paperless state becomes complete? Without records of paper transactions that occurred weeks or months ago, auditors will require new audit procedures to decide whether financial transactions were handled properly.

It is inevitable that these new procedures must allow auditors to perform their tests of transactions as they occur, since there will be no paper record to examine. And if that is the case, better audit planning will be needed so that the many tasks now performed sequentially can be performed more or less simultaneously. Auditors will also have to rely far more on the effective functioning of systems than they do now. Better techniques than we now have for testing such systems must be developed.

With paper transactions virtually eliminated and the auditors checking more into the adequacy of these systems, internal controls will become increasingly important. As many of us know, several organizations, including the AICPA's Commission on Auditors' Responsibilities—the Cohen Commission—have strongly suggested that public interest requires corporate reporting on the adequacy of internal control. In 1979, the Securities and Exchange Commission issued a proposal that would have required the managements of all corporations under its jurisdiction to report on the effectiveness of internal accounting controls and to describe any material weaknesses communicated by independent accountants that had not been corrected. The proposal was withdrawn in 1980 because an increasing number of companies were voluntarily presenting management reports on internal controls in their annual reports to stockholders so there was no apparent need to impose SEC requirements. The AICPA has also issued a statement on auditing standards—number 30, "Reporting On Internal Controls"—that allows the independent accountant to publicly report on a company's system of internal controls when a special study has been performed for that purpose.

With the recent passage of the Federal Managers Financial Accountability Act of 1982, it now seems certain that reporting on internal controls will soon become a reality not only for nearly all companies but also for all levels of government as well. The Act requires an annual report by the heads of all Federal departments and agencies, attesting to the effectiveness of their internal controls or, if necessary, outlining a schedule for strengthening any weaknesses found in their internal control system.

I believe that both internal as well as external auditors will be involved in the process to report annually on their systems of internal control. Internal auditors will be involved because internal accounting control is an area where the corporate internal auditor's depth and breadth of knowledge is superior to everyone else's—inside or outside the company. They will play a role in monitoring the company's internal control system, conducting comprehensive examinations of that system, evaluating it, and making recommendations for modifications.

Evaluating internal controls is going to become a major issue in the future. A difficult problem that must first be faced is that financial controls are changing—radically changing—as the direct result of the use of computers. Many functions performed today both in industry and in government would be virtually impossible without the computer. However, computers have greatly complicated the internal control problem.

One aspect of this problem is the computer's ability to cover distances of thousands of miles in minutes in completing a transaction. A purchase order may originate in New York, the receiving document in California, and the invoice in Washington, D.C.—the transaction being completed before any employee can examine any physical data relating to it. A purchase order is generated by the computer when stocks get too low; the goods are received and the computer is notified; and the computer matches the documents and authorizes a disbursement. Finally, the check is signed by signature insert in the computer and the transaction is completed with virtually no "human" examination.

What we will soon need is a complete new set of accounting controls based on computer operations. Moreover, as our reliance on computers increases, so will the need for these new control systems to be in good working order—for we will have nothing to rely upon to protect against fraud, abuse, and error except the adequacy of the control system.

Perhaps our greatest obstacle in achieving this goal of adequate control is time. While we have had roughly 500 years since the Italians invented double-entry bookkeeping to develop internal controls for manual systems—and even these controls are not perfect—we have had only about 20 years since computers have come into extensive use to adapt the internal control approach to computers—and the computer of today is radically different from what it was only a few short years ago. Much will have to be done to bring the internal controls in such systems to a level where we can feel confident about them, and we will need systems of surveillance to ensure that the controls we generate are used.

Of course, all controls will have to be weighed against the cost involved. A "risk analysis" of sorts will have to be made that assesses the potential damage that the lack of a control might permit and compares it against the potential cost of preventing that damage.

Management must make this decision, just as it must see that all the responsible officials cooperate in setting up the necessary controls and that the personnel resources needed to keep them effective are devoted to the task.

The GAO has been concerned for some time that the audit coverage accorded computer-based systems does not measure up to the quality needed to assure that proper results are obtained. A GAO study led to the development of additional audit standards to provide guidance for auditors involved. These standards became effective in February 1981. They were incorporated into the latest version of the GAO audit standards, entitled "Standards For Audit Of Governmental Organizations, Programs, Activities And Functions."

ASSURANCE OF HIGH PROFESSIONAL STANDARDS

Before leaving this particular discussion, note should be taken of the important steps to assure the public that the auditors are adhering to the highest standards of the profession. I refer to the establishment of the Financial Accounting Standards Board, the Public Oversight Board, the Peer Review System, and to such internal arrangements as the Public Review Board of Arthur Andersen and Company.

All of this is reassuring, but problems remain. How far can we legitimately expect the auditor to go in detecting deliberate efforts to conceal questionable accounting practices by management itself? In recent months, three major firms have acknowledged that some of their employees have done so. Allegations have been made with respect to several other firms. The temptation for abuse is greatly increased in a period of economic recession such as the present. During such a period, there are also pressures to reduce audit fees and audit coverage. This is true in both private industry and in government.

Is there a real danger that auditors may be too anxious to please their clients, willing to accept doctored records as short cuts to increase their own profitability? Detecting fraud is not a responsibility of the auditor by law, but the auditor is usually tainted if fraud takes place. If a business deal goes sour and management is alleged to have paid too much for an acquisition or shows poor judgment, stockholders may presume that the auditor must have known about the facts and should have disclosed these facts to the public or to the stock-holders. This happens with increasing frequency in suits brought before juries usually sympathetic to the stockholders' cause—a jury not knowledgeable and even less interested in the intricacies of what we call generally accepted accounting and auditing standards.

The auditor is thus caught up in what has been described as an increasingly litigious society where increasingly accountability is rendered in the courts rather than through the administrative or the legislative process or by professional standards of ethics and performance. The Carnegie Corporation, in its Annual Report for 1981, concedes that the courts have helped to insure educational equity for minority children and have helped to build minority leadership, but it adds that "use of the courts indicates the failure of the legislative and executive departments of government to deal fairly with the claims of excluded groups. Decisions have been left to the courts by default, and sometimes by design, because of the moral as well as the legal authority of the judiciary." The Manville Corporation, in its announcement of 26 August that it was seeking relief from litigation through Chapter 11 of the Bankruptcy Act, said about the same thing: "No other country uses the court litigation system to provide compensation for occupational disease." It added that the court system with separate individual trials is too inefficient and haphazard for a massive problem involving an anticipated mass of more than 50,000 suits, 20,000 of which have already been filed.

Is all this litigious activity an abuse of accountability, a default on the legislative and executive decisionmaking process, or a problem without a solution?

The auditor's role in fraud prevention and detection is not clearly defined as of today. This is an area where problems have been building in recent years. Some believe the problems first surfaced after Watergate, when investigations made it clear that many corporations had made questionable or illegal payments—including domestic political contributions and payments to foreign officials to obtain or maintain business. These problems, combined with such fraudulent activities as the Equity Funding scandal have made the Securities and Exchange Commission, some members of the Congress, and the public critical of the auditing profession for failing to prevent and detect such irregularities.

Here again is an area with equal applicability to the Federal Government. Concern about fraud, abuse, and error was a major consideration in the creation by the Congress of Offices of Inspector General in the major departments and agencies. That legislation requires the Inspectors General to comply with standards established by the Comptroller General.

Responding to the same concern, the GAO established a Fraud Prevention Task Force within the General Accounting Office in the mid-1970s. It subsequently issued a report, entitled "Federal Agencies Can And Should Do More To Combat Fraud In Government Programs," which pointed out that no one knows the magnitude of fraud and abuse against the Government. Hidden within legitimate undertakings, it usually goes unreported and undetected.

Where management control systems are properly developed and are functioning properly, the possibility of fraud, theft, or error is greatly diminished. Conversely, where the systems do not exist or are not being used properly, the opportunities to defraud the government and the possibility of error increase dramatically.

CONCLUDING REMARKS

I might summarize some of what I have been saying as follows:

- An evolution of the audit function that is already in evidence will continue toward what are called "expanded scope" or "comprehensive audits" where the former refers to any significant expansion beyond the present "financial attest" audit and where the latter refers to a further expansion in which all or any activity of management is comprehended in what is subject to audit, with a resulting report that provides an evaluation of management performance and accomplishments in the selected area. This includes not only selection of the area for audit but also an assumption of responsibility for the report by the auditors to whatever audiences might be pertinent.

- Expansion to audit of planned future activities as well as audit and evaluation of past records and accomplishments will be a part of this evolution. Again, part of this is already occurring with the relaxation of previous AICPA restrictions on audits of financial forecasts, but I see it as evolving to other areas as well, especially those areas where mathematical or computerized models of management activities can or should be used.

- I see these audit extensions occurring in private enterprise as well as public agency audits including extension of audit activities to the presidents' report, or, rather, the whole corporate report, as well as the financial statements and its footnotes even in attest audits. These audits will need to be conducted with third party needs for reports in mind and the reports will need to be designed with a variety of different audiences besides the members of only the financial-investment community.

- More generally we need to do much more in the way of experimentation with new types of government-industry cooperation (witness, e.g., Japan) and related institutional innovations. This needs to be accompanied by vigorous growth (and experiments) in enhanced accountability. Ideally the latter might allow for departures from compliance even with laws or regulations when (a) management can justify such departures and (b) it is virtually certain that effectively functioning accountability systems will require such justifications.

To meet these new challenges the auditors of the future will have to have extensive and continuing education. Auditors will have to be much more proficient in data processing, for example, since virtually all transactions will be handled electronically. Training in fraud prevention and detection will become standard in auditing curricula.

Internal and external auditors will have a closer reporting relationship to audit committees composed of directors outside the organization, thus giving audit a new independence that will improve audit reporting. There will be an increase in the number of audits that involve determining the economy and efficiency of operations and the effectiveness with which governmental and corporate missions are being carried out. Auditors will be involved in social accounting issues and in auditing companies that operate quite differently from those we see today.

Much more information will be included in government financial statements to facilitate better evaluations of their operations. Governmental financial statements at state and local levels will provide improved financial reporting, particularly in the disclosure of unfunded or underfunded pension fund liabilities.

Paper transactions will virtually be eliminated, and auditors will have to review transactions as they occur. Moreover, they will concentrate more on tests of systems than on testing individual transactions.

Internal controls will be better developed and more thoroughly understood by management. However, management will have to increase their reliance on auditors to see that controls are functioning properly.

New auditing procedures will be developed that provide greater assurance against fraud. Auditors who fail to follow these procedures will be held accountable for serious instances of fraud.

In conclusion I return to the illustrations that I referred to in my opening remarks today. Concerns about accountability of individuals and institutions—public and private—will not diminish; they will continue and grow because accountability is basic to democratic society. The accounting and auditing profession can provide much of the creativity and innovation to assure that these concerns are met.

NOTES TO CHAPTER 3

1.   See, e.g., *Kohler's Dictionary for Accountants*. 1983. 6th ed. Englewood Cliffs, N.J.: Prentice-Hall, Inc.
2.   Burton, John, and Patricia Fairfield. 1982. "Auditing Evolution in a Changing Environment." *Auditing: A Journal of Practice and Theory* 1, no. 2 (Winter).

IMPROVED ACCOUNTABILITY AND COMPREHENSIVE AUDIT AS PORTENTS FOR THE FUTURE

Neil C. Churchill

I am in basic agreement with Elmer Staats's paper, and I wish to take this opportunity to compliment him both on his vision and, more importantly, on the role he has played in bringing about many of the developments undergirding the accountability he has described. There are many aspects of his paper I would like to comment upon but I have selected three for my discussion and counterpoint.

ACCOUNTABILITY AS A SUBSTITUTE FOR REGULATION

The first is to point out that accountability, when known in advance, can influence the actions of a business or governmental decision maker toward doing what ought to be done. This is, in many ways, more powerful than writing a number of detailed regulations that prescribe what is and is not to take place. With accountability, a decision maker has a better idea of what should be done than can be written into regulations. Indeed, a study of hospital utilization reviews demonstrated that substituting a peer audit for detailed regulation shortened the length of stay in hospitals for normal patients without hurting the quality of patient care and without requiring much in the way of a bureaucracy.[1] With increasingly complex insti-

93

tutions and rapidly changing contexts, accountability can be, in many instances, much more effective than regulation.

THE INTERRELATIONSHIP BETWEEN AUDIT SCOPE AND AUDIT CRITERIA

My second set of comments point up the interrelationship that exists between extending the scope of audits and developing appropriate audit criteria. Let me do this by first building a model of an audit.

The Audit

An audit involves the following four basic components, with the fifth quite common in most audit situations:

1. A *set of actions*, or evidence of actions, that are to be examined

2. A *set of criteria* held by the auditor against which these actions are compared

3. An *examiner* who makes an objective comparison of actions against the criteria—where "objective" is operationally translated into "independent" and independence is where the auditors penalty/reward structure is affected only by the quality of his examination and not by other possible results of his comparison

4. A *report* of the results of the examination to a third party—neither the auditor nor the auditee—who is concerned with the actions under audit[2]

5. A *set of recommendations* that, if implemented, will move the actions examined into closer correspondence with the audit criteria. Recommendations, by the way, are less extensive in private sector audits than in the public sector.

Utilizing this model or definition of auditing we can see that Dr. Staats is predicting an expansion in the scope of the actions subject to audit. Indeed, instead of narrow financial transactions, auditors are looking at management's strategic and operational decisions and in doing so they are utilizing the following criteria:[3]

- *Compliance* of actions with some preset criteria (either operational or financial)

- *Efficiency* in the quantity and character of the economic resources used or received

- *Effectiveness* of management in both stating its goals or objectives and then in attaining them

- *Propriety*, first of the objectives pursued and second of the methods and processes used.

One interesting examination that illustrates what is now coming to be called a "comprehensive audit" is the General Accounting Office's audit of the Federal Bureau of Investigation in the late 1970s. I quote from *U.S. News and World Report*: "That report [the GAO Audit Report] accused the Bureau of misusing its resources [inefficiencies] by spying on domestic 'radicals' [improper objectives] in ways that were of doubtful legality [propriety of methods] and [fortunately] produced 'few tangible results' [lack of effectiveness]." Note the purpose of the audit—efficiency, effectiveness, and propriety of both methods used and objectives pursued—a far cry from a basic financial accounting audit.

The Interrelationships

This model of the audit process points up the close linkage required between the scope of actions audited and the audit criteria. Any extension of the audit into managerial areas requires quite explicit criteria with which to judge the actions examined or a very knowledgeable (almost a peer) auditor who augments the explicit criteria with his knowledge of the audited area. As the scope of actions audited expands, both the criteria used and the background and training of the auditor must be extended—sometimes criteria leads scope; sometimes scope leads criteria. Let me explicate this point with two of the innovations noted by Dr. Staats—future oriented statements and audits of current values. Both innovations are taken from one annual report—that of Days Inns of America, Inc. 1983[4]—and are an example of what George Kozmetsky called for in his paper (also in this volume) dealing with "the use of present realities to shed light on future developments and problems."

The first involves Days Inns' publication of a report (see Exhibit 3-1) detailing five years of forecasted income and stockholders' equity—a gutsy thing to do—and exemplifies Dr. Staats's com-

Exhibit 3-1. Consolidated Statements of Forecasted Income and Stockholders' Equity.

For the Year Ending September 30,	1984	1985	1986	1987	1988
Net Revenue:					
Lodging	$170,714,000	$195,554,000	$223,925,000	$258,342,000	$300,425,000
Food, gasoline and novelties	68,539,000	80,424,000	94,912,000	111,261,000	130,618,000
Franchise fees	7,976,000	9,424,000	10,811,000	12,161,000	13,362,000
Rental income	2,780,000	2,959,000	3,137,000	3,325,000	3,521,000
Other income	9,205,000	10,464,000	11,430,000	12,516,000	13,746,000
Gains on sales of properties	10,000,000	12,000,000	14,000,000	15,000,000	16,000,000
	269,214,000	310,825,000	358,215,000	412,605,000	477,672,000
Costs and Expenses:					
Cost of food, gasoline and novelties	38,862,000	43,628,000	49,291,000	55,542,000	62,931,000
Selling, general, administrative and operating expenses	151,172,000	176,219,000	204,085,000	236,297,000	274,839,000
Depreciation and amortization	20,501,000	22,311,000	24,802,000	27,983,000	31,945,000
Interest expense, net of interest income	28,674,000	33,271,000	38,296,000	44,475,000	51,911,000
	239,209,000	275,429,000	316,474,000	364,297,000	421,626,000
Income before provision for income taxes	30,005,000	35,396,000	41,741,000	48,308,000	56,046,000
Provision for income taxes	11,502,000	13,025,000	15,541,000	18,141,000	21,178,000
Net income	$ 18,503,000	$ 22,371,000	$ 26,200,000	$ 30,167,000	$ 34,868,000
Stockholders' equity	$ 74,697,000	$ 97,018,000	$123,218,000	$153,385,000	$188,253,000

Exhibit 3-1. continued

Occupancy	70.0%	71.0%	72.0%	72.5%	73.0%
Average room rate	$33.00	$35.25	$37.00	$39.00	$41.50
Number of company hotel/motel openings	12	15	17	19	21
Number of franchise hotel/motel openings	9	8	8	8	8
Number of company hotel/motel sales	8	8	8	8	8
Number of hotels/motels disfranchised	6	4	4	4	4
Total rooms at year end (operating and under construction)	46,500	47,800	49,500	51,300	53,300

Source: Days Inns of America, Inc. 1983 Annual Report.

Exhibit 3-2.   Report of Independent Accounts on Statements of
Forecasted Income and Stockholders' Equity.

To the Board of Directors and Stockholders of Days Inns of America Inc.

The Consolidated Statements of Forecasted Income and Stockholders' Equity of Days Inns of America, Inc. for each of the five years in the period ending September 30, 1988, including the assumptions made by Management in preparation of these forecasts, are Management's estimate of the most probable results of operations for the forecast periods. Accordingly, the forecasts reflect Management's judgement based on present circumstances of the most likely set of conditions and its most likely course of action.

We have made a review of such financial forecasts in accordance with applicable guidelines of the American Institute of Certified Public Accountants for a review of a financial forecast. Our review include procedures to evaluate both the assumptions used by Management and the preparation and presentation of the forecasts. We have no responsibility to update the report for events and circumstances occurring after the date of this report. The summarized historical financial information presented with the forecasts for comparative purposes is taken from the financial statements of the Company for the year ended September 30, 1983, which we have examined and issued our report thereon dated November 18, 1983.

Based on our review, we believe that the accompanying financial forecasts are presented in conformity with applicable guidelines established by the American Institute of Certified Public Accountants for presentation of a financial forecast. We believe that the underlying assumptions provide a reasonable basis for Management's forecasts. However, some assumptions inevitably will not materialize and unanticipated events and circumstances may occur; therefore, the actual results achieved during the forecast periods will vary from the forecasts, and the variations may be material.

Price Waterhouse

Atlanta, Georgia
December 2, 1983

Source: Days Inns of America, Inc. 1983 Annual Report.

ments on the desirability of future-oriented statements. The statements themselves take one page, the company's policy on forecasting one-half page, and then there are two and one-half pages of "assumptions made by management in the preparation of these forecasts." This is followed by the auditor's report on the forecasted information (Exhibit 3-2).

Days Inns also compares this year's actual 1983 income against last year's forecasted income for the same year (Exhibit 3-3). These statements are, in my opinion, close to the ultimate in financially oriented disclosure. What is important to notice is that the necessary criteria have been developed to extend the use of budget versus actual reports; only an audit report on explanations of the deviations is missing.[5] As this series of statements for Days Inns shows, only the (perhaps understandable) reluctance of management in many other companies to have their forecasts disclosed and their performance compared holds back wider adoption of this extension of corporate accountability.

Days Inns also prepares and publishes another statement predicted by Dr. Staats—a complete balance sheet stated in both historical and current value terms (Exhibit 3-4). In this case the scope of what is being audited, complete current value statements, anticipates professional criteria. An examination of the auditor's report on the current value statements (Exhibit 3-5) contains three qualifying paragraphs following the unqualified opinion on historical cost. Incidentally, a statement of the real estate appraisal follows the auditor's opinion. I hope that financial reports such as those of Days Inns stimulate the development of more explicit criteria for inflation adjusted statements. One need only consider the 100+ percent inflation in Brazil and Israel to demonstrate such a need.

Days Inns, by the way, is a privately held corporation that claims to be the sixth largest full-service lodging chain in the United States with 325 lodging facilities in thirty-three states and one Canadian province as of the date of the Annual Report—30 September 1983. Since 1977 it has had a compound growth rate of 14.8 percent in sales and 26.7 percent in before-tax profits.

I have been espousing comprehensive auditing over a broader set of actions, but there is a cost to accountability. That is my third point.

Exhibit 3-3. Comparison of Actual to Forecasted Income and Stockholders' Equity.

For the Year Ending September 30, 1983	Actual	Forecasted	Variance
Net Revenue:			
Lodging	$145,185,000	$143,556,000	$ 1,629,000
Food, gasoline and novelties	63,198,000	63,800,000	(602,000)
Franchise fees	7,820,000	8,233,000	(413,000)
Rental income	1,771,000	2,231,000	(460,000)
Other income	5,675,000	5,811,000	(136,000)
Gains on sales of properties	9,903,000	—	9,903,000
	233,552,000	223,631,000	9,921,000
Costs and Expenses:			
Cost of food, gasoline and novelties	37,477,000	37,767,000	290,000
Selling, general, administrative and operating expenses	127,199,000	131,707,000	4,508,000
Depreciation and amortization	18,695,000	17,819,000	(876,000)
Interest expense, net of interest income	24,036,000	26,182,000	2,146,000
	207,407,000	213,475,000	6,068,000
Income before provision for income taxes	26,145,000	10,156,000	15,989,000
Provision for income taxes	9,725,000	3,859,000	(5,866,000)
Net Income	$ 16,420,000	$ 6,297,000	$ 10,123,000
Stockholders' equity	$ 56,194,000	$ 46,444,000	$ 9,750,000

Exhibit 3-3. continued

Occupancy	69.1%	68.0%	1.1%
Average room rate	$30.06	$29.75	$ .31
Number of company hotel/motel openings	13	8	5
Number of franchise hotel/motel openings	1	0	1
Number of company hotel/motel sales	7	0	7
Number of hotels/motels disfranchised	13	5	(8)
Total rooms at year end (operating and under construction)	45,416	45,300	116

Comments on 1983 Results of Operations

Overview: The Company reported income before provision for income taxes of $26,145,000 compared to a forecast of $10,156,000. The increase in profitability resulted from gains on sales of properties of $9,903,000, higher occupancy, lower administrative and operating expenses as well as reduced interest expense. This favorable performance reflects the impact of several new marketing programs coupled with a resurgence in interstate travel attributable to an improving economy and the opening success of EPCOT. Increases in both occupancy and average room rate, combined with effective cost controls, resulted in earnings well above forecasted levels. Gains on the sales of properties reflect a commitment by management to sell properties not meeting performance objectives or fitting the Company's strategic plan.

Source: Days Inns of America, Inc. 1983 Annual Report.

Exhibit 3-4. Consolidated Balance Sheets (Historical Cost) and Statements of Current Values.

Assets	September 30, 1983		September 30, 1982	
	Statement of Current Values	Balance Sheet (Historical Cost)	Statement of Current Values	Balance Sheet (Historical Cost)
Current assets:				
Cash	$ 2,799,000	$ 2,799,000	$ 2,291,000	$ 2,291,000
Money market investments	20,555,000	20,555,000	9,509,000	9,509,000
Accounts and notes receivable, net of allowance for doubtful accounts of $602,000 and $688,000:				
Franchisees	2,079,000	2,079,000	1,310,000	1,310,000
Refundable income taxes	—	—	1,792,000	1,792,000
Other	6,383,000	6,454,000	4,870,000	4,979,000
Retail inventories and supplies	2,959,000	2,576,000	2,585,000	2,204,000
Prepaid expenses	3,663,000	3,663,000	1,492,000	1,492,000
Total current assets	38,438,000	38,126,000	23,849,000	23,577,000
Property and equipment	592,496,000	396,667,000	446,108,000	332,625,000
Less: Accumulated depreciation	—	(81,568,000)	—	(72,715,000)
Franchisee and other notes and accounts receivable, net of allowance for doubtful accounts of $314,000 in 1982	17,313,000	18,019,000	9,734,000	9,050,000
Franchise agreements	19,993,000	—	20,570,000	—
Deferred charges	7,578,000	7,578,000	6,553,000	6,553,000
Invested bond proceeds	22,203,000	22,203,000	28,359,000	28,359,000
Other assets	3,145,000	2,927,000	905,000	668,000
	$701,166,000	$403,952,000	$536,078,000	$328,117,000

Exhibit 3–4. continued

Current liabilities:				
Notes and bonds payable	$ 14,623,000	$ 13,547,000	$ 9,032,000	$ 11,728,000
Accounts payable	9,301,000	9,301,000	8,480,000	8,480,000
Accrued expenses and other liabilities	12,663,000	12,663,000	9,001,000	9,001,000
Income taxes payable	2,628,000	2,628,000	—	—
Current liabilities excluding deferred income taxes	39,215,000	38,139,000	26,513,000	29,209,000
Deferred income taxes	2,752,000	2,752,000	3,665,000	3,665,000
Total current liabilities	41,967,000	40,891,000	30,178,000	32,874,000
Notes and bonds payable, due after one year	269,590,000	291,124,000	221,508,000	248,704,000
Income taxes on realization of estimated current values	92,581,000	—	68,666,000	—
Real estate commissions on realization of estimated current values	18,172,000	—	13,613,000	—
Deferred income taxes	6,612,000	6,612,000	2,977,000	2,977,000
Deferred income and other liabilities	8,944,000	8,944,000	3,107,000	3,107,000
Minority interest in consolidated subsidiary companies	6,231,000	187,000	1,018,000	516,000

(*Exhibit 3–4. continued overleaf*)

Exhibit 3–4. continued

Liabilities and Stockholders' Equity	September 30, 1983		September 30, 1982	
	Statement of Current Values	Balance Sheet (Historical Cost)	Statement of Current Values	Balance Sheet (Historical Cost)
Stockholders' equity:				
Common stock $.10 per value—1,100,000 shares authorized, 386,805 shares issued	64,000	64,000	64,000	64,000
Capital surplus	8,818,000	8,818,000	8,642,000	8,642,000
Retained earnings	49,846,000	49,846,000	33,796,000	33,796,000
Treasury stock at cost—33,949 and 34,862 shares	(2,534,000)	(2,534,000)	(2,563,000)	(2,563,000)
Unrealized appreciation before estimated costs on realization of current values	311,628,000	—	237,351,000	—
Current value equity	367,822,000		277,290,000	
Less: Potential costs on realizauon of current values:				
Income taxes	(92,581,000)	—	(68,666,000)	—
Real estate commissions	(18,172,000)	—	(13,613,000)	—
Total stockholders' equity	257,069,000	56,194,000	195,011,000	39,939,000
	$701,166,000	$403,952,000	$536,078,000	$328,117,000

Source: Days Inns of America, Inc. 1983 Annual Report.

Exhibit 3-5. Report of Independent Accountants on Historical Cost and Current Value Consolidated Financial Statements.

To the Board of Directors and Stockholders of Days Inns of America, Inc.

Report on Consolidated Financial Statements (Historical Cost)

In our opinion, the accompanying Consolidated Balance Sheets (Historical Cost) and the related Consolidated Statements of Income of Stockholders' Equity and of Changes in Financial Position present fairly the financial position of Days Inns of America, Inc. and its subsidiaries at September 30, 1983 and 1982, and the results of their operations and the changes in their financial position for the years then ended, in conformity with generally accepted accounting principles applied on a consistent basis after restatement for the change, with which we concur, in the method of accounting for capitalization of interest cost on tax-exempt borrowings as described in the Notes to Consolidated Financial Statements (Historical Cost). Our examinations of these statements were made in accordance with generally accepted auditing standards and accordingly included such tests of the accounting records and such other auditing procedures as we considered necessary in the circumstances.

Report on Consolidated Statements of Current Values

In addition to the foregoing examination, we have applied additional procedures in connection with the Consolidated Statements of Current Values of Days Inns of America, Inc., and its subsidiaries as of September 30, 1983 and 1982. Our additional procedures included (1) review of the 1983 and 1982 operating and financial information furnished to Landauer Associates, Inc. for their use in reviewing the Company's estimate of current values, (2) tests of the compilation of the current value data, and (3) discussion with Company officials.

As described in the Note to Consolidated Statements of Current Values, the Consolidated Statements of Current Values provide information about the Company which is not provided by the historical cost financial statements. Such current value information differs from information prepared in accordance with generally accepted accounting principles utilized for historical cost financial statements. Authoritative criteria have not been established for preparation and presentation of current value information.

The Consolidated Statements of Current Values represent the values estimated to be realizable in an orderly disposition of the Company's individual assets and liabilities (after provision for estimated income taxes and real estate commissions) rather than the market value of the Company taken as a whole.

In our opinion, based upon the procedures set forth in the second preceding paragraph, the Consolidated Statements of Current Values of Days Inns of America, Inc. and its subsidiaries as of September 30, 1983 and 1982 have been prepared on the basis described in the accompanying Note to Consolidated Statements of Current Values.

Price Waterhouse

Atlanta, Georgia
November 18, 1983

Source: Days Inns of America, Inc. 1983 Annual Report.

COST OF ACCOUNTABILITY

The Impact of the Evaluation

Whenever the topic of increased accountability is discussed, those opposed cite the deleterious effects of having someone second guess management's decisions and do so with 20/20 hindsight. This, the argument continues, would make management cautious, and in areas where there are risks and where judgment is required, management would take the least risky decisions—ones that would make it less subject to criticism should the chosen course of action fail. Thus innovative leaps of judgment would be obviated, more money would be spent in justifying actions, and the quality of management would decline.

This is an argument that has been used against almost all extensions of accountability—for no one likes to have constraints placed on their actions. Yet in many instances, accountability has produced improved performance and thus countered the argument.

It is unfortunately true that where the criteria for evaluating or taking the actions are ill-specified and where, simultaneously, the auditors are unfamiliar with or unsympathetic to the qualitative and situational aspects of the decision, increased accountability can have pernicious effects that may overbalance its salutory ones. The auditor's criteria must comprehend management's own action criteria for accountability to have maximum effect; and the auditor's report must be sufficiently knowledgeable to use the criteria well. These are appropriate research topics in creative and innovative management.

The Cost of Doing the Evaluation

My final point in evaluating the cost of accountability involves the cost of producing the accountability—the cost of *doing* the audit, of *preparing* the necessary forms, and of *complying* with reporting regulations. These costs, in most cases, are considerably less than the perceived value of holding the decision maker accountable, but too much accountability applied too broadly can be socially ineffective. Currently there is considerable pressure to reduce government-required paper work at the reporting level. I will limit myself, however, to addressing this problem on the audit level.

Two areas of study are currently underway within the accounting profession that focus on small, closely-held companies. The first deals primarily with *auditing* standards and concerns the accountant's overload.[6] The other involves *accounting* standards and is termed "Baby GAAP"—generally accepted accounting principles for smaller, private or closely-held companies.[7] The *accounting overload* comes from the many regulations, disclosure requirements, and auditing procedures that have been designed to ensure adequate financial accountability in giant multinational companies. These include careful disclosure of transactions of interrelated parties, detailed supporting schedule of loans, receivables, pension benefits and the like— audit procedures that are complex, time-consuming and, hence, expensive.

The argument over Baby–GAAP raises a question of whether there can be a conceptual foundation for accounting principles that is different as between small, privately or closely-held companies and larger, broadly-held corporations. And, if so, can it result in a reduction of the very high cost (proportionately) that small companies incur to have "certified accountability." There is a growing feeling that the cost is often not worth the candle.

One theoretical basis for a differentiation might be the familiarity or "proximity" of the recipients of small company statements to the audited entity. These recipients usually know the company, the owner-manager, the geographic and economic setting of the enterprise, the related activities of the owners, their other business investments, and so forth. Indeed, the recipients of the statements are usually either the owner's family or the local or regional bank— both of whom have considerable knowledge of the management, the company, and management's related interests. Further, potential owners of the company are either nonexistent or conduct fairly comprehensive preacquisition studies. By contrast, the owners, or potential owners, of a public company usually know the management only through the newspapers and the annual report and only a few creditors may have extensive knowledge of the company. The others are just part of a lending pool. There are clearly differences in proximity and differences in information needs as between users of these two different reports—as depicted in Figure 3–1.

Whether or not the concept of entity-proximity can differentiate between layers of accountability, or whether other constructs will work, the need to explicitly consider costs with benefits rises as ac-

Figure 3-1. A Portrayal of Differences in Management-Owner-Creditor Relations.

SMALL AND CLOSELY HELD COMPANIES

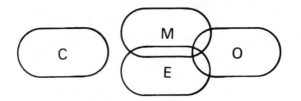

LARGE AND WIDELY HELD COMPANIES

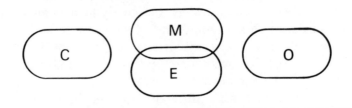

M = Management; O = Owners; E = Enterprise; C = Creditors.

countability *properly* increases in the public and private sector. What is needed is a balanced extension of this most powerful method of dealing with the increased complexity of our society and this in turn requires a better understanding of both sides of the accountability issue.

SUMMARY

I have tried to provide three counterpoints to Elmer Staats' paper: (1) to give explicit consideration of accountability as a substitute for detailed regulation in an increasingly complex society, (2) to point out the intersection of the scope of the audit with evaluative criteria and the need to develop both as accountability expands, and finally (3) consideration of balancing all the costs and benefits of accountability as accountability audits are applied to a wider range of managerial plans and actions.

NOTES

1. See N. C. Churchill, W. W. Cooper and V. Govindarajan, "Effects of Audits on the Behavior of Medical Professionals Under the Bennett Amendment," *Auditing: A Journal of Practice and Theory* 1, no. 2 (Winter 1982): 69–90. These audits also seemed to increase the length of stay (as they should have done) for smaller numbers of patients requiring special attention and treatment—for example, because of multiple diagnoses and/or the advanced ages of these patients.

2. This report can be eliminated and you can still have an audit and produce audit effects, but in practice the third party report is an essential part of accountability. See N. C. Churchill, "Behavioral Effects of an Audit: An Experimental Study" (Ph.D. dissertation, Ann Arbor: Graduate School of Business, University of Michigan, 1962).

3. See N. C. Churchill and W. W. Cooper, "Comprehensive Auditing," Harvard Business School Working Paper, 78–45. Boston: Division of Research, Harvard Business School, 1978.

4. Days Inns of America, Inc., *1983 Annual Report*, 2751 Buford Highway N.E., Atlanta, Ga. 30324.

5. See the comments and explanations provided by management at the end of Exhibit 3–3, which are not audited or at least they are not referenced in Exhibit 3–2. Further discussion of this aspect of such audits of forecasted statements may be found in W.W. Cooper, N. Dopuch, and T. Keller, "Budgetary Disclosure and Other Suggestions for Improving Accounting Reports," *The Accounting Review* (October 1968): 640–48.

6. American Institute of CPAs Special Committee to Study Accounting Standards Overload (New York: American Institute of CPAs. In progress.)

7. American Institute of CPAs, *Report of the Special Committee on Small and Medium-Sized Firms* (New York: American Institute of CPAs, 1980), pp. 11–13.

SOCIOECONOMIC REPORTING AND EXPANDED ACCOUNTABILITY FOR MANAGEMENT ACTIONS

David F. Linowes

INTRODUCTION

The paper by Comptroller-General Elmer Staats is a comprehensive and thoughtful presentation of developments that have been going on in accounting and auditing in recent years. These are developments in which the profession has been moving its horizons for service beyond the traditional "measurement and communication of business and economic data," for accountants, and the attest function for auditors.

We are privileged to have the subject covered for us by the former Comptroller-General of the United States, Elmer Staats. During his fifteen-year tenure at the General Accounting Office, Dr. Staats has done more to broaden the horizons of the accountant and auditor in government than any other person. This, it should be noted, was accomplished by a person who was not originally trained in accounting.

I was especially interested to learn from the paper that today 90 percent of the work of the U.S. General Accounting Office is concerned with matters relating to "economy, efficiency and effectiveness of programs administered." This is a remarkable achievement, for traditionally trained practitioners generally are less than enthusiastic about moving into extended areas of service. I suspect this

111

results from the fact that in most professional accounting firms the fastest career track is with established technical accounting and auditing, traditionally practiced. Nevertheless, the extension of services by professional accountants in the private sector into operational or functional areas has been proceeding through management services departments in the larger accounting firms and by general practitioners themselves in the smaller firms—but at a much slower pace than at the GAO.

INTERNAL AUDITORS AND COMPUTER PROFESSIONALS

The author's suggestion that internal auditors of corporations consider extending their services into matters dealing with descriptions of operational results and including them in financial statement disclosures could have far-reaching consequences and could help the internal auditor hold his own against the rapidly growing "computer professional" who is increasingly becoming the central focus for all internal information. The fact that so many auditors do not have adequate education and training in computer technology and the many opportunities for manipulation of computerized data is becoming of critical concern to all institutions, government and business. As a result, more and more internal information systems are being designed and monitored by computer experts. Yet most computer experts still do not have adequate training in internal control techniques, which are so essential for creditable financial reporting.

In the past, most information systems designed by computer professionals lacked audit trails, but, as a result of some recent major defalcations, more attention is being paid by computer experts to providing audit trails in their software and to designing internal control packages into the systems. The fast-moving area of electronic information systems holds many opportunities not yet fully tapped for the creative accountant and auditor.

Auditing "models of programs," as performed by the GAO—which are so well described in Dr. Staats' paper—is an area that should have priority attention. I cannot constructively add anything to what Dr. Staats has said to emphasize the importance of this topic.

SOCIOECONOMIC OPERATING STATEMENT

When we come to social accounting, the important observation is that accounting traditionally has been economic accounting—that is, accounting for economic activities. In business, we report on profits and losses or numbers of units produced and their values. In government, we report on budgets, appropriations, allocations, expenditures. I submit the time has come for accountants, as the appropriate measurement experts in our society, to recognize that we should be concerned with measuring not only economic data but social data as well. In today's society such social factors are no less important than economic factors.

In my own work in this area, largely to avoid the confusing term "social accounting" described by Dr. Staats in his paper, I have referred to this kind of accounting as "socioeconomic accounting"—that is, accounting that takes into consideration social actions as well as economic actions. In Exhibits 3–6 and 3–7, I give an example from the private sector, on which I might elaborate as follows:

All reporting by business organizations today centers around two basic financial statements: the Statement of Income and the Statement of Financial Condition. Business operations, however, have great impacts on social conditions, such as the general health of a community, the educational level of people, recreational facilities and environmental conditions; in general, matters that in modern-day society are inextricably interwoven with an organization's operations, especially a business corporation's operations. These impacts are not accounted for, however, in the traditional statements I just referred to.

From another point of view, corporations today are essentially quasi-public institutions. No business can thrive over the long term unless the social and political environment is stable. If business organizations contribute to the deterioration of the sociopolitical climate in a particular area, those businesses will find it increasingly difficult to operate profitably and even to attract qualified employees to their premises.

It is ironic, therefore, that in today's enlightened business reporting there is no generally accepted form of reporting for the social actions of the business corporation. I believe the time has come for

Exhibit 3-6. A Socio-Economic Operating Statement.

The various positive and negative social actions and inactions mentioned are classified on the SEOS exhibit into three groups: *Relations with People, Relations with Environment* and *Relations with Product.* The Socio-Economic Operating Statement that I recommend be instituted would then have this appearance:

XXXX Corporation

**Socio-Economic Operating Statement for the Year
Ending December 31, ...**

I. *Relations with People*:
  A. *Improvements*:

1. Training program for handicapped workers	$ 10,000	
2. Contribution to educational institution	4,000	
3. Extra turnover costs because of minority hiring program	5,000	
4. Cost of nursery school for children of employees, voluntarily set up	11,000	
Total Improvements		$ 30,000

  B. *Less: Detriments*

1. Postponed installing new safety devices on cutting machines (cost of the devices)	$ 14,000	

  C. Net Improvements in People Actions for the Year $ 16,000

II. *Relations with Environment*:
  A. *Improvements*:

1. Cost of reclaiming and landscaping old dump on company property	$ 70,000	
2. Cost of installing pollution control devices on Plant A smokestacks	4,000	
3. Cost of detoxifying waste from finishing process this year	9,000	
Total Improvements		$ 83,000

  B. *Less: Detriments*

1. Cost that would have been incurred to relandscape strip mining site used this year	$ 80,000	
2. Estimated costs to have installed purification process to neutralize poisonous liquid being dumped into stream	$100,000	
		$180,000

  C. Net Deficit in Environment Actions for the Year   ($ 97,000)

Exhibit 3-6. continued

III. *Relations with Product*:

A. *Improvements*:

1. Salary of V.P. while serving on government Product Safety Commission	$ 25,000	
2. Cost of substituting lead-free paint for previously used poisonous lead paint	9,000	
Total Improvements		$ 34,000

B. *Less: Detriments*

1. Safety device recommended by Safety Council but not added to product	22,000	

C. Net Improvements in Product Actions for the Year $ 12,000

Total Socio-Economic Deficit for the Year	($ 69,000)
Add: Net Cumulative Socio-Economic Improvements as at January 1, ...	$249,000
GRAND TOTAL NET SOCIO–ECONOMIC ACTIONS TO DECEMBER 31, ...	$180,000

Source: D. Linowes, "An Approach to Socio-Economic Accounting," *Conference Board Record* 9, no. 11, 1972, pp. 60–61.

Exhibit 3-7. Preparing the Socio-Economic Operating Statement.

The SEOS exhibits themselves would be prepared by a small interdisciplinary team headed by an accountant. Other members of the team could include a seasoned business executive, sociologist, public health administrator, economist, or members of other disciplines whose specific expertise might apply to a particular industry or circumstance. Although SEO Statements would be prepared internally by an interdisciplinary group, they should be audited by an outside independent interdisciplinary team headed by a CPA.

Though determination of items to be included in the SEOS is to be based upon subjective judgments, a standard dollar value applied to these improvements or "detriments" would be a combination of what businessmen traditionally classify as capital expenditures and expense expenditures. For example, the full cost of a permanent installation of a pollution control device is included in the SEO Statement in the year the cost is voluntarily incurred, as is the annual operating cost of a hardcore minority group training program. For convenience of reference, the totals could be expressed in Socio-Economic Management Dollars (SEM$) so as to identify all expenditures made voluntarily of a socially beneficial nature.

Specific cost items which would be entered on a SEO Statement as "improvements" or positive actions would include:

1. Cost of training program for handicapped workers.
2. Contribution to educational institutions.
3. Extra turnover costs because of minority hiring policy. (The adverse of this item, the cost of not setting up adequate orientation programs, would be included as detrimental nonactions.)
4. Cost of nursery school for children of employees, voluntarily set up.
5. Cost of reclaiming and landscaping old dump on company property.
6. Cost of installing pollution control devices on smokestacks ahead of legal requirements.
7. Cost of detoxifying waste from finishing process this year, ahead of legal requirement.
8. Salary of vice president while serving on government Product Safety Commission.
9. Cost of substituting lead-free paint for previously used poisonous lead paint.

Contrariwise, these specific costs would be entered on the SEOS as negative or detrimental nonactions:

1. Postponed installing new safety devices on cutting machines (cost of the devices).

Exhibit 3-7. continued

---

2. Cost that would have been incurred to relandscape strip mining site used this year.

3. Estimated cost to have installed a purification process to neutralize polluting liquid being dumped into stream.

4. Cost of safety device recommended by Safety Council but not added to product.

I would emphasize that some of these examples may no longer be includable on a current Socio-Economic Operating Statement, but they serve to illustrate.

---

an appropriate social report to be accepted as a third form of basic reporting, especially for publicly held corporations.

The Socio-Economic Report in Exhibits 3-6 and 3-7 provides one example. It sets forth expenditures made by a corporation for the good of society in three areas: Relations with People, Relations with Environment, and Relations with Product. Annually, expenditures incurred over and above those required by law or contract could be tallied and set forth in such a statement. (The Socio-Economic Operating Statement could be refined further by including charges for social actions that a "socially responsible" management would have undertaken, during the preceding year, but which this management did not undertake.)

SOCIO-ECONOMIC ACCOUNTING IN GOVERNMENT

Applying socio-economic accounting to areas other than business would require that we redefine accounting from the traditional "measurement and communication of business and economic data" to the "measurement and communication of business, economic and *social* data." Those who are trained in accounting are in effect trained in measurement. It need not be argued that accounting is the only measurement discipline, but there is reason, nonetheless, for accounting professionals to extend their expertise into assisting members of other professions with their measurement needs. Sociologist Professor Bertram Gross, formerly of Syracuse University and more recently at the State University of New York, has been urging the accounting profession to move into this area for over twenty years. In 1968, Professor Daniel Bell, social scientist at Harvard University, addressed the Annual Meeting of the American Institute of Certified Public Accountants urging CPAs to move into social measurement.

Such measurement need not be confined to financial (dollarized) magnitudes. Here is a simple, stripped-down example in the field of health where quantifiable dollarized data are not available: When a physician examines a patient, the physician classifies that individual as being in either excellent, good, fair, poor, or critically ill health. This provides a rank order which also lends itself to objective measurement along with the more common dollars and cents (or units of production) that accountants are accustomed to.

Applied to a government program that is designed to improve the health of 1,000 children, the accounting might be made as follows: If at the beginning of the program 20 percent (200) of the youngsters are determined to be in excellent health and at the end of the program 60 percent (600) of the subjects are determined to be in excellent health, it is fair to conclude that the program has had a significant beneficial impact on the health of the subjects.

At the present time, most government agencies charged with improving the health of children make no attempt to evaluate whether their programs are effective, often because no determination of the condition of the health of the entire group of youngsters is made when the program begins and ends.

ACCOUNTABILITY VS. ACCOUNTING

The foregoing observations discuss "accountability" as though it were synonymous with "accounting." Although accounting is a basic tool of accountability, when the term "accountability" is used by management it generally relates to the fixing of responsibility for job performance.

A broader meaning for accountability may be important when considering creativity and innovativeness in management. Such discussions have been stimulated in recent years because of our declining rate of productivity and our slippage in international trade. These discussions have often centered on doing something different, such as molding Japanese management techniques into our own industrial enterprises, adopting West German or Swedish management-labor participation arrangements, or intensifying the application of our own scientific personnel management techniques. In these various approaches, the concern is often with the management of accountability—whom we hold responsible for various elements of an operation and how we do it—and this, too, is a subject in need of creative and innovative attention.

CONCLUSION

In conclusion, in addition to the excellent points made by Dr. Staats, I believe we should recognize that:

- The inroads being made by the rapidly developing computer profession—that is, those computer experts who are competently and broadly applying their strong background in computer programming and technology to the information systems of all organizations.

- The important need for business organizations to adopt a third basic report—namely, a social report such as the socio-economic operating statement.

- Accountants should involve themselves in the measurement needs of the other professions, especially social scientists.

- There also needs to be a recognition that accounting is only one tool of the broader aspect of accountability, albeit a vital one; and that the broader aspect of accountability is also going through major changes.

PRIVATE SECTOR MANAGEMENT AND POLICY ISSUES

4 CREATIVE MANAGEMENT IN MATURE CAPITAL INTENSIVE INDUSTRIES
The Case of Cement

B. Collomb
J. P. Ponssard

INTRODUCTION

Basic industries have received much attention in recent years. After all, the automobile industry with its related traditional products such as tires, the building industry with cement and wood—others, too, such as glass, steel, and copper—still represent a significant portion of the social infrastructure of industrialized countries. The public image of these industries is, however, often poor. They are seen as facing shrinking markets, possessing large overcapacity, and experiencing fierce competition as a result. Indeed, some sectors, such as steel, the situation seems so dramatic that government intervention is constant (large subsidies and even crisis cartelization in Europe, along with trigger price mechanisms and quotas in the United States).

The opinion that these are industries of the past, while telematics and aerospace are industries of the future, is reinforced by the spreading use of "portfolio approaches" to strategic management. In these techniques as described in the concluding section of this paper, the weaknesses of these industries cumulate: no demand growth or even negative demand growth, no opportunity for product differentiation, numerous competitors with small individual market shares, high capital intensity combined with huge bulk investment requirements. Under these circumstances typical recommendations under

123

portfolio approaches to strategic management would suggest milking or quick divestment whenever possible.

This paper is a reaction against this last set of tendencies. First, a number of businesses that might fall into this category may enjoy reasonable profitability. This seems to be the case for float glass, cast iron, plaster, or cement—at least in some countries. What factors can explain these contrasting results? A detailed comparative study of the evolution of the cement industry for the United States and France will provide some answers.

Our interpretation will lead to a reassessment of the way these strategic tools have been used. Rather than discrediting these tools, our empirical study will suggest that they can provide a basis for creative and innovative management as long as three essential ingredients are kept in balance: (1) cost dynamics and steady selective investment, (2) imperfect competition with a special focus on structural change rather than on short-term collusion, and (3) financial and economic evaluations that emphasize long-term effects.

It appears particularly crucial to find ways to integrate these three elements in the case of mature capital intensive industries with stagnant markets. Management is often dominated by a simplification of one of the three aspects almost to the point of caricature. It is the role of creative and innovative management, however, to scrutinize each dimension fully and to provide a globally constructive synthesis. After presenting our analysis of the cement industry, we shall come back to these more general points.

THE CEMENT INDUSTRY: AN INTERNATIONAL COMPARISON

General Background

The cement industry provides an example of a mature capital-intensive industry that has undertaken significant changes, despite its lack of glamour for addicts of the portfolio methods.

Let us recall the basic steps of cement manufacturing: Natural raw materials, basically limestone and clay, are crushed and mixed, to be burned at $1450°$ C in a kiln, to supply a material called clinker, which must, in turn, be ground and mixed with gypsum and other additives to produce a fine powder called cement.

At its origin (1830), the cement industry was very much like the ancient lime industry: Small vertical kilns were scattered about various limestone deposits with very limited production and used numerous workers for stone-crushing, transportation, bagging, and the like. But at the start of the present century, the cement industry underwent several significant changes (rotary kiln, wet process, use of new fuel sources, new machinery, and, later, automation) that gave this industry its current shape.

At present the main characteristics of this industry are the following:

- Energy content: Each ton of cement produced requires 75 to 150 kilograms of fuel oil or an equivalent fueling amount (depending on the cement variety and the process used).

- A homogeneous product: Although produced from natural raw materials that are different in each plant, cement can be considered a standard product—there are only a few classes of cement (two or three classes account for 80 percent of sales in France) and in each class, products from different producers can generally be substituted. Therefore, price is the most important sale parameter; quality premiums exist but are rather limited.

- A process and capital intensive industry: With the development of modern automated machinery and continuous material handling devices, the cement industry has become a process industry, which mainly uses skilled labor in limited amount. A modern plant is usually manned by less than 200 people. Capital intensity is very high: The capital investment required to produce a ton of cement annually is at least three times the sales price of this ton. When we take the definitions used in PIMS,[1] capital intensity ratios are in the order of 55 percent for investment/sales, 95 percent for investment/value added and 50 percent for gross book value/sales. According to PIMS findings, this would cause ROI (return on investment) to fall 16 percent behind the average industrial ROI were other variables held constant (which, fortunately, does not—or need not—occur in practice).

- A cheap and heavy product: The price of cement is approximately ½ cent a kilogram. But transportation costs are significant, and one used to say that cement could not be economically hauled beyond 100 or at most 200 miles. Bulk shipping has changed that, however, and it is now cheaper to cross the Atlantic Ocean with 35,000 tons of cargo than to truck it 200 miles. But within a country like the United States or France, transportation costs normally cluster the markets into regional areas, with the exception of a few long-distance transfers (on the Mississippi River, for example).

- A mature product: Demand for cement (which was first produced in the early 1800s) increased considerably in the twentieth century, reflecting the development of industry and of urban areas. Consumption in the industrialized countries has been multiplied by four since World War II. After the end of this reconstruction effort, however, the growth rate has declined steadily. There have, to be sure, been ups and downs in the 1960s and the 1970s in the United States, and in Europe, but growth ended with the oil crisis in 1975—with a subsequent decline of 20 to 40 percent in various countries (Figure 4-1).

  Cement consumption can even, in a way, be taken as an index of industrial and urban development. Cumulated consumption in various countries relates rather well to GNP per capita, as Figure 4-2 shows. The shape of the curve indicates that the industrialized countries have reached a point where not much demand expansion can be expected.

Despite this seemingly dull and unattractive background, an industry has developed in various countries to a point where shareholders and financial analysts consider cement stocks with considerable interest. Although this development has been uneven among different countries and companies, the three largest world cement groups have been developing steadily in the last fifteen years (see lower portion of Table 4-1).

The first group, Holderbank, is a Swiss-based company with interests in twenty-two countries selling 38 million metric tons and grossing $1.5 billion in 1980. Next is Blue Circle, a British group with about the same gross dollars sales on a volume of 27 million tons, followed by a French group that has been able to achieve significant developments in North America, as well as diversification in other construction materials and, more recently, in biotechnology (chosen as a new growth area for the long term). This group, Lafarge Coppée, grossed $2.5 billion in 1981.

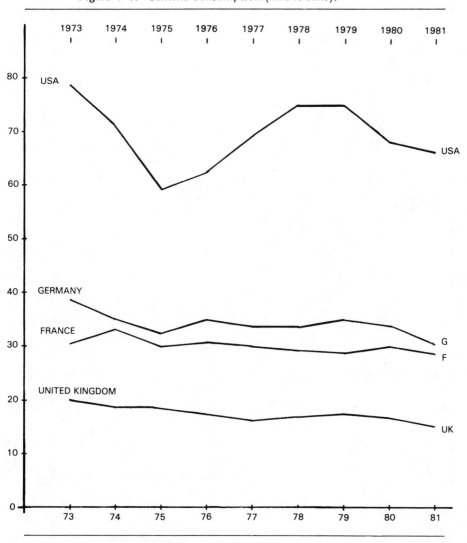

Figure 4-1. Cement Consumption (*metric tons*).

Source: CEM Bureau and Portland Cement Association.

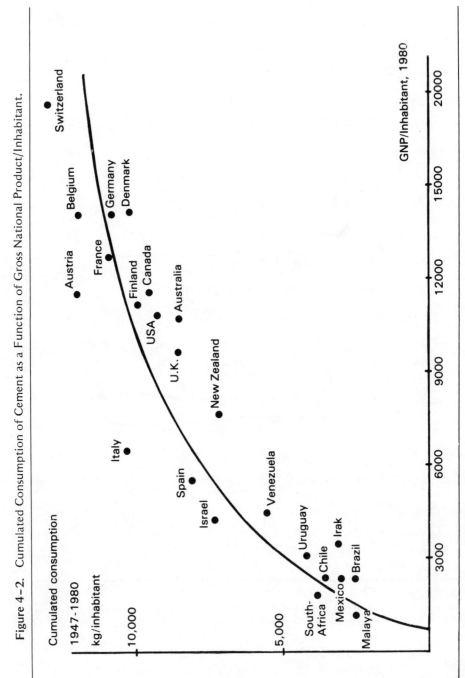

Figure 4–2. Cumulated Consumption of Cement as a Function of Gross National Product/Inhabitant.

Source: Lafarge Coppeé, internal document.

Table 4-1. Development of U.S. and European-Based Cement Industries.

	Development of the U.S. Cement Industry (million metric tons per year)		
	1964	1980	Percent Increase
Ideal Cement	6.80	5.50	-19
Lone Star	6.46	8.14	26
General Portland	4.66	6.16	32
U.S. Total	51.70	72.40	40
	Development of European-Based Cement Industry		
	1964	1980	Percent Increase
Holderbank	11.60	38.50	232
Blue Circle	14.50	27.30	88
Lafarge Coppée	9.00	26.30	192

Source: Cembureau and Portland Cement Association.

Although direct comparison is made difficult by differences in the currency and accounting methods used in recent years, these three groups have displayed profitability ratios that look satisfactory enough. In the Fortune list, for example, they show a return on equity of 13 to 14 percent, except for the British group whose replacement cost depreciation policy—allowed under British accounting rules—reduces the apparent return on equity to 6 percent instead of 21 percent on an historical cost accounting basis.

In smaller countries such as Greece or Spain where companies have remained more of the family-owned type, we have less information on financial results, but they have been able to develop worldwide exports and to overcome the difficulties of the oil crisis much better than other industries in their own countries.

In contrast, in the United States old, established cement companies have been experiencing difficult times since the 1960s. After a period of overcapacity and fierce competition, the price controls imposed by the government in 1971 froze profits at a very low level. Profitability was better—although varying widely among companies—only in the years 1977-1980, before falling again with the current recession. At the same time, first in Canada, and then in the United States, European-based groups were acquiring a significant share of the industry (30 percent as of 1982). In 1973 and 1979 the United States experienced cement shortages in several states, with imports of cements from Canada, Japan, or Europe representing the only way of satisfying these local demands and with very high selling prices being experienced in those areas as a consequence.

This short description shows that the fate of the cement industry did not depend only on simple factors such as market growth or capital intensity but also depended on country and company strategies that allowed some firms to develop while others could not overcome difficult times or changing market conditions.

Key Factors and Key Strategies

Success or failure in an industry such as cement evidently depends on recognition of a few key factors and on an ability to respond to these key factors in a given environment through appropriate strategies. The key factors that we shall now list and discuss are basically related to technical and industrial competitiveness and to market situations.

1. *Technical Change and Investment Policies:* It is obvious that investment cost is a prominent factor. We noted earlier the high capital-cost ratio. Furthermore, this ratio has a tendency to increase as greater emphasis is placed on pollution control, quality control, working conditions improvement, and technical sophistication. In such situations there are two possible responses: either try to increase the life of costly equipment with a strong maintenance policy but with little emphasis on technical progress, or, on the contrary, increase efficiency through continuous technical innovation and introduction of new processes, while accepting the corresponding increase in capital costs.

A policy of the second type has been followed by many European or Japanese firms, under the pressure (or with the help) of specific conditions in their own environment. Thus, attention given both in Europe and Japan to energy dependence, even before the oil crisis, led to significant progress in calorific consumption. Figure 4–3 shows trends in France, the United Kingdom, Japan and the United States. The large differences that are apparent in this figure point to

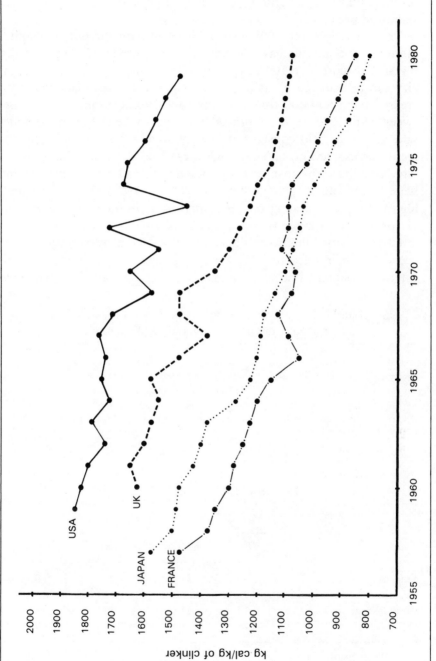

Figure 4-3. Evolution of Calorific Consumption.

Source: CEM Bureau and Portland Cement Association.

the possibility of benefits from technical change even in a seemingly stabilized process.

These changes required an aggressive investment policy. Capital intensity did not increase, however, as economies of scale allowed investment cost increases to be controlled: Unit cost per ton of capacity can be reduced by as much as 20 percent when plant size is increased from 500,000 tons per year to 1,500,000 tons per year. Between 1960 and 1980, it proved possible to keep the investment/sales turnover ratio constant at approximately 2.9, excluding investment for extraction, only through a twofold increase in plant capacity. This aggressive investment policy had a positive influence on the scale factor and on productivity (see Tables 4-2 and 4-3). Technological progress, scaling-up, and increased productivity were joint factors participating in this progress.

Large rotary kilns were limited in the 1970s by technical difficulties in their refractory-brick coating, which made it uneconomical to go beyond one million tons per year capacity. The Japanese

Table 4-2. Labor Productivity in the Cement Industry Measured as Number of Kilos of Cement Produced Per Working Hour.

	1970	1975	1980
France	1141	1445	1671
U.S.	1066	1049	1206
Germany	989	1206	1378

Source: Cembureau and Portland Cement Association.

Table 4-3. Number of Kilns and Capacity of Average Kiln, 1976.

	Number of Kilns		Capacity of Average Kiln[a]	
Country	Dry	Wet	Dry	Wet
France	60	35	400	210
Germany	98	11	423	385
United Kingdom	18	64	383	188
U.S.	176	211	224	200

a. Million metric tons per year.

Source: Cembureau, U.S. Bureau of Mines, EEC Reports.

responded to this, however, by trying to go beyond this limit when environmental and land-availability constraints prevented them from building new sites. And, thanks to the so-called precalcining process (where a substantial part of the process is carried out before the material goes to the kiln), they found a way to increase the capacity of a given rotary kiln by a factor of two or three.

2. *Concentration:* Of course, increasing plant sizes means accepting more transportation cost and/or reducing the number of plants. In markets of average density, it is possible to show that transportation cost increases are limited—that is, the cost increments in transportation are outweighed by the economies obtainable in the production stage. In fact, a rough economic calculation shows that, in a country like France, if the industry were to be rebuilt from scratch, ten to fifteen plants would be optimal as compared to the more than fifty that presently exist.

Concentration is therefore necessary and, indeed, essential if market growth is limited. This is the second key factor noted above for this industry. In countries like France, leading companies were able to buy out (or merge with) smaller competitors and close down some small plants which were becoming noncompetitive on a long-term basis (even though they were still able to make some money in the short term). In the United States, however, the process was made more difficult by antitrust legislation and regulation. For example, in France the industry had more than thirty companies in 1960, but now has only five industrial groups, the first two of which account for more than 60 percent of total capacity. In the United States, by comparison, the number of firms has remained roughly constant at an average of fifty since 1964. In 1980, for an output level three times that of France, the four major U.S. firms accounted for only 30 percent of total capacity with eleven U.S. companies, representing 10 percent of total capacity. Five of these still operate on a single plant basis and have a capacity of less than 1.5 MMTPY (Million Metric Tons per Year) versus none in France in either category. This concentration process was triggered not only by the need to achieve economies of scale but also because it could have a significant impact on the market situation. Far from excluding competition, as standard economic textbooks or FTC rulings would suggest, it creates situations where the long-term horizon is taken into consideration and "potential competition"—a concept now apparently being "discovered" by economists[2] but well-known to industrialists— remains strong and prevents undue exploitation of situations of local dominance.

It is of interest to elaborate this particular point since a "heavy industry" and a "heavy product" give market competition some special features. First, competition in such cases is basically in regional markets; second, fixed costs, whether capital costs (investment and financial expenditures) or fixed operating costs (labor and part of maintenance costs), represent a substantial share of the total cost of the product.

In every country the industry started with family-owned single plant companies and with a rather large number of competitors in each regional market. Such a structure cannot lead to a stable market equilibrium in this type of industry. Investment lifetimes are very long (over thirty years with proper maintenance). Overcapacity can easily appear when minimum efficient plant size requires lumpy investments and when many competitors are present in a slowly growing or declining market. With little opportunity for product differentiation, competition is mainly focused on price, which is therefore very sensitive to market conditions. Seemingly reasonable short-term behavior for a single plant company is, therefore, to maximize short-term return by pushing market share at the expense of prices.

Figure 4–4 shows the sensitivity of unit cost to the capacity utilization rate, and the difference between total and variable costs. Furthermore, when inflation enters the picture, its impact on an historical accounting system reduces the weight of capital cost, which is no longer adequately taken into account by depreciation allowances.

It is, therefore, practically impossible to reach a stable competitive equilibrium when a large number of one-plant companies are competing in the same market. The probability of at least one of these competitors pushing prices down to increase sales volume is very high. Of course, this leads to a situation in which every company in this market does not obtain high enough financial returns to allow the replacement of plant when age, technical change, or size inadequacy make this necessary. But this threat is too remote (10 or 20 years ahead) to alter competitive behavior significantly. We are thus in a situation where the theoretical adjustment process described in economic textbooks does not work due to economies of scale (increasing returns) and the long time lags associated with the survival of ailing firms as long as they do not need substantial new investment.

Figure 4-4. Estimated Cost Per Ton of Cement (*modern plant MMTPY*).*

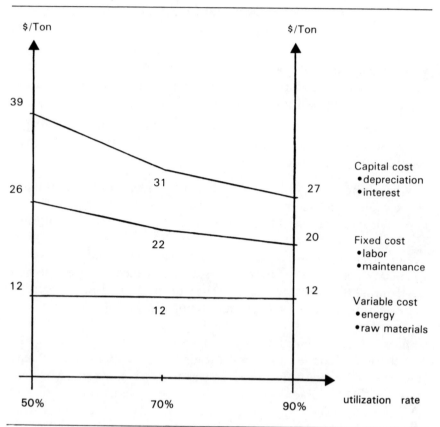

*MMTPY—Million Metric Tons Per Year Capacity.
Source: Lafarge Coppeé Internal Document.

How can a firm—or an industry—react in such an environment to control the destabilizing and destructive effects of short-term competitive behavior? The concentration process is one of the keys to a more stable structure.

The acquisition of single-plant, family-owned companies by larger multiplant firms has several effects:

• When concentration is legally possible on the same regional market, it reduces the number of competitors and fosters the construction of larger plants even without market expansion.

- Behavioral patterns change: As multiplant companies are likely to have regular investment needs, they cannot ignore the impact of fixed costs, and they know they cannot operate very long on a marginal cost basis. Large companies have greater incentives to base their pricing policies on long-term optimization.

- Competition between large companies is not confined to only a single market, and a balance of strengths can be achieved through retaliation capabilities in other markets.

- The social impact of technical change can be better managed when people working in obsolete plants can be transferred to new plants where production is concentrated.

When concentration is not legally permissible, the process is likely to be more chaotic. It may be abruptly triggered by new technical and environmental conditions. For instance, when new antipollution regulations were introduced in the United States in the 1970s a number of plants were forced to shut down, since they did not have the financial capacity to make the investments needed to meet the new regulations. Similarly, if energy prices in the United States were to increase substantially, a large number of old wet plants, which still represent 50 percent of capacity (as compared to 10 percent in France), would at once be obliged to stop operating.

This type of sudden adjustment leads to shortages and subsequently very high increases in prices, as was the case in several American states in 1973. Table 4–4 shows the range of variation of prices in different countries. The volatility of prices in U.S. markets is striking. One can also see that concentration in European industries did not lead to substantially higher price levels. On the contrary, despite the impact of fuel costs, which are still much lower in the United States, the selling price in 1981 was higher in many American states than it was in Western Europe (excluding Great Britain).

Excessive competition does not actually lead in the long term to a minimum price; its negative impact on technical progress and productivity can lead to higher costs which, even with strong competition, will result in higher prices.

3. *Vertical Integration:* Another subject of interest is vertical integration. In this respect strategies and situations are also very different. The main fields for vertical integration of cement manufacturers are ready-mix concrete, aggregates, and precasting businesses. Ready-

Table 4-4. Delivered Cement Prices at Selected Locations in the U.S. and Europe 1977–1982.

	Delivered Cement Prices in Some U.S. Urban Areas ($/short ton)						
	MAR. 77	FEB. 78	FEB. 79	JAN. 80	JAN. 81	JAN. 82	AUG. 82
Chicago	39.00	42.50	56.00	58.00	57.00	51.00	51.00
Cleveland	41.65	47.00	55.00	59.50	62.50	56.00	56.00
Denver	44.20	47.80	51.30	60.00	60.50	73.30	73.30
Detroit	34.60	39.78	48.18	56.17	53.17	55.04	55.04
New York	40.00	38.63	47.70	50.30	53.72	61.02	54.00
Philadelphia	39.00	33.98	43.90	44.30	48.31	53.42	59.42
Pittsburgh	41.94	42.80	51.30	51.89	56.79	62.36	62.36
San Francisco	44.30	62.40	62.66	68.90	71.27	72.04	72.86
Seattle	51.85	58.20	63.90	68.30	68.30	78.50	78.50

Average Delivered Cement Prices in Urban Areas: International Comparison ($/short ton)[a]		
		Type of Cement[b]
	JAN. 81	JAN. 82	
U.S. high	48.31	51.00	OPC
low	71.27	78.50	OPC
France	48.90	44.25	CPJ 45
Great Britain	81.65	71.95	OPC
Germany	50.96	47.84	PZ 35
Switzerland	53.61	55.34	OPC

a. Currency rates are taken at each point of time.
b. Technical specifications may not be exactly equivalent from one country to another.

mix concrete is a channel through which a substantial part of concrete is produced (from 30 percent to 70 percent, depending on the country). Precasting activities represent another way of manufacturing concrete for the final user (from 10 percent to 20 percent of concrete). In all cases, aggregates that are needed to prepare concrete are becoming more or less scarce materials near urban markets due to growing environmental constraints and reduced availability.

Integration has been viewed differently in various countries. We will restrict ourselves to the ready-mix business and give only a few examples:

In Great Britain, where a cement company reached a position of quasi monopoly (65 percent market share), another industrial firm took an early lead in the ready-mix industry acquiring a dominant position in its domestic market and then expanding internationally.

In Canada, where more than 60 percent of cement goes to ready-mix, the cement industry acquired substantial interests in the ready-mix industry at an early date and the competition between cement producers was often more apparent at the level of ready-mix operations.

In France, cement companies concerned with maintaining a low level of buyer concentration reacted to the aggressive entry of the British ready-mix group by developing their own interests in the ready-mix industry. Currently, approximately 40 percent of the industry is controlled by cement companies, with regional positions roughly similar to those achieved on the cement market.

In Germany, where the British ready-mix group was able to develop more freely, it eventually clashed with the cement producers, and integrated itself by setting up a cement plant. This was one of several factors which led to serious instability in the cement industry in northern Germany during the last twenty years.

The situation in the United States seems similar to that of Germany with several cases of backward integration by ready-mix companies. There the problem is even more difficult for cement producers since by a 1967 FTC ruling they are basically barred from acquiring ready-mix companies.

While vertical integration has primarily been viewed as a way to control the market, it has certainly also had positive effects on efficiency. Large investment plans are more easily developed when there is a reasonable amount of captive demand. Furthermore, integration has entailed diversification into different businesses where capital intensity and cash requirements are much lower. But it can hardly be said that reduction of capital intensity or portfolio diversification has been the aim of the integration strategy.

4. *Product Quality and Specifications:* Another marketing strategy where management decisions had to be made relates to product quality and specifications. Innovation has occurred not only in the manufacturing process but also in the product itself and in its uses. Concerns about energy saving in some countries triggered the use of available byproducts (slag, fly-ash, puzzolanic stones, and so forth) as additives to pure Portland cement.

Here again the behavior of various companies or industries was different and was not necessarily related only to the physical availability of byproducts (see Table 4–5). Three basic strategies have been used with differing success. Some companies thought their best interest was to promote their original product, pure cement, with high value added, by maintaining strict and traditional specifications. Others thought that the byproducts would be used in any case by the concrete manufacturers and that these byproducts would also be pushed with the help of governmental agencies implementing energy-saving programs. These companies promoted new specifications that allowed "mixed cements" with reduced energy content and still satisfactory performances. Admittedly this strategy was more easily developed when demand growth and price control provided incentives for producing larger quantities of lower cost cement with the same clinker capacity, as was the case in France in the 1960s. Finally, some companies (especially in the United States), tried to secure positions as traders, taking control of the byproducts supply and delivering these byproducts, in addition to cement, to their clients. After a number of years, as can now be seen, the companies which have been reluctant to develop mixed cement are in serious danger of

Table 4–5. Average Content of Secondary Material in Manufactured Cement in Selected Countries.

Year	France	Germany	United Kingdom	U.S.
1980	24%	8%	0%	1%

Source: OECD Report on Energy Consumption in the Cement Industry in the Year 2000.

losing revenues to outside byproduct suppliers. Furthermore, partial integration in ready-mix and aggregates appears to yield substantial advantages in terms of overall economic optimization in production of the final product.

Summary

To summarize this comparative discussion of current strategies in the cement business, we may emphasize four points where textbook solutions were probably not those that were best designed to serve the future of the companies involved:

1. *Capital Investment:* The first of these relates to capital investment. Strategies designed to reduce capital intensity (according to PIMS recommendations) or to use the business as a cash-cow with minimum investment, maximum lifetime, and without technical change could lead to obsolescence and lagging productivity growth. The best course was, on the contrary, to rely on technical progress and competitiveness. Not only did the companies who made this choice perform well in their own countries but they were also able to draw on their technological know-how to take advantage of growing markets elsewhere—for example, in developing countries. Of course, the choice to be made was not independent of each company's specific environment. And it should be noted that a realistic energy-pricing policy or government energy-saving subsidies in some countries encouraged the cement companies to go as far as possible in technical progress. In other countries, like Japan, the weight of environmental constraints did add momentum to this effort.

2. *Concentration:* The strategic choice to reach a significant size by acquisition or merger is a classical move in portfolio theory, where relative market share is often considered as a key to success. But the reasons underlying the need for concentration that we have examined are not related to the classical experience curve theory. Concentration does reduce cost when it allows firms to take advantage of economies of scale, but its effect on short-term versus long-term competitive behavior and on investment policies is more significant. Finally, as we have seen, legal constraints that provide obstacles to this concentration process may significantly alter the long-term efficiency of an industry.

3. *Vertical Integration:* Here again the motivation for these moves was not portfolio analysis but rather the need to control and stabilize the market. However, and interestingly enough, one can notice that capital integration reduces the capital intensity of cement companies which, according to some authors, should allow better returns. This is true, indeed, but only when the stabilization effects resulting from large-scale integration lead to higher returns in downstream business. Otherwise, the available evidence shows that ready-mix concrete activities, an industry with low capital requirements, can have worse financial returns than cement.

4. *Product Strategy:* The fourth and last choice we examined was product strategy and the extensive use of byproducts. This is actually a way to reduce capital intensity and to produce cement with less investment. It is also a strategy to limit the possible impact of materials that can be substituted for cement in concrete utilization, and a way to change a threat into an opportunity.

A REASSESSMENT OF THE PORTFOLIO APPROACH

We would like to conclude this paper by offering some general remarks on the portfolio approach that will take advantage of what we have said about the experience of the cement industry. In this case we have a typical situation in which a routine application of these techniques would lead to a milk or divest quickly strategy. Indeed, the market of industrialized countries is stagnant due to such factors as the end of the reconstruction period, demographic reasons, general recession, and high energy content. The industry has a very high capital intensity and requires huge bulk investment to recoup some gains through economies of scale. Portfolio management techniques strongly discourage investments in new plants when demand can be satisfied through existing ones and productivity gains or technical progress are difficult to forecast. Finally, in this industry the product is virtually undifferentiated so that competition can easily take the form of ruinous price cuts.

Under this apparently uniformly detrimental context a detailed comparison of the strategies followed in Europe and in the United States provides striking differences. These differences may, at first sight, be reduced to local responses of the cement industry to specific national conditions. In this respect it is tempting to attribute a large part of the impact to the different attitudes toward financial concentration. By focusing on the potential for short term collusion, U.S. antitrust policy probably did not promote the long term efficiency of this specific industry. But this factor should not be overemphasized, and some authors have indeed highlighted the general decline of U.S. manufacturing activities by attributing it to an overemphasis on short-term financial considerations in management.[3]

Paradoxically, we shall argue that European firms implicitly followed a strategy based on a good "creative" understanding of the portfolio approach. Indeed, the cement industry offers a good basis for the reappraisal of these strategic management techniques. Let us, therefore, briefly sketch out what would be a creative use of these tools.[4]

First—in our opinion, one of the reasons for the initial success of the portfolio approach—the growth/market share matrix[5] provides a synthetic view of three essential aspects of management: cost dynamics, imperfect competition, and financial analysis. For the first time one could systematically develop comprehensive reasoning using a simple matrix representation. But this comprehensiveness is bought at a high price. Cost dynamics are reduced to the "experience curve." Imperfect competition is schematized as a homogenous market with stable price leadership. As for the financial aspect, it is reduced to the needs for growth and cash flow generation depending on market position, where the balancing aspect is described as a "pipes and taps" problem between industrially independent activities.[6]

It is very tempting in this framework, first, to underestimate the role of these simple underlying assumptions and blindly follow the generic strategies that they suggest; and, second, to focus on only one dimension, gaining insight in that dimension but completely bypassing the other two.[7] A creative use of this approach is based on simultaneously balanced analyses of these three dimensions.[8] In this respect the case of the cement industry shows the interaction between financial concentration, competitive behavior, and improved efficiency in investment planning and productivity. Similarly, product modification through the use of byproducts, as well as vertical integration, reduce capital intensity but can hardly be dissociated from an analysis of the competitive forces that structure the sector. Thus, in the case of a French cement company that we have been able to study, the different divisions (either geographical or product-based) are not viewed as industrially independent entities but with the objective of achieving a global sustainable position in the basic building material industry. But, "the proof of the pudding is in the eating." In the contrasting pictures we have used, it is arguable whether environmental conditions or internal strategic choices had the major influence. In any case, European-based companies are now operating on a large scale in the North American scene, and processes similar to what were seen in Europe are taking place in the United States; so the interaction between environment and strategies will continue to be interesting to watch in the coming years.

NOTES TO CHAPTER 4

1. PIMS = Profit Impact of Market Share, a commercially available data base with accompanying mathematical models, which was originally developed by the General Electric Company but is now available from the Institute of Strategic Planning in Cambridge, Massachusetts. See M. Lubatkin and M. Pitts, "PIMS: Fact or Folklore," *The Journal of Business Strategy* 3, no. 3 (Winter 1983): 38–43.
2. See W. J. Baumol, J. C. Panzar and R. D. Willig, *Contestable Markets and the Theory of Industry Structure* (New York: Harcourt, Brace, Jovanovich, Inc., 1982).
3. See R. H. Hayes and W. J. Abernathy, "Managing Your Way to Economic Decline," *Harvard Business Review* (July–August 1980): 67–77.
4. See J. P. Ponssard and J. Sarrazin, "Fondements des Nouvelles Méthodes d'analyse Stratégique — le critère de la part de marché relative," *Annales des Mines* (Juillet–Août 1981) and contrast this with the tendency toward destructive criticism of these ideas as in, for instance, the four-part series on strategy by W. Kiechel in *Fortune* (Oct.–Nov. 1981).
5. See D. Abell and J. S. Hammond, *Strategic Market Planning* (Englewood Cliffs, N.J.: Prentice-Hall, 1979).
6. Surprisingly, capital intensity does not appear as a key factor in the initial matrix — a gap quickly filled by the PIMS approach.
7. Typically, the competitive dimension is the one that used to be neglected. See M. Porter, *Competitive Strategy* (Glencoe, Ill.: The Free Press, 1981).
8. For a general discussion of implementation, see G. Y. Kervern, J. P. Ponssard and J. Sarrazin, "Proposition for a Relational Conception of Strategic Planning: Adaptation of the Past and Integration of the Future," in P. Lorange, ed., *Implementation of Strategic Planning* (Englewood Cliffs, N.J., Prentice-Hall, 1982).

CREATIVE AND NONCREATIVE USES OF PORTFOLIO PLANNING TOOLS AND STRATEGIES

Maurice Saias

I agree with the remarks by Drs. Collomb and Ponssard about the need to be creative in our uses of the presently available tools for strategic planning. I would also say that we need to be creative about the tools. The same is true for the concepts used. In the last twenty-five years we have not improved much. We are still guided by a planning concept in which we try to find the best match between our capabilities on one side and what the environment is likely to require on the other side. This is too mechanistic. Creativity in strategic planning should really start in an analysis of environmental factors and the discovery of ways in which they might be changed, and then go on to consider imaginative and innovative ways in which our capabilities can be used.

A creative manager should be able to take a problem and convert it into an opportunity. This is exactly what the cement producers like Lafarge Coppée have been doing in France. I suppose we also ought to have a class called anti-managers, who take an opportunity and turn it into a problem. This is what a lot of other managers have been doing.

Figure 4-5 is one portrayal of the kind of portfolio planning that Drs. Collomb and Ponssard are discussing.[1] Using the terminology of the Boston Consulting Group we refer to the products in a portfolio as "cash cows" and "dogs," respectively, when they occupy positions in the lower portion of the diagram. Those in the upper por-

Figure 4-5. Product Portfolio Matrix.

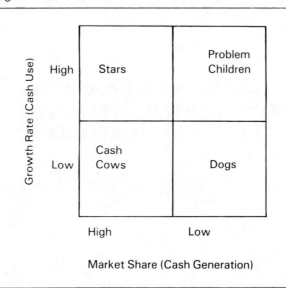

tion of the diagram we refer to as "stars" and "problem children"—although I prefer the term "dilemmas" since I do not really think that the term "problem children" is appropriate.

The problem children, as you can see, have a relatively low share of a fast-growing market. This often means that competitive pressures will tend to push profits to fairly low levels, and, at the same time, large influxes of cash will be needed to maintain or increase market share.

Cash cows, on the other hand, have relatively high market shares in low-growth markets and therefore generally generate more cash than they can invest. A generally recommended strategy is one that would invest this excess cash in some of the problem children in an attempt to convert them into stars.

The stars, as shown in Figure 4-5, have relatively large shares in high-growth markets. This may mean that additional investments will also be needed for them to meet competition and increase or hold market share. However, in time, as things settle down and growth slows, we may expect these stars to become cash cows. In other words, the cycle is complete: from cash cows to problem children to stars and back to cash cows.

Dogs are to be avoided or eliminated—for example, through divestment or sale—if possible. They generally do not require significant amounts of cash, or significant amounts of attention from top management. Hence, dogs tend to stay on in the portfolio with, at best, only modest amounts of capital investment needed from time to time.

Now what is it that Drs. Collomb and Ponssard say that Lafarge Coppée did? They say it "short-circuited" the whole thing and moved from dogs to cash cows by creatively obtaining high market share in low-growth industry. Moreover, Lafarge Coppée is doing more of the same by using the resulting cash "throw off" to invest in the U.S. cement industry, which is also in the dog category.

I will not repeat what Drs. Collomb and Ponssard have recounted as to how this was done with large added investments, merger and elimination of smaller firms, and so forth. What I will say instead is that, as a result, Lafarge Coppée was able to grow to a larger market share and, in the process, avoid the intense competition and long waiting periods involved in going from problem child to star and back to cash cow. Lafarge Coppée also reduced its unit costs through the route of economies of scale (rather than the "experience curve")[2], and they also introduced a variety of product and process innovations.

Thus, Drs. Collomb and Ponssard showed that portfolio analysis could be *made* wrong. On the other hand, they were careful to point out that they were mainly criticizing just a mechanistic use of this planning tool. I would also add that this tool, the so-called matrix portfolio representation, is quite old—going back to at least the early 1970s via work by the Boston Consulting Group. A lot of other, more sophisticated, tools are now available, although none of them seem to know quite how to deal with creativity.

Another way of looking at the matter is to say that Drs. Collomb and Ponssard showed that we have to look for creativity and innovation possibilities in every one of the cells of the matrix. Now this is very important for France. Only 20 percent of our exports originate in other than our traditional industries. This is to say that most of our exports come from cash cows and dogs. In addition, it is the traditional industries that are the large employers, and so, in a country like France, one simply cannot play the game the way a mechanical use of the portfolio approach to strategic planning would suggest.

There is also the question of structure—not only business structure but also social structure—where we have to be creative and innovative. The U.S. Federal Trade Commission, as Drs. Collomb and Ponssard have noted, is no longer well adapted to dealing with the widened (international) scope of competition in the 1980s. If it keeps on its present track this Commission will help the Japanese to realize their dream of becoming "number one" not at the end of the century but by the end of the 1980s.

We need to be pragmatic and innovative, but when we move into social structure we have to take a lot more into account, as Dr. Kirby noted elsewhere in this volume. We also need to alter our business education programs, as Dr. Kozmetsky has noted, so that our graduates will be able to help bring these kinds of altered social and business structures into existence and manage them well.

There is also a merging of private and public interests to be dealt with. We need to be good job providers, and so even a socialist government in France wants business to be profitable. (The government also collects more taxes in this way.) In any case, socialist government or not, there is no way in which private business can survive on the basis of purely economic considerations only. Just as Dr. Kirby talked about constituencies in the public sector, so we now also have to manage with the interests of many different constituencies in mind in the private sector. Here again our management education is less than adequate, and we need to bring far more into it about managing with such constituencies. Creativity and innovation should receive a prominent place, especially in considering different ways of organizing and regulating the activities of *both* public and private organizations.

How shall we go about this and how soon will we need to get started? I am reminded in this connection of the story of two Frenchmen who went to take pictures of African wildlife. A hungry lioness had other ideas about what they should be doing. In the resulting encounter one of the Frenchmen made it up toward the top of a very large and thick baobab tree, the only tree in the vicinity, while the other was able only to scurry around the tree with the lioness in hot pursuit. The one in the tree thought he ought to do what he could to help his friend and so he shouted down in an agitated manner, "Hurry, Jean, hurry! The lioness is just behind you." The other replied, in a very cool and collected manner, "Don't worry, I am still one jump ahead!"

NOTES

1. Adapted from Derek Abell and John S. Hammond, *Strategic Market Planning* (Englewood Cliffs, N. J.: Prentice-Hall, 1979).
2. See Abell and Hammond, *op. cit.*, pp. 110 ff. for a discussion of this aspect of portfolio planning.

OLD AND "NEW" CONCEPTS OF COMPETITION AND CONCENTRATION

Claude LeBon

The paper by Drs. Collomb and Ponssard emphasizes something with which I would agree, and so would almost anyone else—namely, a superficial rote use of portfolio analyses and planning approaches can discredit the cement industry as a possible outlet for investment. The same would hold for almost any other basic industry.

Reasons why the cement industry will not classify well under the portfolio approach include examples like the following: (1) no growth in demand and, indeed, fairly stable and saturated demand; (2) no real opportunity for product differentiation—after all, cement is cement; and (3) as a result of all this, competition is likely to be based on price only.

Additional reasons why the cement industry is unattractive would include the following: (1) the presence of many competitors, both in Europe and the United States; (2) the fact that business is capital intensive and, indeed, requires large capital outlays; and (3) the fact that the cement industry has now been submitted to many regulations ranging from pollution control to control of working conditions and product quality.

All of the above should lead to divestment or the milking of a so-called cash cow in the portfolio approach to strategic planning. As Drs. Collomb and Ponssard show, however, some subdivisions of the cement industry have exhibited innovation in both processes and products and have also been able to widen their markets—for example, by discovering new possibilities in less developed countries. They

151

have even been able to respond quickly to the energy crisis by reducing the calorific requirements of their outputs (inter alia, there have been capacity increases and innovations in product use as well).

I have no quarrel with the paper's criticism of mechanical uses of portfolio approaches to strategic planning. I also agree that creative and innovative management has played an important role in the cement industry and can do so in other basic industries as well.

My main qualification to what Drs. Collomb and Ponssard are saying lies in their discussion of integration and concentration as a source of these responses. The basis of their comparison rests on what happened in Europe and the United States. The former, we are told, has replaced the old concept of competition with the newer one of potential competition, and this can be relied on to prevent exploitation of consumers.[1] Furthermore, with fewer competitors, it is possible to plan larger plants that will provide access to economies of scale that are not otherwise available. In addition, larger companies are better at managing social changes by transferring people to new plants when this is required by technical progress or market changes. Finally, larger companies can base their policies on long-term optimal considerations and in this way avoid "dirty little price wars" with accompanying volatility and uncertainty in these markets.

I am not certain that big companies are better behaved than small companies in all these respects. To be sure, the cement situation has been chaotic in the United States in recent years. It went from overcapacity to shortages, and vice versa, in fairly short intervals of time. On the other hand, a great many other things have also been going on in the U.S. economy, and until these have been pretty well sorted out one cannot conclude much more than something like "small is vulnerable" instead of "small is beautiful."

The paper by Collomb and Ponssard provides some good examples of vertical integration as well as concentration. Suppose, however, that concentration is in the hands of the buyer rather than the seller of cement. Would Drs. Collomb and Ponssard regard this with equal favor? In their analysis of the aggressive entry of the British ready-mix group as potential buyers, that appears in their section on vertical integration, Drs. Collomb and Ponssard speak about the need for maintaining a low level of buyer concentration. In other words, they are saying that seller concentration is to be encouraged, but not buyer concentration.

Large investment plans, they say, are more easily developed when there is a reasonable amount of captive demand. When I see terms like "reasonable amount of captive demand" I grow worried since I do not think I would like to be a reasonably captive customer. Anyway, this needs to be spelled out in more detail. When I see a word like "reasonable" I am reminded of the question posed by a British professor to a candidate defending his thesis. In the manner of economists everywhere, the candidate said, "It seems reasonable to assume. . . ." "Well," replied the professor, "if it seems reasonable, then why don't you reason it!"

Whether speaking of buyer concentration or seller concentration, one has to recognize that concentration is power. This naturally points in the direction of regulation and control whether by the U.S. antitrust laws or by other approaches.

I think the paper by Collomb and Ponssard leaves that question open. It also leaves open a variety of other questions. Consider, for instance, the issue of economies of scale. I would like to obtain an answer to the question, How Much—in particular, how much concentration do we need to get these economies of scale? Do we need 95 percent concentration in two companies, for example, or would some other number of companies get us most of the benefits we would like from such economies of scale? Similarly, even if vertical integration in a single industry provides high levels of output from concomitantly large investments, we also need to consider other things such as the outcomes we are likely to confront in the face of an industry downturn. Faced with large fixed costs and resulting leverage, such companies may be forced to cut back sharply. That is what has happened in the automobile and steel industries, and I believe a pretty good case can be made for the fact that these industries should have diversified, as in a standard portfolio analysis, instead of investing in large plants, as they did in prior years. Maybe the real trouble was that these decisions were made by managers whose entire experience was in a single business. Thus, one might reasonably conclude that portfolio analysis or other approaches were needed to get these managers to look systematically at other possible alternatives for their investment decisions!

NOTES

1.   Baumol, W. J.; J. C. Panzar; and R. D. Willig. 1982. *Contestable Markets and the Theory of Industry Structure.* New York: Harcourt, Brace Jovanovich, Inc.

5 RISK MANAGEMENT

Karl O. Faxén

INTRODUCTION

By "Risk Management," I mean methods to deal with uncertainty in collective wage bargaining, energy contracts, and other business agreements. I do not mean protection against fire, sabotage, and similar problems.

In the United States, escalator clauses are common in collective wage agreements. Profit sharing is also widespread. These types of contracts can be seen as partial solutions to risk management problems. The development of the price level is uncertain. A wage agreement without escalation would, therefore, have to be rather short. For instance, in Sweden one quarter of a year became common practice during the 1917 inflation. Escalation was then introduced in order to obtain advantages from longer contract periods.

In profit sharing, it is not risks from general inflation as much as uncertainty about markets and sales of individual firms that are shared. Risks can be shared in energy contracts. For instance, an electric utility can make a contract with an aluminum manufacturer linking the price of electricity to the price of aluminum. In this way, the uncertainty of the aluminum price is shared between the aluminum manufacturer and the electric utility.

SOURCES AND EFFECTS OF INCREASED
UNCERTAINTY

Uncertainty in economic life has increased. It is now significantly higher than in the 1960s. The two oil price shocks in 1973 and 1979 were dramatic expressions of this increased uncertainty. But the oil price shocks are not the only causes. In fact, uncertainty increased before the first oil price shocks.

For practical businessmen it is more important now than during the 1960s to find creative and innovative methods to manage uncertainty. Contracts may have to be made more complicated. Contingencies, like price links and escalator clauses, are justified more often now than earlier. Hence, I will argue that a considerable amount of creativity along such lines is needed in order to expand business under present conditions.

The increased uncertainty stems from the macroeconomic system, not from changed conditions for individual businesses. It is, therefore, necessary to discuss macroeconomic problems in order to understand the character of the uncertainties that confront business today and will continue for a long time.

Let us first look at Figure 5–1, which describes inflation and unemployment in the OECD area as a whole since the mid-1960s. Along the vertical axis inflation is measured by increases in a consumer price index and unemployment as a percentage of the labor force is measured along the horizontal axis. As we see, the development has followed three loops, each loop being wider than the preceding one. It is not a very stable situation.

If you look at Figure 5–2, you will see a so-called "Phillips Curve." Inflation is again represented on the vertical axis and unemployment on the horizontal. The Phillips Curve was invented in 1958 by an Australian economist and dominated macroeconomic discussions during the 1960s. The one in Figure 5–2 is the Phillips Curve for the United States up until 1969, taken from Arthur Okun's book, *Prices and Quantities* (Washington: The Brookings Institution, 1981). As you can see, there was a stable relationship between unemployment and inflation. You could make demand management policy a bit more expansive and get less unemployment and more inflation. You could make demand management policy a bit more restrictive, getting more unemployment and less inflation. In most

Figure 5-1. Unemployment and Inflation in OECD 1965-1984.

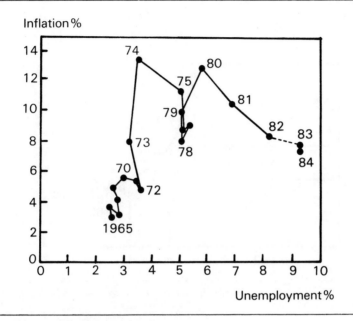

Inflation = Consumer price increase, percent.
Unemployment, percent of labour force, standardized.
Source: *OECD Economic Outlook*, December 1982, Tables R10 and R12 and estimates made from other tables.

countries left wing parties advocated less unemployment and were willing to accept more inflation. Right wing parties took the opposite position: less inflation at the price of more unemployment. The important thing was that this relationship was stable. It did not shift during this period.

What happened during the 1970s? Figure 5-3, again taken from Okun's book, portrays the development in the United States up to 1981. The relationship of the 1960s exploded. In the 1970s there was no longer any Phillips Curve. You see just a cluster of points.

As I have already noted, uncertainty in economic life has increased since the 1960s. One measure of this is provided by the surveys of consumer price expectations that are made by the Survey Research Institute at the University of Michigan. Figure 5-4 illustrates the development of actual price increases and of price expectations in the United States. The actual rate of inflation plotted in the upper part

Figure 5-2. Phillips Curve U.S.A. 1954-1969.

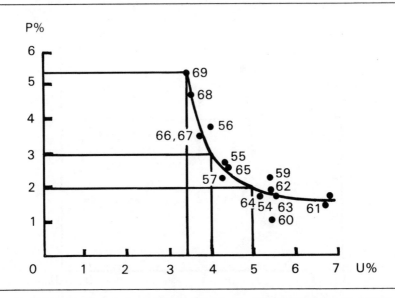

P = Percentage change in implicit GNP deflator; U = Unemployment rate in percent of labour force.

Source: Arthur M. Okun, *Prices and Quantities: A Macroeconomic Analysis*, Figure 6.3 page 238, Washington, D.C.: The Brookings Institution 1981.

of the figure clearly shows the two oil price shocks and the deceleration period in between.

The middle figure shows the relationship between the actual price development and consumers' expected price development four quarters earlier. First, the oil price shocks were unexpected. Actual price development was much higher than expected price development. There is one peak in the fourth quarter of 1973 and another peak in the fourth quarter of 1979. The peak in the second oil price shock was lower than in the first. The second, still more important observation is that during the deceleration period—from 1975 to 1978— price expectations were as a rule lower than actual inflation. In other words, high price expectations cannot have contributed very much to the "stagflation" problem during that period.

In the bottom third of Figure 5-4 one may see the variance of consumers' inflationary expectations. Different consumers had different inflationary expectations, and a measure for these differences is shown. The measure, variance in the expected rate of inflation,

Figure 5-3. Phillips Curve U.S.A. Exploded 1970.

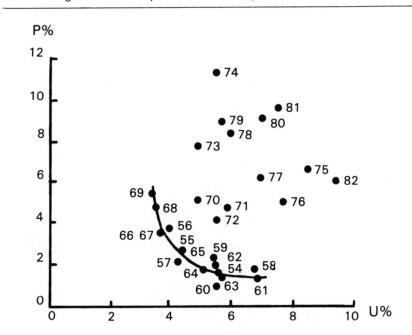

Source: A.M. Okun, *Prices and Quantities: A Macroeconomic Analysis*, (Washington, D.C.: The Brookings Institution 1981), Figure 6-4, page 240. Data for 1980, 1981 and 1982 from *OECD Economic Outlook*.

may be taken as an index for uncertainty about inflation among consumers in the United States. Again one may see that uncertainty increased dramatically in the two oil price shocks. This may not be surprising, but it is nevertheless of interest to observe that uncertainty was consistently higher between the two oil price shocks than in the period before. I will come back to this point later.

Similar surveys of households have been made in the EEC countries from 1973 onwards.[1] The general picture is the same as for the United States. The oil price increases were unexpected. As in the United States, price uncertainty increased dramatically in Europe during the two oil price shocks. In most EEC countries, between the two oil price shocks, expected inflation was lower than actual inflation, as it was in the United States. Unfortunately, because of lack of data, we cannot make any comparison with the period before 1973, as we did for the United States.

Figure 5-4. Actual and Expected Rates of Inflation, U.S., 1971-1982.

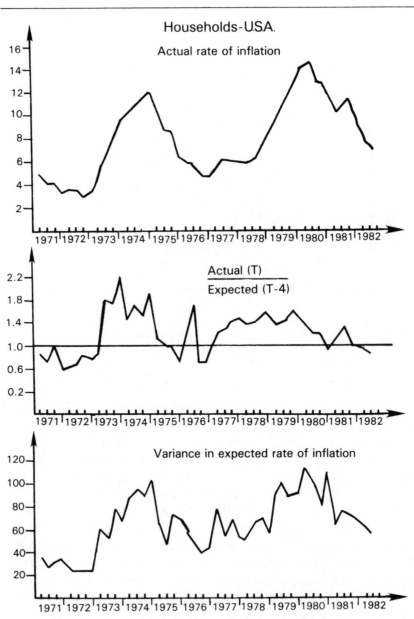

Source: Graphs are based on data from surveys by the Survey Research Center at the University of Michigan.

Roy Batchelor of the City University of London has studied business expectations in five EEC countries for the period 1965–1979. His data indicate that in all five countries the first oil price shock was as unexpected among businessmen as it was among consumers.[2] Also, in all five countries, price uncertainty among businessmen increased significantly during the period of shock. In Italy and in the United Kingdom, business price uncertainty also increased around 1970. This did not happen in the other three countries. In Belgium, France, and Germany, after 1975, business price uncertainty decreased to levels below those of the years before 1973. This is in contrast to what happened among U.S. consumers as shown at the bottom of Figure 5–4. Only in the United Kingdom and in Italy did business price uncertainty after the first oil price shock behave like it did among U.S. consumers.

To sum up, two observations can be made. The first is that in some countries there was already an increase in business price uncertainty around 1970. Thus, the oil price shocks were not the only source of increases in business price uncertainty in Europe. The second observation is that there was, in two European countries, more price uncertainty between the two oil price shocks than before 1973. The opposite was true in three other European countries.

Let us now return to the United States. In Figure 5–5, we see the "Expectations-Augmented Phillips Curve" for the United States. On the vertical axis we no longer have price increases. Instead, the variable on the vertical axis is actual price increases, symbolized by P_A, divided by expected price increases, P_E, four quarters earlier. Unemployment is plotted on the horizontal axis line as a percent of the labor force, just as before. The horizontal line in the body of the graph indicates where the actual price increase is equal to the expected price increase four quarters earlier—that is, this line indicates where expectations are fulfilled on the average. Above this line, inflation is higher than expected. This should mean that demand is also higher than expected, which means that business firms should try to increase employment more than expected, and so on. Below this horizontal line expected inflation is higher than actual and the opposite should be true, at least in theory.

Thus, according to economic theory, one would expect unemployment to be lower the higher the actual price development is in relation to the expected price development. Using this as a guide we no longer have only an unorganized cluster of points. In contrast to

Figure 5-5. Expectations-augmented Phillips Curves, U.S.A.

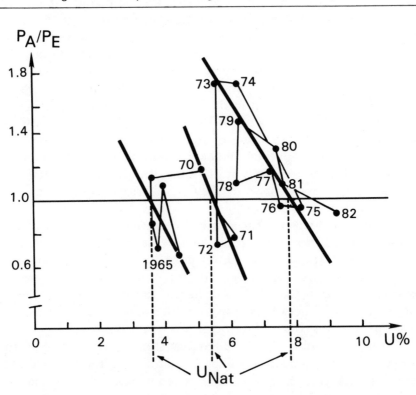

U = Unemployment; P_A = Actual price increase; P_E = Expected price increase year before. The three solid lines are "Expectations-augmented Phillips curves."

Source: K.O. Faxén, Stability in Economic Growth Under Uncertainty, in *Policy Making in a Disorderly Global Economic System*, (Stockholm: Industrial Institute for Economic and Social Research, 1983).

Figure 5-3, this figure has a structure. But the "Expectations-Augmented Phillips Curve" did shift twice—the first time around 1970 and the second time during the first oil price shock in 1973. Remarkably, it has stayed constant for almost ten years since then.

The level of unemployment where the "Expectations-Augmented Phillips Curve" intersects this horizontal line is called "Natural Unemployment" by Milton Friedman.[3] Economic policy can temporarily bring unemployment below this level by means of an expansionary monetary and fiscal policy—but only temporarily. Sooner or later expectations will adjust to actual inflation and unemployment will be brought back to its "Natural Level." Now, as you see from the figure, "Natural Unemployment" in the United States was around 3.5 percent in the late 1960s, increased to about 5.5 percent in the beginning of the 1970s, and now for ten years has been a little under 8 percent. Because actual inflation has been higher than expected most of the time, actual unemployment has been below its "Natural Rate." All that U.S. monetary and fiscal policies have been able to do from 1973 on is to travel up and down along this curve. They have not been able to move it to the left, toward the origin.

This is remarkable. Even more remarkable is the fact that this theory was formulated by Friedman, and Phelps, before 1970—that is, before the phenomenon we are studying here existed.

Now let us return to the topic of uncertainty. Uncertainty increased from the late 1960s to the early 1970s and from the early 1970s to the last ten-year period. The cause for the shifts in the "Expectations-Augmented Phillips Curve" in the United States has been increased price uncertainty. What can lead to such a conclusion? Paul Wachtel[4] has used Survey Research Center data for the period 1955-1973—that is, before the second shift of the curve on Figure 5-5—to study the effects of price uncertainty upon wages, prices, and interest rates. His regression results support the view that uncertainty is a major factor behind the shifts we observe in Figure 5-5.

Roy Batchelor[5] also made an analysis of the U.K. Expectations-Augmented Phillips Curve and found a significant influence of price uncertainty among U.K. consumers. The U.K. has a more open economy than the United States, and so Batchelor had to add a few variables, including the exchange rate. His main results are that (1) a 1 percent increase in the standard deviation of inflation expectations among U.K. consumers increases unemployment by 0.75 percent and (2) that unexpected inflation reduces unemployment by 0.25 percent for every 1 percent that inflation exceeds expectations among U.K. consumers. In other words, other empirical studies also indicate a relationship between increased uncertainty and shifts in the Expectations-Augmented Phillips Curve.

On the theoretical side, the empirical relationship is supported by "search theory." Search theory was introduced into economics beginning in the 1970s to help explain labor market search among the unemployed. Search theory can be equally well applied, however, to any form of market search—be it the markets for consumer goods, intermediate goods or raw materials, financial markets, markets for corporations, and the like. The central idea is that search takes time and involves costs. It also involves risk and uncertainty in that continued search will not necessarily produce better alternatives and also already discovered alterations may be lost. A buyer or a seller has to consider these costs when deciding whether to accept an offer or to continue searching. When search costs are high, it is better to make an early contract rather than to continue search. If uncertainty is high, it may pay to continue searching at given costs rather than to make an early contract. If more precise information can be expected later, making it possible to make a better deal, it may pay to acquire such information, even at a cost.

This means that high uncertainty will lead to long search times and low-capacity utilization. It might be added that it will also lead to high unemployment (caused by the low-capacity utilization). This theoretical conclusion is confirmed by Batchelor's empirical findings. In all four countries investigated (Belgium, France, Germany, and Italy) Batchelor found a significant lagged relationship between business inflation uncertainty and capacity utilization. An increase in inflation uncertainty will cause a decrease in capacity utilization and, at the same time, cause an increase in unemployment.

For some countries and periods of time, there are measurements of uncertainty among consumers. Uncertainty among businessmen has also been measured for other countries and periods of time. I would regard such measures as indicators of the degree of uncertainty in the economy in general and not exclusively related to either consumers or business.

By intuition, uncertainties in different markets are related. For instance, uncertainty about the oil price spreads to related markets: to the labor market, to investment in the energy sector, to other investments in transport and manufacturing, and so forth. Search theory is not yet very much developed on this point, it is true, but some work is going on in Stockholm at the Institute for Economic and Social Research. Jim Albrecht and Bo Axell of Columbia have investigated search market equilibrium for a two-market economy—one commodity and one kind of labor.[6] For the time being, however, we will have to rely mostly upon intuition as a basis for the conclusion that uncertainty in different markets is interdependent.

As an indication of the importance of uncertainty let me quote a few passages from what is presently the latest GATT report, *International Trade 1981-82*. This report distinguishes four main forms of increased economic uncertainty.

The first is the uncertainty persisting since 1973 about the future availability and price of energy. Since energy enters into all economic activities, energy price uncertainty impinges on all investment decisions.

The second main form of uncertainty, according to GATT, is the uncertainty generated by inflation. It affects business planning in two distinct ways. Business decisions are based primarily on information conveyed by changes in relative prices. Inflation introduces severe irregularities into relative price behavior and thus impairs the information function of the price system. This is the first way uncertainty affects business planning.

The third way that uncertainty affects business planning is that the unpredictability of price behavior and the generally high inflationary expectations are a source of the present high level of interest rates, at least according to the GATT report. Because inflation in different national economies is proceeding at different and varying rates, GATT finds uncertainty about future exchange rates inevitable. This uncertainty arising from international economic relations enters the domestic price structures in different countries, and I believe that this, too, is a major factor behind the 1970 increase in general economic uncertainty that we saw in Figure 5–5 for the United States, and which Batchelor found for the United Kingdom and Italy.

Fourth, and finally, according to GATT, a distinct type of uncertainty that has been felt within the financial system emanates from the perceived deterioration in the quality of bank assets. In addition, decreased equity/debt ratios in corporate balance sheets have added a company risk to the country risk mentioned above.

Thus, in addition to the oil price shocks, the irregularity of inflation, the unpredictability of foreign exchange rates, and the increasing uncertainty in financial markets constitute an increasing challenge for business to be creative and to find new forms of risk management. In addition, there may also be intrinsic causes for more uncertainty in the real economy in the real growth process itself.

GROWTH AND ECONOMIC PROGRESS

As I have observed several times, the first oil price shock did not start the process I am examining. Something had already happened around 1970. I will now venture the hypothesis that the increased uncertainty in economic life during the 1970s was due to endogenous fac-

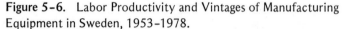

Figure 5-6. Labor Productivity and Vintages of Manufacturing Equipment in Sweden, 1953-1978.

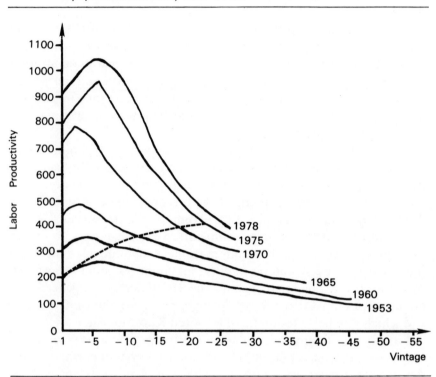

Source: Pehr Wissén, *Wages and Growth in an Open Economy* (Stockholm School of Economics, 1982).

tors occurring in a rapidly growing economy. As we know, the first post-war decades were unparalleled in economic growth. Never before 1940 did the industrialized world experience such a long period of relatively high and stable growth. My hypothesis is that growth breeds its own destruction—that is, stagflation.

Let us look at Figure 5-6. It is taken from a study in which Dr. Pehr Wissén[7] at the Economic Research Institute of the Business School in Stockholm has made simulations of the structure and age composition of equipment in Swedish manufacturing during the post-war period. In 1953—the lowest line on the figure—labor productivity on different vintages of equipment was described by a rather flat and long curve. As a result of a high investment rate and

Figure 5-7.   Changes in Swedish Employment in Response to Changes in Wages, 1953–1978.

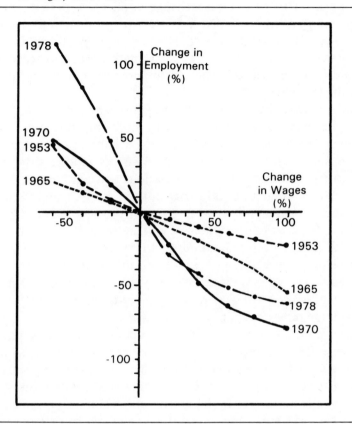

Source: Pehr Wissén, *Wages and Growth in an Open Economy* (Stockholm School of Economics, 1982).

high technical progress during the post-war years, combined with strong wage pressures, this curve became shorter and more peaked. In 1978, machinery was scrapped about twice as fast as in 1953. Slack in the use of capital was much smaller in the 1970s than immediately after the war. This made the economy more sensitive to disturbances in 1978 than in 1953.

Turning to Figure 5-7, we see the sensitivity of employment to a change in wages. In 1978, a 20 percent increase in real wages would have decreased employment around 30 percent, compared to less than 10 percent in 1953.

The same holds for cost disturbances other than wage increases—for instance, an oil price increase. The economy was much more sensitive in the 1970s to a sudden change in oil markets than it was in the beginning of the 1950s. Now, if we expect a certain frequency of disturbances of a certain size, the effects of given disturbances will become stronger and stronger as the growth process proceeds. Furthermore, one disturbance will add to another, reinforcing the next link in the sequence.

Similar results have been obtained by simulations of another model, the micro-macro model of the Industrial Institute for Economic and Social Research. Thus, these results are not dependent only on some special feature of Dr. Wissen's model, although we must remember these are only simulations and not empirical observations. When simulating industrial output, profit margins, and unemployment for the period 1977–2027 (fifty years) Gunnar Eliasson found that high utilization rates of existing capital and fast restructuring led to a tailspin reaction after thirty years.[8] Fifteen years of complete stagnation followed. Less stress during the first thirty years led to stable growth. Another important observation was that simulated slower market adjustment regimes led to more stable growth at lower average rates of capacity utilization.

We can now formulate the relevant hypothesis in a consistent way as follows: There were systematic factors arising from a long period of high and stable economic growth that increased the probability that a disturbance beyond a certain size would create a serious disruption in the economy. If this is true, the two oil price shocks were endogenous in a stochastic sense. Unpredictable market changes of different kinds can be expected to create new and serious disturbances in the 1980s, as they did in the 1970s. Business must understand this and learn how to live in this type of surrounding.

LABOR NEGOTIATIONS AND BARGAINING

After this discussion of the macroeconomic causes of increased uncertainty, let us return to a more practical business level. I am not a businessman. I am an economist and have spent my professional active life advising the Swedish Employers' Confederation. Against this background, I might ask: How did bargaining change from the relatively stable and predictable conditions before 1970 to the uncertain 1970s and 1980s? Did we, from 1970 onwards, make more long-term contingency contracts—making active attempts to stabilize the economy—or did we resort to short-term and less complex agreements?

When centralized agreements were introduced in Sweden in the mid-1950s, we inherited escalator clauses from the war. Wage escalation was phased out in a number of steps. The last contract of this type was the two-year agreement for 1957 and 1958. It contained a cost-of-living reopener. After 1958, there was a common opinion—shared by the union side—that wage escalation should be avoided. For instance, we made a three-year agreement for 1966–68 without any cost-of-living guarantee.

In 1969, the salaried unions proposed a five-year agreement on the basis of a fixed annual percentage salary increase. By this action, the question of risk sharing was again raised. In order to reduce inflation, both sides wanted to make the five-year agreement on a lower percentage increase than would have corresponded to the average salary increase during the 1960s. Salary escalation was considered undesirable, both by the employers' side and the unions' side. The idea was to take account of macroeconomic effects, as could be done under Swedish labor-bargaining arrangements, and to help stabilize the economy by making a fixed agreement for five years. The 1966–68 three-year agreement had worked satisfactorily. Risk sharing was, therefore, limited to the fourth and fifth year in the contract period. Instead of cost-of-living index numbers, the contingency clause was tied to the shares of salaries, wages, and operating surplus in the amount of value added for manufacturing and building. If you like, you may say that it represented a kind of macrolevel profit sharing.

When we wrote that agreement in December 1969—covering the years 1970–74—we believed it to be crystal clear. However, as a security measure we introduced the possibility of arbitration, a rather unique feature for Sweden. When 1973 arrived, we could not agree upon the interpretation because of statistical difficulties. The case went to arbitration and an agreement was reached.

I think this experience is not unusual when long-term and complex contingency contracts are used for the first time. The agreement was certainly creative, in the sense of being new for Sweden, but a number of unforeseen difficulties arose during the contract period. In theoretical terminology, the contracting costs turned out to be prohibitive. Both sides burned their fingers.

I do not think it can be said that this five-year agreement with the salaried unions contributed very much to stabilization of the Swedish economy between 1970 and 1974. It created a lot of difficulties in our relations with the manual workers' trade unions. It did not prevent the first oil price shock from creating serious disturbances in the Swedish economy.

Let me pass over the shock years of the mid-1970s, which are best described as being confused. We experienced a cost explosion, we lost international competitiveness, and wage policy was a disaster.

In the fall of 1976, the time was ripe for a wage and salary policy that could help in reducing inflation. This meant that the advantages of a low base increase had to be weighed against the disadvantages of contingency clauses. The union side could not accept the risk that a low wage and salary agreement might fail to lead to a corresponding deceleration of inflation. In 1977, we had limited indexing, and in the two-year agreement 1978–79, there were cost-of-living reopeners for both years. The price ceiling was broken in August 1979 because of the second oil-price shock. An agreement was reached on 5 December 1979 after serving notice of mutual strikes and lockouts, overtime bans, and similar limited action. Thus, the experience of this kind of contingency clause was not very positive. In the two-year agreement 1981–82 we again had wage and salary escalation above a price ceiling. It was broken in September 1982. The reason was higher interest rates, and the high interest rates had their roots in U.S. monetary policy.

What I want to illustrate with this long story are the swings between the efforts to find some kind of risk-sharing arrangement as part of a program to stabilize the economy and a more laissez-faire attitude, which asserts that things are better with uncomplicated, short-time, "best-possible" contracts.

RISK SHARING ARRANGEMENTS

This experience also demonstrates that it is by no means self-evident that contingency contracts—which both parties find advantageous—also have stabilizing effects upon the economy.[9] For instance, when a reopener has been invoked, special factors enter the bargaining. The union side takes a more legalistic position and forgets macroeconomic consequences. This can be destabilizing. It is remarkable that this is true also in economy-wide collective bargaining. In this bargaining situation, macroeconomic considerations enter much more than in long-term contracts between business firms as, for example, in energy contracts.

As we have learned during the 1970s, price relationships in the energy field are highly uncertain. Profits in the 1990s—the period when equipment decided upon now should earn profits and pay back its investment costs—will be highly dependent upon the price relationships between the major sources of energy: oil, coal, gas, and nuclear input. How does this uncertainty enter the planning process in business corporations? How can one cope with these difficulties?

Figure 5-8, taken from *Shell Briefing Service*, provides an example of cost estimates for various sources of energy. The range can be taken as an expression of uncertainty, as seen from the buyer's point of view. The buyer could be an electric utility. Middle East oil is in a cost range by itself. After that you can see, in a second group, North Sea oil, coal mined in the United States, coal imported into Northwestern Europe or mined there, and nuclear input. For electricity generation, coal and nuclear energy are—at least in Europe—the relevant alternatives. Oil will, in the 1990s, be used primarily when coal is not technically possible.

I do not want to go into a lengthy technical analysis of relative costs. I only want to make one point. What made energy a major source of uncertainty since 1973 was not any of the cost factors. It was the change in the market regime for crude oil. In order to move from the estimated cost ranges in this figure to relative prices in the 1990s, assumptions about market regimes for coal, nuclear input, and the like are needed.

When will the exhaustability of a low-cost energy source be discounted to a point where the price level will be determined by the costs on the next step in the staircase that we see in the figure? What role can cartels like OPEC play in this process? Can this type of uncertainty be described by means of probabilities?

The mutual interest in reducing uncertainty has made long-term contingency contracts common in coal. During part of the contract time, the price is linked to some suitable index or some similar arrangement is made. For the remainder of this time, prices are to be negotiated between the contracting parties on the basis of an agreed

Figure 5-8. Comparative Energy Costs.

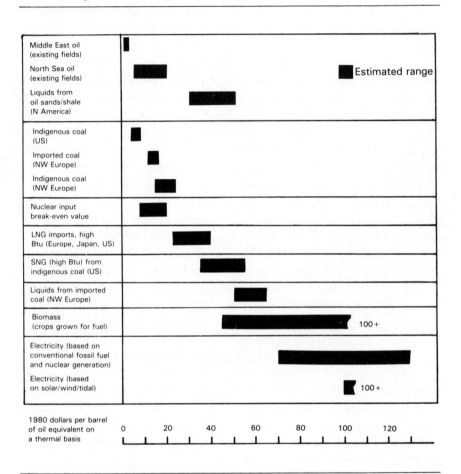

Source: Shell Briefing Service (London: Shell Oil Co., 1982).

list of determining factors. This facilitates investment decisions by reducing uncertainty. The reduction is primarily on the volume side. The main part of long-run price uncertainty remains.

In conclusion, I would like to make only one more point. It is by no means certain that a more extended use of contingency contracts in wage determination, in energy and in other fields will increase macroeconomic stability.

GAIN SHARING

In an article in a recent issue of *Challenge*, Daniel Mitchell[10] proposes a wider use of "gain sharing" as an antiinflationary reform. What is gain sharing? Mitchell says that "The essential feature of any gain-sharing plan is a linkage between the wage and the economic health of the employer, the industry or even the national economy. This linkage would make wage-setting responsive to the business cycle and, therefore, to monetary policy." Thus, Mitchell sees gain sharing as the addition of a second contingency clause to long-term collective agreements in the mutual interest of both parties, at the same time as the macroeconomic performance of the economy is improved. The United States has a tradition of contingency clauses since COLA (cost-of-living allowances) were introduced in the beginning of the 1970s. Gain sharing would build upon that tradition.

For a number of years the Swedish Employers' Confederation has promoted gain sharing on an experimental basis, particularly for small and medium-sized business. Positive experiences are reported from more than one hundred cases. Only recently has Mitchell's idea brought our attention to the possibility of positive effects upon wage rigidity and the macroeconomic performance of the economy from a general acceptance of gain sharing.

There is, however, a counterexample. In Iceland, fishing constitutes 70 percent of the competitive sector. Fishing has, by tradition, used gain sharing as a method of sharing risks between the owners of the boat and the crew. The sheltered sector has indexed wages and salaries that are linked to the pay levels in the competitive sector. The experience of this system is not stagflation but strong inflation (50–80 percent annually) and full employment. Risks in fishing—from variations in catch and from market fluctuations—are shared and transmitted via institutional arrangements in wage and salary formation in such a way as to constitute an engine for inflation. But Iceland is, as far as I know, the only high standard of living, full employment economy with high inflation.

Neither does it seem that the well-known biannual bonus system is the root of the substantial wage flexibility in Japan. True, bonuses are paid mostly according to value added per hour worked at plant level, but average bonuses form a constant percentage of total pay even during periods of rapid wage deceleration. Flexibility is in base pay, not in bonuses, when the entire manufacturing sector is considered. Britain and Japan have about the same wage flexibility, in spite of their widely different wage formation systems. Thus, it does not follow that a particular form of gain sharing will improve the macroeconomic performance of the economy only because it is mutually advantageous to employers and employees at the micro level. It has to meet certain requirements as to the lag structure, among other things. All forms of risk-sharing long-term contracts that can be agreed upon do not contribute to the solution of the stagflation problem.

CONCLUSION

This leads me to conclude that in the world in which we live, Pareto's grand principle for a stationary economy with perfect foresight does not hold. When the kind of uncertainty that I have discussed is introduced, it no longer seems to hold that a mutually advantageous contract between two parties is always good for society.

The OECD economies have demonstrated their sensitivity to market regime shocks such as accompanied the 1973 oil price and supply cutoff. "Regime" shocks in macroeconomic monetary and fiscal policies should also be added to this list of disturbances. I have not dealt here with this aspect of the problem, since the emphasis has been upon possible action in the business community itself, including its wage-setting methods. But this does not preclude the possibility that improved predictability in government monetary and fiscal policies over periods of several years, perhaps five years or more, is what we should aim at during the next few years. Such words as confidence, credibility, and consensus should be used more often. We have to find a compromise between an active countercyclical monetary and fiscal policy and the inflexible monetary targets that have lead to unpredictability in interest rates (even in real interest rates). Otherwise, monetary policy will contribute to high uncertainty for business, not decrease it, as was the goal. In conclusion we can return to Figure 5-5 and see that the Volcker years are on the same curve as was established in 1973. Strict adherence to fixed monetary targets as undertaken by the U.S. Federal Reserve System under Paul Volcker did not reduce uncertainty and shift the curve toward the origin, as was hoped. A more flexible monetary strategy that could reduce interest rate uncertainty appears to be called for. But this topic cannot be addressed here. It is a large one and would be a subject for another paper.

NOTES TO CHAPTER 5

1. F. Papadia and V. Basano, "EEC–DG II, Inflationary Expectations. Survey-Based Inflationary Expectations for the EEC countries," *EEC Economic Papers* 1 (May 1981).

2. R. A. Batchelor, "On Three Conjectures by Friedman" (Paper for Tenth Money Study Group Conference, Oxford, September 21–23, 1981). (Mimeo). Also R. A. Batchelor, "Expectations, Output and Inflation. The European Experience," *European Economic Review* (1982): 1–25.

3. Milton Friedman, "Inflation and Unemployment," (Nobel Lecture) *Journal of Political Economy* 3 (1977): 451–471. The "Expectations-Augmented Phillips Curve" can be traced back to Milton Friedman, "The Role of Monetary Policy," *American Economic Review* 58 (1968): 1–17, and E. S. Phelps, "Money Wage Dynamics and Labor Market Equilibrium," in E. S. Phelps, ed., *Microeconomic Foundations of Employment and Inflation Theory* (New York: Norton, Inc., 1970).

4. Paul Wachtel, "Survey Measures of Expected Inflation and Their Potential Usefulness," *Studies in Income and Wealth*, vol. 42, *Analysis of Inflation, 1965–1974*: 361–395.

5. R. A. Batchelor, "A 'Natural' Interpretation of the Present Unemployment" (Paper for the City University Conference on Monetarism in the United Kingdom, September 23–29, 1981). (Mimeo).

6. James W. Albrecht and Bo Axell, "General Search Market Equilibrium," Working Paper No. 63, The Industrial Institute of Economic and Social Research, Stockholm, Sweden, 1982.

7. Pehr Wissén, *Wages and Growth in an Open Economy* (Stockholm School of Economics, 1982).

8. Gunnar Eliason, "On the Optimal Rate of Structural Adjustment" in *Policy Making in a Disorderly World Economy* (Stockholm: The Industrial Institute of Economic and Social Research, 1983), pp. 269–323. Cf. especially pp. 313–317 and Figure 5 in that book.

9. For a discussion of this issue based upon risk theory (not uncertainty), see Jo Anna Gray, "On Indexation and Contract Length," *Journal of Political Economy* 1 (1978): 1–18.

10. Daniel J. B. Mitchell, "Gain-Sharing, An Anti-Inflation Reform," *Challenge* (July/August 1982): 18–25.

UNCERTAINTY AND THE NEED FOR INNOVATION IN MANAGEMENT TECHNIQUES AND METHODS

Bertil Naslund

The Institute of Management Sciences organized a conference in 1979 with representatives from Europe, Asia, Australia, and the United States to discuss the most important problems facing management in the 1980s. It yielded a consensus that management would have to deal with more turbulent environments, more shocks, more risk. Therefore, I think that the presentation of Dr. Faxén and his suggestions address a problem that is clearly perceived by many to be very important.

THE REASONS FOR TURBULENCE

One major point that Faxén makes is that this higher uncertainty is endogeneous and is the result of the growth that we have experienced since the second world war. This growth will create uncertainty and a turbulent environment.

Others (e.g., Drucker) have argued that the post-war period has been the most abnormal period in economic history with its long and uninterrupted growth. Turbulence is the "normal" state of affairs seen in a larger perspective. Since the mid-1970s we are returning to the normal, to a state of affairs with high rates of demographic changes, transnational production sharing, unions fighting for survival, and revolutions in information technology and its applications.

177

It may seem startling to many that the restructuring of several industries that have been stable since World War II should be something natural, especially as both higher education and managerial instruments have been designed and refined under the assumption of more or less unbroken stability and growth.

THINGS OTHER THAN RISK SHARING AND CONTINGENCY CONTRACTS WERE IMPORTANT

Higher uncertainty requires innovative management techniques and Dr. Faxén suggests two forms, namely (1) contingency contracts and (2) profit sharing or gain sharing. These are ways to diversify risks among different parties to help facilitate the making of longer contracts.

In order to find out how business firms responded to the turbulent events in the 1970s, I have been responsible for a research project trying to determine how firms responded to some of the main uncertainties during the 1970s (e.g., the oil price shocks and rapid exchange rate variations) and, in particular, to find out in what ways they tried to adapt to this new situation.

The study involved extensive interviews with presidents of twenty-five Swedish firms. Many things came out as a result of the study; in particular—in connection with contingent claims and risk sharing—the firms considered it to be more important in the face of unforeseen events to create an openness and willingness to accept changes in the organization. These executives did not see high turbulence as necessarily bad. They noted that it also creates opportunities and that it is important to grasp these opportunities as they occur. Therefore, the prime objective is not to aim for passive risk diversification and longer contracts but rather to maintain flexibility.

SEARCH IS NOT SO IMPORTANT

I have also been going over the material from my research project to see whether the responses by firms indicated that search times had gone up and thus empirically verify Faxén's suggestion that increased search could be the cause of the higher natural unemployment. The firms reported that search *was* affected, but, even more important, the search was mainly of a new kind and directed toward objectives besides the one of obtaining more facts, as described by Faxén. These firms now believe it to be necessary continuously to question and audit frames of reference. Hence their searches were also directed to ensuring that alternative hypotheses would be continuously generated in areas affecting the corporation's present and future behavior.

If search time is not increased very much, we need to look for something else that can explain Figure 5-5 in Dr. Faxén's paper? In research and development it is well known that faced with, say, twenty projects to choose from, one can either search and collect data and eventually start, say, twelve, out of which perhaps ten will succeed. Alternatively one might start all twenty at once and then see what happens. In the latter instance ten might fail but the firm might still end up with ten successful ideas.

If one response to higher turbulence is to undertake less search and to use smaller, more flexible units with the anticipation that more units than before will fail on the average, the result will be that the economy will (also on the average) have more idle resources and thus more unemployment. This alternative explanation cannot be ruled out as a possible source of the behavior observed in Figure 5-5 of Faxén's paper.

RISK SHARING HAS OTHER EFFECTS

When uncertainty increases it becomes more important to distribute it optimally in society. In addition to what Dr. Faxén mentions about profit sharing, I would like to add that it might provide workers with opportunities to take risks and obtain their most preferred balance between risk and return. The owners of capital can, in principle, invest in many different companies, in different assets, in different countries, and thereby obtain an income that reflects their willingness to take risk. The workers do not have the same opportunities. Hence, part of what is needed, in principle, is to provide every worker with an opportunity to receive the present value of his lifetime salary when he enters the labor force. He can then invest that money in accordance with his risk preference. If risk-sharing arrangements are thus organized, workers can take more risk and thus increase the supply of risk sharing in society and this will, in turn, reduce the cost of risk bearing.

NEW PLANNING METHODS NECESSARY

Some of the difficulties that Dr. Faxén discusses in the energy sector and in wage bargaining have to do with unforeseen events that make even probability estimates less useful. I believe that these difficulties are very real and that we have to develop new planning tools. Such tools, including the search theory referred to by Faxén, have been developed recently in operations research. Another new set of models is also now being explored where the aim is not to maximize expected profit but to obtain a satisfactory profit on as many future states of the world as possible. This redirection of what is being optimized involves a refocusing of both public and business planning that is important when uncertainty is high, and I believe that we must develop and refine such methods even further. Hopefully, this conference will help point us and others to these possibilities for research into the development of new and badly needed tools.

UNCERTAINTY AND THE OPPORTUNITIES FOR INNOVATION AND INVESTMENT

Sten Thore

Dr. Faxén has provided us with a penetrating and original analysis of current economic problems in the Western world. In his view, it is the increased uncertainty in economic life that is responsible for stagflation. The argument goes like this: Increased uncertainty leads to longer search times, both in labor and product markets. Longer search times mean lower capacity utilization and more unemployment.

As illustrations, Dr. Faxén has discussed the role of uncertainty in the labor and energy markets. The key idea is that it might be possible by new and imaginative forms of bargaining and designs of contracts to contain some of the increasing uncertainty. In particular, Faxén proposes that a suitable form of gain sharing might reduce uncertainty in labor markets, and he also mentions the possibility that long-term contracts with contingency clauses might stem some of the uncertainty in energy markets.

I find this analysis appealing, but there is an important proviso. What is the origin of the increased uncertainty that we are talking about? Note that increased uncertainty can indeed cause longer search times, but it can also be the other way around: Longer search times mean more uncertainty. Rising unemployment in itself brings more uncertainty into the labor markets. The still-employed workers may become more concerned about their ability to hang on to their present jobs, and the unemployed will face stiffer competition in their search for available job openings. Similarly, growth in unused production capacity can increase uncertainty in product markets. The prospects of again starting up production at a steel mill that has been shut down are less favorable if there are many other steel mills sharing the same fate. Uncertainty can be both a cause and an effect of unemployment and unused capacity. Uncertainty can be both exogenous and endogenous to the economic system.

I would like to mention here a few examples of exogenous risk. My first example is "regulation risk." In planning for the future, the executive of a company has to take into consideration not only current government regulations of productive processes but also the possibility that new regulations may be introduced in the future. Many regulations were introduced in the 1970s for the purpose of abating pollution, or for worker health and safety protection. Regulations lower the net return on existing industrial capital. Perhaps the most important observation to be made in this connection is that the implementation of government regulations requires the discretionary judgment of an administrator, and there will often be some element of uncertainty in the mind of corporate planners as to the outcome of an administrative evaluation. When the automatic mechanisms of the marketplace are replaced by administrative review and control, new uncertainty that did not exist before is bound to be created. Indeed, as the government sector of the economy expands, there is more risk.

My second example is the energy markets. Here I feel very comfortable with Dr. Faxén's analysis. The increases in risk in the energy markets are exogenous: The pricing policies of OPEC constituted an abrupt change of market regime.

My third example is the financial markets in the United States after 6 October 1979. On this date the Federal Reserve Board changed its procedures for conducting monetary policy. The earlier policies, which aimed at stabilizing interest rates, were abandoned and new procedures were instituted that were designed to control the money stock. As is well known, this shift of policy led to volatile interest rates and a considerable amount of uncertainty about the future course of interest rates both in the short run and in the long run. In the view of many monetary analysts,[1] this increased uncertainty has also caused interest rates to be much higher than they would otherwise have been, and there is presently built into interest rates in the United States a risk premium that compensates the lenders for the increased short-term volatility of interest rates.

To follow through Dr. Faxén's analysis, it is interesting to note that the real estate industry in the United States is now experimenting with new forms of mortgage financing (e.g., so-called variable-rate financing). The purpose of such new contract forms seems to be to shift some of the increased financial risk over to the homeowner.

The examples that I have discussed illustrate the proposition that exogeneous increases of risk lead to longer search times. But does it follow that they also lead to unemployment and unused capacity? From the point of view of the private corporation, all the uncertainty elements reviewed here constitute risks of reduced profits. More government regulation, higher and more volatile energy prices and interest costs all lead to lower profit streams and capital values. Thus the increased uncertainty that we are talking about is not symmetric — the probability distribution of profits and capital values is slanted toward the negative side.

To my mind there is nothing wrong with risk or even more risk in the business sector, as long as opportunities for innovation and expansion blend with the dangers of failure. In a sense, one could even argue that the capitalistic system thrives on risk. It is a great virtue of the capitalistic system that it tends to transfer the ownership and control of productive resources to those who perceive and are able to sustain the most efficient use of those resources so that technological advances, advances in industrial organization and in marketing, may evolve from a process of selection among uncertain and risky alternatives. The managers who succeed are rewarded. Those who fail are penalized. My own concern is, therefore, not so much that risk may be on the increase but rather that the opportunities to make the profits and capital gains that counterbalance the risk may be waning. Creativity and innovative management must be rewarded in the marketplace if all such efforts are not to come to nothing for the ultimate beneficiaries of these activities.

NOTES

1.   Milton Friedman, *Newsweek*, 28 June 1982.

IV ACADEMIC RESEARCH IN PSYCHOLOGY AND ARTIFICIAL INTELLIGENCE

6 PSYCHOLOGY AND MANAGERIAL CREATIVITY

Wayne H. Holtzman

Psychology is a relatively young science, having existed in its modern, experimental form for only one hundred years. Astute observers of human behavior and of the mind go back many centuries before the advent of scientific psychology. Even today, psychology can hardly lay any special claim of deep understanding much beyond the accumulated collective wisdom of our culture. Nevertheless, the use of scientific methods of investigation and the continual dialogue between behavioral scientists, practitioners, and the general public have led to the development of fresh points of view, new insights, and major technologies, particularly within the past thirty years. Some of the most successful applications of psychology have been within the fields of industrial organization, personnel assessment and training, human relations within social organizations, and the understanding of creativity, intelligence, and personality within various social contexts. Before examining in more detail the relationships between some of these psychological technologies and managerial creativity, let us first take a closer look at general creativity.

WHAT IS CREATIVITY?

When most people use the term "creativity," they are referring to some kind of socially recognized achievement in which there are

187

novel products or ideas to which one can point as evidence of a creative process. Inventions, theories, paintings, and novel methods of problem solving are but a few of the forms of divergent thinking that yield some kind of highly valued product or idea. One common method of studying creativity is to select individuals who are judged to be highly creative in their particular field of science, art, engineering, management, or whatever field is of special interest to the investigator.

Studies of highly creative adult artists, scientists, mathematicians, and writers generally find them scoring high on tests of general intelligence. Once you drop below the very highest levels of such creativity, however, the relationship between measures of tested intelligence and indices of creative achievement or reputation is only weakly positive at best. In other words, even in such fields as artistic and scientific creativity, the degree of tested intelligence above a certain level seems to make little difference. Highly intelligent individuals may be quite unable to use their intellectual abilities for creating novel solutions to difficult problems or for creating unique products and ideas that are deemed valuable. Likewise, individuals of only ordinary intelligence may indeed have special talents or be so highly motivated that they are able to achieve truly creative products.

Most of the research in the field of creativity has revealed a fairly stable set of core personality characteristics related to creative achievement and activity. Among these are high valuation of aesthetic qualities in experience, broad interests, attraction to complexity, high energy, independence of judgment, autonomy, intuition, self-confidence, ability to resolve apparent contradictions or to accommodate apparently conflicting traits in one's self-concept, and a firm sense of oneself as being creative (Barron and Harrington 1981). A productively creative person is also one who is strongly driven to achieve an artistic expression, to solve a complex problem, or to hold in mind seemingly contradictory ideas in spite of the tension that may arise.

One of the psychological techniques often used in a battery of assessment methods for the study of creativity is a projective test such as the Rorschach or Holtzman Inkblot Technique (Holtzman, Thorpe, Swartz, and Herron 1961). Early studies by MacKinnon and his associates (1965) at the Institute for Personality Assessment & Research in Berkeley focused in particular upon mathematicians, engineers, creative artists, and physical scientists, using a variety of personality measures, performance in laboratory-type tasks, and problem-solving tests. His work suggested that creative striving and production required different characteristics and involved different processes, depending upon the field of endeavor.

Using rigorously selected artists, architects, and engineers, my colleagues and I studied creativity in three contrasting modes of visual experience and their psychological correlates (Holtzman, Swartz, and Thorpe 1971). Showing a person a series of otherwise meaningless inkblots and asking him to use his imagination in telling you what he sees, is a good way to study creative expression in fantasy. Objective scores measuring a number of different aspects of personality, perception, and cognition provide a quantitative basis for comparing different kinds of individuals. As one would expect, creative, abstract artists are less concerned with the structural characteristics of the inkblots and are more likely to draw upon their own inner feelings and fantasies, often resulting in deviant and bizarre verbalizations, as contrasted to mechanical engineers who pay much more attention to the form and structure of the inkblots. The creative architect combines and integrates parts of the inkblot and shows sensitivity to the harmony and proportion of the visual design more than either the artist or engineer. Quite clearly, creativity is a complex mental activity that is expressed differently in one field than in another (Gilchrist 1972).

What do we mean by managerial creativity? A manager is someone who leads others in a common social endeavor to achieve a goal. Of particular interest to us are managers within complex social organizations, such as industrial plants, business firms, government agencies, educational institutions, or military units. The management of human behavior for group achievement of stated goals has been an essential leadership activity within social organizations since the first collective behavior of mankind. Managerial creativity is expressed when a manager comes up with a novel way of dealing with the organization and direction of individuals to achieve a previously unrealized goal.

Can psychological tests be used to predict a criterion of managerial creativity? In spite of many hundreds of studies in personnel assessment and prediction, no one has come up with a very good psychological test for predicting high levels of creativity, managerial or otherwise. Of course, you can increase significantly your chances of finding a highly creative manager by eliminating many individuals who do not have sufficiently minimal levels of intelligence, special talents, or the personality characteristics mentioned above that generally form the core characteristics related to creative achievement. Beyond this minimal set of personal characteristics, situational factors play a far greater role than personal traits. Probably one of the best methods of selecting creative managers is to look carefully at their past performance in similar situations as an indication of their future prospects.

Since all managers express their creativity through some social organization involving other people, a search for situational factors conducive to managerial creativity should begin at the level of the social organization. Psychology and the related behavioral sciences concerned with organizational behavior and development have made great progress in the past generation. The nature of these situational factors within social organizations will become more apparent after first examining key findings in organizational behavior and development.

ORGANIZATIONAL BEHAVIOR

Among the more particularly active areas of psychological research on organizational behavior are such topics as managerial personality, job attitudes, motivation, leadership, group dynamics, role theory, communication, task design, decision making, power, and politics. A search for environmental or situational factors within an organization that are conductive to managerial creativity would require careful study of all these topics and then some. Only a select few can be covered here. Let us first look at those that focus more on the individual and then turn to human relations and social factors.

Achievement Orientation and Locus of Control

The two individual variables that have received most attention are achievement orientation and locus of control (Mitchell 1979). High achievers stay on the job longer, perform better, and respond more positively to criticism. Managers with a high degree of achievement orientation are most likely to show candor, openness, receptivity, the use of participation, and concern for people when dealing with the organization. Locus of control refers to a basic attitude about the control of events in one's life. An individual is said to have a high amount of internal control if he believes that he is more or less master of his own destiny and that success or failure is largely dependent upon his own ingenuity and efforts. A person is characterized as having a high degree of external control if he believes that he is at the mercy of uncontrollable events outside of himself and that success or failure is largely a matter of luck. Most people fall between these two extremes. Recent research on locus of control has shown that managers with strong internal orientation have lower stress levels, cope better with stress, and have better jobs, higher pay, and more job satisfaction than do individuals with external orientations.

Attitudes Toward Work and the Organization

Job attitudes such as satisfaction, commitment to the organization, and willingness to become deeply involved in the organizational effort are obviously important factors in any social organization. A recent review of the job satisfaction concept by Locke (1976) indicates that a high degree of satisfaction is generally due to some combination of good working conditions, good opportunities for promotion, high and equitable pay, and challenging jobs where there is a great deal of autonomy, stimulation, responsibility, and variety of assignment. These results should surprise no one, and yet too often we fail to give them the serious attention they deserve. It is interesting to note that with high job satisfaction, people are also more satisfied in general with their lives, tend to have better physical and mental health, and are more likely to dedicate themselves to their jobs than those who are dissatisfied with their jobs.

But satisfaction alone is not enough. Personal commitment to the organization, with a strong degree of personal loyalty and involvement, is equally important in managers and other employees alike. A manager deeply committed to the organization will tend to remain task oriented in the face of conflict or uncertainty, leading to a more creative and constructive resolution of the inner tension often present in a challenging assignment.

Goal Setting and Motivation

The setting of goals is an important step in achieving higher performance within a social organization. Up to a point, the more specific
the goal, the better. A number of studies in a wide variety of field
settings as well as laboratory experiments consistently demonstrate
that having specific goals results in higher performance than not having them. Setting difficult goals, as long as they are accepted by the
group responsible for achieving them, will result in higher performance than setting fairly easy goals. Group participation in goal
setting always leads to higher satisfaction but may not necessarily
produce higher performance, depending upon the kind of task being
undertaken (Mitchell 1979). Group participation in goal setting may
actually increase the difficulty of the set goals, thereby resulting in
higher performance in many situations. Probably goal setting combined with incentive systems, appraisals, and feedback is the best
way to increase and maintain high levels of performance.

Goals and their achievement are a major source of motivation for
individuals at work. Quite often, the process is one that feeds upon
itself in a positive manner. The setting of goals results in increased
effort that, in turn, is reflected in higher individual performance that
leads to greater organizational success. The achievement of success
for a committed group member increases self-esteem which, in turn,
strengthens job involvement and results in the setting of even higher
goals the next time.

Leadership

The very nature of the managerial process implies leadership on the
part of the manager. The nature of leadership—how to define it,
assess it, select individuals for leadership roles, and train individuals
to become more effective leaders—has been a major topic of concern
to psychologists for the past century. Over 3,000 references are listed
in Stogdill's comprehensive *Handbook* (1974). The major theory that
has dominated leadership thinking in recent years is the contingency
model (Fiedler 1967), which suggests that group performance is a
function of both the leader's motivation and the amount of control
and influence that is available to the leader in the situation. Fiedler's

own work indicates that leaders who are highly motivated to achieve a task are more effective in situations where the leader has either high or low control. Leaders who are more motivated by interpersonal concerns within the group are most effective in situations of intermediate control. As might be expected, these results are sufficiently specific and controversial that they have generated a good deal of additional research. Teaching a leader how to assess his or her own leadership style, how to determine the amount of situational control present, and, most importantly, how to alter the situation so that it will match the leader's personal style has been developed by Fiedler and his associates in a training manual (Fiedler, Chemers, and Mahar 1976).

Another interesting idea recently advanced for improving leadership is the Path-Goal approach proposed by Evans (1970) and House (1971). This theory is built on the important principle that the role of the leader is to provide subordinates with coaching, guidance, and reward necessary for satisfaction and effective performance. As in the case of Fiedler, the specific style of leadership behavior best suited for increasing motivation depends upon the situation. In the Path-Goal approach, the situation is broken down into two parts: (1) the personal characteristics of subordinates in the group, and (2) the amount of environmental pressures and task demands confronting the group. Two different leadership styles are contrasted: (a) the extent to which the leader shows personal consideration for the subordinates in the group, and (b) the extent to which the leader concentrates on initiating the structure of the task. Both consideration for group members and structuring the situation to provide guidance are essential qualities of a leader. An emphasis upon consideration for group members generally leads to higher subordinate satisfaction. Structuring the behavior in a highly directive manner, however, is often irritating and tension producing, particularly when personal consideration is low. The theory makes several specific predictions about the way in which consideration and structuring interact with different kinds of tasks and environmental pressures, but as yet there has not been sufficient research to substantiate them firmly.

Personality factors of the manager and the manager's attitude toward the task at hand—particularly the degree of job commitment and involvement, the extent to which the manager sets goals in a participatory manner with others whose involvements are essential to the task, and the extent to which leadership factors of the kind outlined above are really taken seriously—will determine, to a large degree, the success of the manager. Managerial creativity is most likely to be expressed when the manager takes all of these psychological factors into account in a novel way to achieve a valued goal, to produce a new set of ideas, or to develop a totally new product.

The psychological factors reviewed thus far deal primarily with managerial performance in relatively small organizations or task-oriented goals within large, complex organizations. What about the human factors and psychosocial technologies that can be applied in large-scale, highly complex organizations, such as major corporations, universities, or government agencies? And how about factors beyond the organization itself, such as cultural features of the larger society or nation as a whole? Let us first look at human factors within large social organizations and then examine briefly the cultural milieu within which the organization must exist.

HUMAN RELATIONS IN THE ORGANIZATION

It was not until the middle of the 1930s that a clear understanding of the importance of human relations with respect to productivity was clearly recognized. In 1927, Elton Mayo and his Harvard colleagues were invited by the Western Electric Company to study variations in worker output at the Hawthorne Plant in Chicago. Management at Hawthorne had obtained very puzzling results in studies of variations in lighting upon worker output. A monumental series of experiments was launched in which working conditions were systematically varied. The results were disconcerting. The workers steadily increased their output regardless of the working conditions. The more production increased, the more positive became the women's attitude toward their work. Intensive interviews and subsequent studies at the Hawthorne Plant revealed that a strong, informal organization developed among the women and their supervisors that was characterized by trust, friendship, and high morale. When these studies were finally published by Roethlisberger and Dickson (1939), they created such a sensation that the debate about their validity and significance still continues.

Parallel to the work of Elton Mayo and his school was the series of experiments by Kurt Lewin et al. (1939) demonstrating that a democratic style of leadership was more effective in increasing both group productivity and satisfaction with work than either an authoritarian or laissez-faire style. Immediately after World War II, these major theoretical and practical movements were drawn together by Douglas McGregor, Rensis Likert, and others in new centers for group dynamics, first at the Massachusetts Institute of Technology and then at the University of Michigan. Many of the outstanding leaders in the fields of industrial social psychology and human relations in industry over the past thirty-five years grew up in this exciting post–war period in Cambridge or Ann Arbor.

One of the most prolific writers and articulate spokesmen of the human relations point of view with respect to industry has been Chris Argyris (1957, 1962, 1964). He and his followers have pointed out quite convincingly that social organizations in nearly all economic enterprises run counter to the psychological needs of mature adults. There is a basic incongruity between the two sets of requirements, human and organizational, that often leads to resentment, sabotage, alienation, and stunted personality development.

The rapid dissemination of these ideas, together with the development of new technologies for changing individual and group behaviors through group dynamics, quickly led to various kinds of human relations training by applied behavioral scientists using T-groups, sensitivity training, encounter groups, and a wide variety of other techniques for increasing the self-awareness of participants, improving interpersonal relations within small groups, and releasing new potentials for creative activity. The more zealous practitioners, the uncritical initial acceptance by many beleaguered administrators, and the extreme, sometimes bizarre variations that blossomed under the umbrella of humanistic psychology in the 1960s gave human relations training a bad name that it did not fully deserve. The more thoughtful practitioners and scientists have moved far beyond the naive ideas of solving the human relations problems of industry by sensitivity training in small groups.

ORGANIZATIONAL DEVELOPMENT AND SOCIAL CHANGE

Today the human relations movement has evolved largely into concern with organizational development that takes into account technology and structure, as well as people. Organizational development is at once a field of interdisciplinary academic study and a recognized profession with accredited practitioners. A variety of techniques are employed by the practitioner for optimizing human and social improvement on the one hand and task accomplishment by the organization on the other. The strong resistance and failure of earlier efforts to deal with only the organizational structure or only the technology of the organization or only the human being with his values and needs has accelerated the evolution of a total systems approach wherever possible.

The objectives of the organizational development specialist are largely colored by his personal values. The more humanistic and democratic approaches to organizational development have been stated explicitly in the literature. Among the more popular are those stemming from the Theory Y assumptions of McGregor (1960). He argued that much that was important about a manager could be learned by determining what the manager's underlying assumptions were concerning human nature. A manager with Theory Y assumptions believes that in general people are hardworking, responsible individuals who need primarily to be supported and encouraged. A Theory X manager would assume the opposite, namely that people are basically lazy, irresponsible, and need to be watched constantly. Among the stated objectives of practitioners are the creating of an open problem-solving climate, building trust and collaboration, supplementing the authority of role and status with the authority of knowledge and competence, developing a reward system that recognizes both the organizational mission and the growth of people in it, helping managers to manage according to relevant objectives rather than past practices, and increasing self-direction and self-control for people within the organization (Argyris 1970).

When asked in to help solve a problem or to improve the effectiveness of an organization, the practitioner may find himself in conflict between the organization's need for more effective and efficient use of its resources and the individual's needs for personal growth and development. At the crux of the value disputes is the problem of power and what role the practitioner can best play as a consultant to the organization. The techniques of organizational development have been applied in an amazing variety of organizations—multinational industrial organizations, urban police departments, community health care organizations, public school systems, religious communities, prisons, and even in a futile attempt to resolve the conflicts among warring groups in Northern Ireland (Alderfer 1977). Interventions employed as techniques to bring about improvement in social organizations include team building, survey feedback, intergroup problem solving, skill building, job enrichment, and altering major structural properties within the organization, such as territory, technology, and time.

One of the more interesting techniques from the point of view of managerial creativity when faced with a completely new challenge or an apparently intractable problem is the development of a collateral organization. Establishing a new satellite organization that coexists with the older one is especially well-suited for solving ill-structured problems (Zand 1974). Completely new combinations of people and new ways of viewing old ideas can be a highly creative solution that circumvents the parent organization's formal and informal structure with its status network, power centers, and bureaucratic inertia.

Organizational development as an applied behavioral science is not without its critics. Burke (1977, 1980) has pointed out that all too many practitioners pay only lip service to the trinity of technology, structure, and people. Too little attention has been paid to industrial engineering, job design, and the whole area of sociotechnical systems. In a major review of research evidence concerning the accomplishments of organizational development interventions, Porras and Berg (1978) found little systematic evidence concerning its value. They concluded that such interventions do not often make people happier or have a truly significant impact on the overall organizational process. Of all the techniques employed in the published studies they reviewed, sensitivity training groups, encounter groups, and T-groups showed the lowest percentage of any reported change.

While much of the research on organizational development is rather critical of current practices, research dealing with the improvement of the quality of work life is on the rise. A good example is the major program for organizational assessment developed at Michigan's Institute for Social Research (Seashore et al. 1983). Supported by both the Ford Foundation and the U.S. Department of Commerce, this research program includes a number of quality-of-work-life projects representing an effort unprecedented in scope, magnitude, and sophistication. Work experiments of this type are generally carried out on factory workers who participate directly in the change program. Various experimental techniques are tried, such as forming autonomous work groups, rotating workers through different tasks to provide enrichment and variety, providing special training in inter-personal skills, giving a feedback of results as the changes are imple-mented, creating quality circles, altering the physical or technical setting in order to form whole task groups, and changing the reward system to reinforce group performance. It requires a great deal of patient persistence and flexible willingness to consider new organi-zational structures and decision making processes if major changes are to be implemented. Most case studies that have been reported stressed the importance of union-management collaboration and em-ployee participation.

CULTURAL DIFFERENCES IN ORGANIZATIONS

In many ways, the human relations movement as it has evolved into contemporary theory and practice for organizational development is largely a North American and British creation. As Faucheux, Amado, and Laurent (1982) have pointed out in their excellent review of recent work in organizational development and change, the strategies developed in the United States, in Great Britain, and in the industrial democracies of Northern Europe simply do not work well when ap-plied in other cultures. Even in the Latin countries of Europe such as France or Italy, managerial ideologies and cultural premises underly-ing industrial organizations and bureaucracies are very different. While American managers generally view an organization as an instru-ment through which a set of tasks can be achieved, French managers tend to think of organizations as a collectivity of people. These major cultural differences are not reduced within large multinational companies, a fact that often disillusions the top management of one country when it tries to implement a satellite organization in an-other. As Faucheux, Amado, and Laurent (1982) point out, power and its distribution is of greater significance in Latin cultures where the influence of Roman Law and the lack of a consensual basis in society strengthen state centralization of authority and power. McGregor's Theory Y approach to management is more suited to the Protestant ethic of North America. In a study of fifty industrial plants in five countries—Austria, Israel, Italy, the United States, and Yugoslavia—Tannenbaum et al. (1974) found major differences in the degree of hierarchy and management practices that were related to cultural and ideological differences among the five nations.

When the technique of management by objectives was introduced in France ten years ago, it failed to take hold because managers thought of it primarily as an additional control procedure by which they could exert their authority (Trepo 1973). In applying his theory of bureaucratic organization to French society, Crozier (1964) saw the organization as a power structure consisting of a number of hidden games organized around uncertainty areas that individuals would try to control for their own goals. Any intervention based on a purely voluntary process of information sharing would be doomed to failure. Viewing the human relations movement as naive, Crozier and his coworkers have developed a system called strategic analysis for analyzing power structures and organizational games (Crozier and Friedberg 1980).

The cultural milieu within which the organization functions is too often neglected by managers who are otherwise highly competent. American organizations are particularly blind to such factors, often making serious mistakes when they extend their organization into unfamiliar territory. Earlier this year I was approached for advice through an intermediary by a subsiduary of a major American company with a large assembly plant in Monterrey, Mexico. Top management of the plant consisted of English-speaking Anglo-Americans. Middle management had been recruited from moderately bilingual Mexican-Americans, and all of the workers were Spanish-speaking Mexicans. The plant was getting into serious trouble because top management failed to realize that the Mexican-Americans they had trained as supervisors were markedly different in culture and language from the Mexican workers themselves. Studies that Diaz-Guerrero and I had done in Mexico and the United States for a number of years on values, attitudes, personality characteristics, approaches to problem solving, and family life-styles consistently revealed major differences between Mexicans, Anglo-Americans, and Mexican-Americans that are directly related to managerial performance and style within social organizations (Holtzman, Diaz-Guerrero, and Swartz 1975).

The growing competition between business and organizations in Japan and the United States, together with the realization that the quality and efficiency of Japanese productivity have overtaken the United States in areas such as automobiles and electronics, has raised a question in the minds of many Americans, How did the Japanese do it? The recent best-seller, *Theory Z* by Ouchi (1981), provides a fairly convincing answer to this puzzling question of why productivity in Japan is so much higher. Concentrating primarily on the organizational and behavioral side of management in the tradition of the human relations movement, Ouchi proposes Theory Z as an adaptation of the best in Japanese and American management ideas. Productivity is seen as a problem of social organization under a management style aimed at enhancing trust, loyalty, and commitment throughout the organization.

After many years of careful case studies in Japan and the United States, Ouchi places a high value upon collective decision making with individual final responsibility as a way of promoting greater trust and reducing internal competition; upon strongly egalitarian wholistic concerns by management while maintaining hierarchical control modes within the organization; and, most important of all, upon a series of activities aimed at socialization of all members toward a common philosophy and set of goals for the organization. Within the United States, companies such as IBM, Hewlett-Packard, Proctor and Gamble, and Eastman Kodak are seen as outstanding prototypes of Theory Z organizations. Ouchi goes on to suggest a series of steps that must be taken to change an organization in line with his Theory Z concept, starting with top management and union representatives and working down through the organization over a period of several years. An interesting example of these ideas in action is the new program at General Motors with the explicit goal, not of increasing productivity (although such an outcome is anticipated), but of improving the quality of work life.

Theory Z is based directly upon the earlier work of McGregor, Argyris, Likert, and other behavioral scientists working in the human relations field. As a national best-seller, *Theory Z* has been enthusiastically endorsed by an impressive array of leaders in business and industry. The time may indeed be right for truly major changes in the way in which people are organized and managed at work.

FUTURE PROSPECTS

Most of the work to date dealing with organizational development and managerial creativity is concerned with familiar organizations in government, industry, education, or the military services. It is generally well recognized that most of these organizations, as well as the society within which they operate, have been changing more rapidly in the past few years than at any previous period. What about the future? Can we make any speculations based upon trends in society and technology as to where the greatest challenges confronting managers will arise in the next twenty years?

In his imaginative essay on the reflections of a twenty-first-century manager, Kozmetsky (1969) pointed out how a manager's responsibilities would change drastically with the profound transformation of industry itself. Developing organizations engaged in nonroutine industries would make up a major part of government, industry, and education. A primary characteristic of these new industries would be the mission of working on problems that required new orders of solutions for which previous answers were inadequate. These nonroutine industries would be based upon high technology, calling for managers of intellectual resources quite unlike those traditionally found in mass-production industries. Top managers would have more time for strategic planning and would have a high degree of authority and control made possible by the information technology available to them. When not engaged in planning, the manager would be studying in a wide variety of fields with assistance from an administrative aide. Advances in the psychology of motivation and cognition, coupled with new information technology, would provide the twenty-first-century manager with powerful tools for dealing with human factors in the organization.

Envisioned thirteen years ago, the broad outlines of Kozmetsky's fantasy concerning the manager of the future have already been confirmed by trends that are in evidence today.

The three areas of high technology that will have the greatest impact on industrial organization and the role of the manager are communications, computers, and robotics. High-technology products now (May 1982) constitute one-half of business purchases of capital goods, as compared with only one-third in 1977 and one-quarter in 1972. The high-technology revolution is affecting all aspects of our society. The social and psychological significance of this revolution is still only poorly understood. A brief look at education, the field with which I am most familiar, will illustrate these points.

In the late 1960s, a number of us in psychology, computer sciences, engineering, and education became deeply involved in experi-

mental programs using computers for everything from the management of instruction to the microunits of the curriculum itself (Holtzman 1970, 1976). While many of these exciting ideas were stalled
during the 1970s because of excessive cost factors and inadequate
technology, they are now finally beginning to come into their own.
Powerful, low-cost microprocessors are now moving into literally
millions of homes, schools, industrial and government settings. When
coupled with interactive video devices, communications technology,
and new advances in the fields of artificial intelligence, cognitive processes, and instructional psychology, computer-based educational
systems will finally make it possible to provide enriched learning on
an individualized basis at a time and place most suitable for the
learner (Simon 1979). The social organization of schools, colleges,
and other traditional learning centers will be profoundly transformed
to take advantage of these new technologies. A great deal of managerial creativity will be required to bring about the need transforma-
tions and to manage educational systems of the future.

Since more effort will have to be expended on research and development, both to advance the new technologies and to implement the
organizational restructuring to maximize their benefits, the special
case of management within a research organization is worth examining. What are the kinds of social environment that are likely to foster
a high level of scientific effectiveness?

In their study of eleven research and development organizations in
industrial, government, and university settings, Pelz and Andrews
(1966) found plenty of evidence to support the view that creativity
in this environment requires the presence of two somewhat contradictory conditions. First, there must be some source of security for
the individual scientist, special conditions and management relations
that protect the scientist from distracting demands. A major source
of such security in many institutions is permitting the scientist a
large amount of freedom in determining the direction of his work.
The second condition essential for creativity in this environment is
the presence of a major challenge to the scientist that presents a
burning desire for achievement. The challenge can come from others
within the organization, from management, from external forces, or
even from intrinsic motivation. The most effective scientists were
those whose technical tasks were established in consultation among
four sources: themselves, their immediate chief, their colleagues, and
higher executives or clients. The effective scientist confronts a diver-

sity of viewpoints in these multiple channels of decision and evaluation. Where a supervisor alone has the major voice in deciding a scientist's assignments, the scientist's performance is poor.

A number of American corporations are on the cutting edge of high technology. Several were singled out by Ouchi as examples of his Theory Z approach to management and organizational development. The largest of these corporations, IBM, is deeply involved in all three of the high technology areas — computers, communications, and robotics. As a consultant to IBM and director of one of its subsidiaries, Science Research Associates, I have been impressed by the extent to which these technologies are being integrated within the daily activities of the corporation. Everything from industrial production to continuing education, from managerial control and decision making to social interactions among workers is being altered.

The importance of psychological factors in the social organization of the future, regardless of its mission, will increase as the social transitions called for by Theory Z and the new technologies take place. The manager of the future will indeed be challenged greatly if the transition is to succeed without being derailed by an Orwellian future. Both the risks of failure and the opportunities to advance mankind compel us to move quickly in adopting new perspectives and managerial roles to match the new technologies. Whether or not we are up to this challenge remains to be seen.

REFERENCES

Alderfer, C.P. 1977. "Organization development." *Annual Review of Psychology* 28: 197–223.

Argyris, Chris. 1957. *Personality and Organization: The Conflict between System and the Individual.* New York: Harper.

Argyris, Chris. 1962. *Interpersonal Competence and Organizational Effectiveness.* Homewood, Ill.: Dorsey.

Argyris, Chris. 1964. *Integrating the Individual and the Organization.* New York: John Wiley & Sons, Inc.

Argyris, C. 1970. *Intervention Theory and Method.* Reading, Mass.: Addison-Wesley.

Burke, W.W., ed. 1977. *Current Issues and Strategies in Organization Development.* New York: Human Sciences.

Burke, W.W. 1980. "Organization development and bureaucracy in the 1980s." *Journal of Applied Behavioral Science* 16: 423–38.

Crozier, M. 1964. *The Bureaucratic Phenomenon*. Chicago: University of Chicago Press.

Crozier, M., and E. Friedberg. 1980. *Actors and Systems*. Chicago: University of Chicago Press.

Evans, M.G. 1980. "The effects of supervisory behavior on the path-goal relationship." *Organization Behavior and Human Performance* 5: 277–98.

Faucheux, Claude; Gilles Amado; and Andre Laurent. 1982. Organizational development and change. *Annual Review of Psychology* 33: 343–70.

Fiedler, F.E. 1967. *A Theory of Leadership Effectiveness*. New York: McGraw-Hill.

Fiedler, F.E.; M.M. Chemers; and L. Mahar. 1976. *Improving Leadership Effectiveness: The Leader Match Concept*. New York: Wiley.

Gilchrist, M. 1972. *The Psychology of Creativity*. Melbourne: Melbourne University Press.

Holtzman, W.H.; J.S. Thorpe; J.D. Swartz; and E.W. Herron. 1961. *Inkblot Perception and Personality*. Austin: University of Texas Press.

Holtzman, W.H., ed. 1970. *Computer-Assisted Instruction, Testing, and Guidance*. New York: Harper & Row.

Holtzman, W.H.; J.D. Swartz; and J.S. Thorpe. 1971. "Artists, architects, and engineers—three contrasting modes of visual experience and their psychological correlates." *Journal of Personality* 39: 432–449.

Holtzman, W.H.; R. Diaz-Guerrero; and J.D. Swartz. 1975. *Personality Development in Two Cultures*. Austin: University of Texas Press.

Holtzman, W.H. 1976. "Education for creative problem solving." In *Individuality in Learning*, edited by Samuel Messick and Associates. San Francisco: Jossey-Bass, Inc.

House, R.J. 1971. "A path goal theory of leadership effectiveness." *Administrative Science Quarterly* 16: 321–38.

Kozmetsky, G. 1969. "Reflections of a 21st Century manager." *Bell Telephone Magazine* (March–April). (Reprinted in Schoderbek, P.P., ed., *Management Systems*, 2nd edition, pp. 543–546. New York: Wiley & Sons, 1971.)

Lewin, Kurt, Ronald Lippit and Ralph K. White. 1939. "Patterns of aggressive behavior in experimentally created 'social climates.'" *Journal of Social Psychology* 10: 271–299.

Likert, Rensis. 1967. *The Human Organization: Its Management and Value*. New York: McGraw-Hill.

Locke, E.A. 1976. "The nature and causes of job satisfaction." In *Handbook of Industrial and Organizational Psychology*, edited by M.D. Dunnette. Chicago: Rand McNally.

MacKinnon, D.W. 1965. "Personality and the realization of creative potential." *American Psychologist* 20: 273–81.

May, T., Jr. 1982. "Fortune forecast: shackles on growth in the eighties." *Fortune* (October 4): 51–52.

McGregor, Douglas. 1960. *The Human Side of Enterprise.* New York: McGraw-Hill.

Mitchell, T.R. 1979. "Organizational behavior." *Annual Review of Psychology* 30: 243-82.

Ouchi, W.G. 1981. *Theory Z.* Reading, Mass.: Addison-Wesley.

Pelz, D.C., and F.M. Andrews. 1966. *Scientists in Organizations: Productive Climates for Research and Development.* New York: Wiley.

Porras, J.I., and P.O. Berg. 1978. The impact of organizational development. *Academy of Management Review* (April): 249-66.

Roethlisberger, F.J., and W.J. Dickson. 1939. *Management and the Worker.* Cambridge, Mass.: Harvard University Press.

Seashore, S.E., and Edward Lawler, ed. 1983. *Assessing Organizational Change: A Guide to Methods, Measures and Practices.* New York: Wiley.

Simon, H.A. 1979. "Information processing models of cognition." *Annual Review of Psychology* 30: 363-96.

Stogdill, R.M. 1974. *Handbook of Leadership: A Survey of Theory and Research.* New York: Free Press.

Tannenbaum, A.S.; Bogdan Kavčič; Menachem Rosner; Mimo Vianello and Georg Wiesner. 1974. *Hierarchy in Organizations: An International Perspective.* San Francisco: Jossey-Bass.

Trepo, G. 1973. "Management style á la française." *European Business* 39: 71-79.

Zand, D.E. 1974. "Collateral organization: a new change strategy." *Journal of Applied Behavioral Science* 10: 63-89.

POWER MAPPING AND THE PRACTICE OF INNOVATION IN MANAGEMENT

Lester A. Fettig

PSYCHOLOGICAL UNDERPINNINGS: TAKEN AS A GIVEN

What Wayne Holtzman has done for us is to give us a smorgasboard of what we think we know about creative people and the environments in which their creativity is enhanced. He has reviewed for us the research and findings to date on personal traits and characteristics such as IQ, broad interests, attraction to complexity, candor, openness, self-recognition, intuition, self-confidence, and so forth. Beyond noting those personality profiles, I am going to leave it right there and not try to fathom how we create or induce that kernel of creativity in the individual, that hidden mystery of what causes the "Eureka!" I have concluded that we do not really know how to duplicate, manipulate, or otherwise "create creativity."

THE CREATIVE MANAGEMENT CHALLENGE: EXECUTION IN A FRACTURED ENVIRONMENT

This leads to the key point I want to develop. The essence of the creative and innovative management problem, it strikes me, is not so much that we need to enhance individual creativity per se but rather that we need to enhance our ability to execute and implement creative ideas—which is, by definition, management. In his commentary on Dr. Staats, Jack Borsting referred to the long list and tall pile of studies and creative managerial attacks on problems that have already been made by individuals, groups, and task forces. Dr. Staats has also contributed a paper to this volume. He and I go back to 1969 together on the Commission on Government Procurement where we attacked, among other things, managerial problems in our Major Systems Acquisition process, a specialty of mine. We came up with some very creative and innovative solutions—and, I might add, some of them have actually found their way into widespread practice today.

My point is that we are not at a loss for creative ideas by any means. We are blessed in this country to have a rich base. But the essence of the problem of innovative management, I think, is our ability to execute and implement creative ideas within what is increasingly becoming a fractured and complex bureaucratic environment. So, if I could reformulate the noble goal that Dr. Kozmetsky has for the University of Texas and its activities here, it is to achieve a higher aggregate creative performance in actually implementing creative and innovative ideas within the complex American infrastructure, both public and private.

This is the classic creative managerial problem, implementation of innovative and new ideas. If we want to enhance aggregate managerial performance, the first specific opportunity that suggests itself is to give students here and in the future some new tools to rely on.

To use the terminology in the following paper by Allen Newell, we seem to be in a mental rut by not thinking of some new combinations of knowledge that offer new solutions to the problem of management implementation. Or, at least we have failed to consider all the possible permutations of management techniques. This failure, as Dr. Newell framed it, is a failure of one essential element in managerial creativity—namely, the lack of a properly broad assemblage of possible combinations for management attention.

In my speech at a California conference, without thinking about this one, I explained the failure of the management initiatives under Secretary Carlucci in the U.S. Department of Defense as due in part to the tools selected. As with so many past traditional approaches, the current Defense Department leadership has chosen to emphasize orders from on high, in the form of memos, directives, regulations, and other standard bureaucratic techniques. They are not working because—as any true bureaucratic practitioner will tell you—those tools cannot be effective in implementing new, creative, and adaptive solutions to management problems. The reasons are simple and cultural.

The people who are, in the main, responsible at high levels for implementing these new ideas may soon be moving on to new positions. These people are transients. The people who are at the next level in the permanent bureaucratic structure realize that the top-level initiators, the creative people who want to see innovation come about, will all be leaving soon; as a consequence, the people at this next level in the permanent bureaucracy become anesthetized when they see a package of management improvements being proposed from new sources year after year after year.

The real tools for penetrating this bureaucratic structure are not often exercised, despite the fact that there is almost a standard set of these more effective techniques. They include management compliance, linkage to budget approval, and linkage to personal evaluation and promotion standards. These primitive tools go more directly to the motivations and performance of the actors in our scheme of highly developed bureaucratic organizations.

THE NEED FOR A NEW SUBDISCIPLINE: POWER MAPPING

I think there is a new subdiscipline that must be taught for creative and innovative management. I do not know what name to give it, but mentally I have come to refer to it as "Power Mapping." Perhaps the work by Crozier and others, to which Dr. Holtzman refers covers the topic, but I think of bills, legislation signed into law, and administrative regulations (including those for which I was responsible). These are things I think people like Lyndon Baines Johnson do intuitively. The point is that these techniques are here. Let us not forget the very recent history of Mr. Johnson during the 1960s when we *had* a forceful example of successful national management, agenda setting, *and* implementation. For better or worse, depending on your political ideology, we *did* put a "Great Society" program into effect.

The way I think it can be done more regularly—with aggregate improvement in our management innovation—is to teach a careful and methodical analysis of those fractured centers of power that a manager must deal with, whether within a government bureaucracy or an industrial one. It is certainly no good simply to put on blinders and blame the world for not coming to take, and implement, the best new creative ideas.

To use a private sector example, one of my clients, a shipbuilder, was working on the front-end of a bid to build a brand new concept for a ship. The president let his program manager, a very creative fellow, run with the idea. I spoke with the president recently to ask how it had gone. He reported that it had been killed by the Board of Directors, that there was to be no more investment in this activity. "What happened?" I asked. "It was a unique and promising approach." In essence the president's response was as follows: "Although the program manager was creative, he failed in implementation. He did not take everybody along with him. He did not keep [the president] informed of what he was doing. He did not keep the Board informed of what he was spending and for what. He did not realize that the Comptroller was gunning for him."

Many stories of badly needed creativity that fail for lack of that special kind of bureaucratic execution are embodied in this response. The subdiscipline to be developed must first ask, Who are the players within my universe?

In a Washington setting, I have actually done this with legislation— laid it out on a piece of paper. You must first ask which committee chairmen, which ranking members can help or hinder; similarly for the elements of the executive branch bureaucracy: ONR (Office of Naval Research), OSD (Office of the Secretary of Defense), and the like. You have to check in with Jack Borsting in the Comptroller's shop of DOD, but you also have to cover the Under-Secretary for Defense Research & Engineering. Any one of these can spell the difference between innovation successfully implanted or thwarted. But the total picture for any given initiative is manageable, and such a mapping can portray the dimensions of necessary action.

Next you must analyze each of the key players in the power universe of interest: Who are your potential allies, who will likely remain neutral, who is going to give you a great problem? A lot of successful, creative, and innovative managers owe their success to intuitive manipulation of the environment in this manner. I think the essence of their managerial creativity was in implementation of new ideas or programs in a complicated, fractured power environment. To use a celestial analogy, they were intuitively able to say, in their universe, who were the "red giants"—those people and power cen-

ters who cast a presence across a great swath of bureaucratic operations—and who were the "white dwarfs," people with very intense
power but in a narrow regime. The latter may even be more dangerous and difficult to deal with than the red giants when it comes to
innovative managerial programs.

At any rate, you can see the pattern. First map the universe of
power centers involved in a given management innovation—whether
internal to a company or in the Washington sense—and also develop
a handy genealogy to categorize them by types. Then ask, How do I
cope with each?

The techniques to be applied include outright swapping and extend to simple, outright flattery, appeals to logic, threats of a down-
side consequence, and emotional attacks that recall past unpleasant
experiences and, if one has the power to do it like Lyndon Johnson,
annihilation.

Whatever the full set of possible tools, this is the second part of
power mapping: After you lay out your universe and identify the
power centers who influence its behavior—all the red giants, white
dwarfs, and black holes—you must then make book on the attributes
of each and select the manipulative tools most appropriate for each.
Note the importance of making book. Every good Senator knows
and does this. They know how to approach each member, what obligations each member is carrying and what points of appeal would be
most effective to gain a vote or an action.

At any rate, I would suggest strongly from my own empirical base
of evidence that, as I have framed it, the crucial problem in creating
an aggregate improvement in America's infrastructural managerial
creativity—and this applies equally to public and private organizations—involves developing a supplementary discipline directed to
being able to analyze and manipulate a fragmented power structure
that is, in the end, very human. As I have also emphasized, however,
I think there is already a body of evidence and experimental history
to enable us to formulate such an approach to explain, predict, and
manipulate managerial outcomes in complex organizations.

7 ON COMPUTERS, CREATIVITY, AND MANAGEMENT

Allen Newell

I have not given attention to the problems of management science in twenty years at least—not since 1961 when I moved from the Graduate School of Industrial Administration down to computer science at the other end of the (then) Carnegie Tech campus. But the opportunity to address old friends on topics that still fascinate me, if not occupy me professionally, could not be missed. Still, the undeniable problem remained of finding something to say that would address the topic of this conference—creative and innovative management—in a way that would be worthy of the intellectual attention of my management colleagues.

In the intervening years I have paid considerable attention to the nature of human cognition, hence by extension to creativity. Similarly, I have paid considerable attention to the nature of the computer, hence by extension to the computer in management, which by yet further extension might reach to innovation. Unfortunately, my concerns have been focused almost completely on the individual—both the individual human and the individual computer. This leaves

This research was sponsored by the Defense Advanced Research Projects Agency (DOD), ARPA Order No. 3597, monitored by the Air Force Avionics Laboratory Under Contract F33615-78-C-1551.

The views and conclusions contained in this document are those of the authors and should not be interpreted as representing the official policies, either expressed or implied, of the Defense Advanced Research Projects Agency or the U.S. Government.

a substantial gap to be bridged to contact the real concerns of management. As the other papers at this conference amply reveal, this concern is with organizations, markets, industries, and economies. Still, the obvious topic for my address is computers, creativity, and management.

THE QUESTION OF A TITLE

If I may stay in the historical mode for a moment longer, the considerations above left me only with a topic, derived impeccably perhaps, but hardly with a solid core of content. I needed some point of view on that topic, some vector that I could follow to generate a talk. Instinctively, I reached for a title to the talk. A title would announce both to my audience and myself where I was going and what we might both expect. Immediately, I thought, "The Nature of Computers and Creative Management." That seemed a reasonable view: how to apply computers to manage creatively.

No sooner had that title occurred to me than so did "Creative Computers and the Nature of Management." This was not bad either: The flavor of how the use of computers in new ways affected the nature of managing but with no implication that these ways added up to creative management rather than simply more effective management. But then occurred "Computer Management and the Nature of Creativity." This had the flavor of using artificial intelligence to manage the creative process. And thereupon instantly emerged "The Creative Nature of Managing Computers." This seemed a little far out and perhaps contained a bit of special pleading. Still it might also do.

What was going on here? Well, there are four words: *nature, computer, creative* and *management.* That meant that there could be $4 \times 3 \times 2 \times 1 = 24$ possible titles. I begn picking titles at random. Every one worked! For instance, I obtained "The Computational Nature of Managing Creatively." This is a real thesis—one that most of my audience would no doubt disagree with. It is not clear I could maintain it, but it would certainly make an interesting talk.

My imagination raced on. I imagined myself giving twenty-four talks. Perhaps I would give a course or go on a speaking tour. Why not increase the number of words in the title, say, to five? Then there would be 5! or 120 different titles, hence different talks. I imagined typing the 120 titles on bits of paper, putting them in a hat and letting each member of the audience draw one. They each could give a different talk, but on the same topic. I would only have to listen. Would we then have exhausted what was to be said on the topic? But why stop at five? Six key words would yield 6! or 720 talks, and beyond that many ways exist to select the key words. So perhaps I could form a new company—call it WORDS FOR HIRE—whose slogan would be: You give us the topic, we give you the title and the talk. Surely some venture capitalist could be found to support such an enterprise.

Reveries end, of course. And in this case, as in most others, all the real work remained to be done. The talk had still to be invented and written. Perhaps, however, the fantasy can be of use. We can learn from it a little bit about the nature of creativity and its role in management.

THE NATURE OF CREATIVITY

As background to this small inquiry into the nature of creativity, there are two questions, not one. The first is how managers might be creative and whether that is in fact an important dimension for managers. The second question is whether computers might be creative and, if that is possible, how that might affect the task of management or indeed the creativity of managers.

As background, also, an almost infinite amount of attention has already been paid to the nature and circumstance of creativity (Arieti 1976; Gardner 1982; Hadamard 1945; Koestler 1964; Kubie 1958; Perkins 1981; Polya 1965; Stein and Heinze 1960; Taylor and Barron 1964) and from points of view almost infinitely diverse. It follows, conventionally, that there has been little decisive issue from all these investigations and reflections, although of course much is known empirically about this and that aspect, and even more is known about the difficulties of the more obvious conceptual approaches. However, as we shall see, the situation is not hopeless.

Consider, then, the creativity involved in the little episode just related. Of course, it is possible that it does not seem at all creative to see in the dice-roll of titles a whole population of talks. However, I must confess that I found myself rather pleased with the whole thing. There was a sudden emergence, without preparation, of a novel point of view, one that was in fact of importance to my (difficult) task of inventing a talk in an area in which I had thought hardly at all for years. That is not at all a bad characterization of a creative act. Perhaps it was a small thing, but it was at least mine own. In any event, I will ask you to see in this episode a smallish act of creativity, which we can dissect with profit.

Point 1: An Irrelevant Generation of Possibilities

The most prominent feature of this event was the generation of possibilities—the twenty-four titles. This was, in fact, quite mechanical. It could easily have been done by a computer. We should not let the mechanical aspect per se get in the way. What is striking about the generation is its *irrelevancy*. Nothing in the process bears any organic relation to the demands of the task. Indeed, it is just this irrelevancy that makes us uncomfortable with a chimpanzee painting a picture, however similar in surface appearance the product is to some varieties of abstract art. The chimp's behavior is irrelevant to the artistic enterprise and we never forget it.

Yet the irrelevancy is essential. Without it there can be no creativity. Let me illustrate this with an example from my own ongoing research. Elaine Kant, a computer scientist at Canegie-Mellon University, and I are trying to understand how algorithms are discovered (Kant and Newell 1983). Computer science, as a body of knowledge, is in substantial part composed of algorithms for doing this or that: for sorting items (e.g., Quicksort); for solving equations (e.g., Newton's method); for solving linear programming problems (e.g., the Simplex algorithm); and on and on. An important area of research in artificial intelligence is to construct computer systems that can themselves discover algorithms and program them. In our attempts to do this, we have been exploring how humans discover algorithms, as an aid in building such artificial intelligence systems.

In the particular fragment of interest, a subject is trying to discover an algorithm for finding the convex hull of a set of points. Consider the points, A, B, C, D and E in the left side of Figure 7-1. The convex hull are those points on the outside (here A, C, D, E), such that the polygon comprised of these points includes all the other points in the set (here, B is the only interior point). This is shown in the center of the figure. The problem for the subject is not to find the convex hull (that's easy—he can just see it), but to create

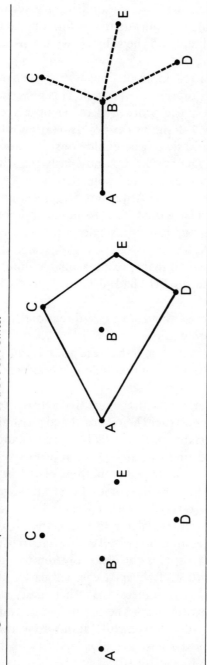

Figure 7-1. Example of the Convex Hull of a Set of Points.

an algorithm which, when given an arbitrary set of points (say their (x, y) coordinates), will output the points on the hull. The latter is a much harder problem and the subjects we use in this work are Ph.D's in computer science.

One subject started in an obvious way: to generate each point and then to test if it is on the convex hull. This puts the whole burden on discovering the test. He proceeded to set up a specific test case (the left side of Figure 7-1 shows the points he drew). He started with the first point (A) and asked if he could construct a test to tell if A is on the convex hull. The answer was obviously negative: no information was available about an isolated point (such as A) from which to determine a test for whether A was on the convex hull. He realized that the input to the test would have to be all the points that had been generated so far, not just the single point. He thus considered successively, (A), (A, B), (A, B, C), asking at each stage whether there were enough points to make up a reasonable input to the test case to start to design the test. He had just considered whether three points is enough:

"Now I can go in any one of three directions from this point [B]."
Then he immediately said:

"I conjecture that if it's the case that I can choose two points, such that I can go on either side of the given line, then this line can't be on the convex hull."

Thus, he simply announced the test. In fact, the test was correct and he proceeded to construct the rest of the algorithm using it.

Now, an important point for us from this example is that the subject was trying to find one thing—an appropriate input for his testcase investigation—and found something else—the actual test that he was hoping would be the outcome of that investigation. In the event, of course, the investigation never occurred; he simply went on to solve the larger problem of constructing the algorithm. The finding of the test is a genuine nontrivial act of creativity. Unlike my little title-finding incident, it is the clear solution to a problem of genuine intellectual difficulty. It bears clear hallmarks of the creative act: It appeared suddenly, unheralded. The result strikes the observer as quite unobvious (it is not the usual sort of test one sees). In fact, we were baffled for quite awhile about how the discovery of the test occurred; it stood as a major mystery in this protocol. And finally, the result is of high social utility (it is the key to the whole algorithm).

Just to avoid details, I will leave some of the mystery intact and not take you through exactly how the discovery was made. The point for us is that there was an *irrelevant* generation of possibilities—(A B C), (A B D) and (A B E)—that created the conditions in which the test could be seen as obvious. We show this at the right side of the figure. This generation, although embedded in a fluid problem-solving situation, is just as mechanical as the generation of my titles. The subject only wants to find out the remaining possibilities for extending the input to three points. Yet that generation produced the pattern without which the test would not have been discovered.

Point 2: The Recognition of Appropriateness

It is not enough just to have a combinatorial process that generates possible situations. There must be a *recognition* that a case is appropriate to the ultimate task—that is, to the task that the creative result will ultimately serve. Given a variant sequence of words, produced by the throw of my mental dice, I had to see it as an appropriate title, not just as another sequence of words. Furthermore, that recognition had to occur in an instant. It could not be a deliberate judgment. If the sense of appropriateness had not occurred in a hurry, the erstwhile title would have been gone, replaced by some other thought.

The same thing is true of our subject's discovery of a test for being on the convex hull. The pattern made by the three options—(A B C), (A B E) and (A B D)—was available as a total pattern only adventitiously within the subject's short term working memory for a few tens of seconds. If the relevance was not noticed right then, the pattern would have disappeared. After all, there was no reason for this particular pattern to stay around. It, like an indefinite number of other patterns, was just flowing by. Suppose an elaborate judgmental process were required to determine that this pattern was relevant. Such a process would have to be applied to all the other adventitious combinations that were continually occurring and which could have been relevant. The subject could not have known they weren't relevant prior to applying the judgmental process, for *ex hypothesi* that is what the judgment was for. But, however fast basic cognitive processes might be, there is not time enough to apply a time-consuming judgmental process to *everything* in sight.

Figure 7–2. Basic Architectural Organization of the Computer (left) and the Human (right).

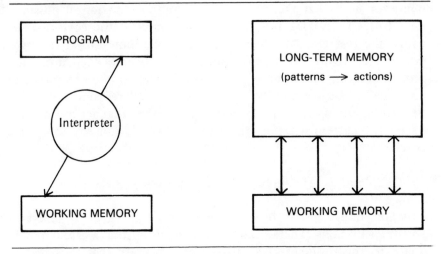

The process under discussion reflects the well-known aphorism that chance favors the prepared mind. In both cases, me at my titles and my subject at his diagram, although the generator of possibilities is irrelevant, the context is saturated with concern with the ultimate task. Not only is the goal of solving the task (inventing the talk, discovering the test) well established as a higher level goal, but the general substance of the situation, if not its detail, is relevant to the task.

The view that the required process is an immediate recognition, not a deliberate judgment, accords well with current conceptions of human cognition. There is much evidence that humans are organized as recognizers. There is a nice contrast here with the basic organization of computers. On the left side of Figure 7-2 we see the basic structure of a computer, which has an interpreter that keeps one pointer into the program and another pointer into the temporary data being processed. Its operation is described by the well-known "fetch-execute cycle," which moves the upper pointer to fetch the next instruction from the plan and then executes that instruction on the data by means of the lower pointer. On the right side of the figure is a plausible basic model of the human cognitive architecture. Its operation is described by the "recognize-act cycle." The long-term memory holds a collection of patterns, each of which links to some action. The working memory holds the representations that comprise the awareness of the current situation. All the patterns in long-term memory continuously attempt to recognize themselves in the working memory. At each moment, one such satisfied pattern fires its action (in some schemes, more than one). This changes the contents of working memory, which leads to another recognition, hence another action, and so on.

This view of the human versus the computer shows one basic reason why the computer and the human seem in some respects quite different information processing systems. The computer, viewed this way, seems a device for making deliberate judgments (i.e., for following explicit instructions), whereas the human is always producing new things with its recognition process. A moment's consideration, of course, reveals that these are equally deterministic ways of organizing information processing and that machines can be built that operate in the manner of the right side of Figure 7-2, as well as in the manner of the left side. Indeed, many such systems exist, although they are realized mostly as software (Waterman and Hayes-Roth 1978).

Point 3: Recognition is Also Not Enough; There Must be Problem Solving

The recognition that a configuration is appropriate to a task is only the beginning. All the recognition can accomplish is to bring the ongoing behavior to a screeching halt. In fact, the recognition can be viewed as being specialized to the task of interrupting and redirecting. Given the title, it is still necessary for me to come up with a talk. This latter task, however, is no longer one of creativity. Rather, it requires extended "problem solving," as that term is used in psychology. The context has now become sufficiently definite that the usual processes of problem solving can be used. "Invent a talk" and "invent a talk with the title of 'Computer Management and the Nature of Creativity'" are significantly different tasks. In the latter case, there is immediately much to think about and do.

The same holds true of our subject who has just creatively recognized that, with lines branching off to points C and D, line segment (A B) cannot be on the convex hull. He still has problems to solve. For starters, he must be able to articulate the test, not just recognize it. In fact, in the little quote from his protocol, we can see that he took on the linguistic mantle of the mathematician—"I conjecture that . . ." and "if . . . such that . . . then. . . ." He was indeed formulating a precise condition, which was certainly not given immediately in the recognition. The subject must also determine whether the test is correct. Indeed, the careful reader will have noticed that the test is not for a *point* being on the convex hull, which was what was called for, but for a *line segment* being part of the convex hull polygon. A subtle but real redefinition of the task took place in the heat of discovery. Thus, the subject must ascertain by analysis what his creativity has delivered to him and adapt his further progress to the circumstance.

Whereas the recognition is all but instantaneous, the problem solving may be extended and drawn out. From a management viewpoint it can even be delegated to others. There may, of course, be other difficulties that are encountered along the way in working out the details, and these may require additional acts of creation.

Point 4: The Task Need Not Be Difficult

Calling the long second phase problem solving suggests that mountain ranges of difficulties always remain to be surmounted. Such a suggestion goes along with the common notion that acts of creation are related to difficulty. The greater the difficulty o'erleaped by recognition, the greater the act of creation.

My little title episode suggests it might be otherwise. After all, I found a talk for every title. Surely the problem of finding the talk could not have been very hard. In fact, it looks like solutions were everywhere to be found. This suggests that difficulty may not be the key issue in creativity. (It can only suggest it, of course, since it itself is only a baby example.) The key issue is in gaining the right context with the right goal in the background. The creative leap (the recognition) lands you in some mental territory, far away from where you were the moment before. With luck it lands you in territory where no others have been as well. There will certainly be details to be filled in. But whether these are easy or difficult (or even impossible—there is nothing in this picture that guarantees success), it is quite independent of the original leap.

Summary

We have milked my example for all that it is worth (possibly, a good deal more), and have managed a rather substantial characterization of the creative process. You must be prepared, with the goal sitting in the background. You must be doing the right thing for the wrong reason. That is the irrelevant generation. There must be an instantaneous recognition of the appropriateness of what you have generated. This implies a memory chock full of potential connections. There must be problem solving to follow up on the recognition. That is the 99 percent perspiration that follows the 1 percent inspiration. And finally, the creativity of the recognitional step does not necessarily relate to the difficulty of the subsequent problem solving.

THE NATURE OF THE COMPUTER

Now that we have a grip on the nature of creativity, let us move on to the computer. For many reasons it intrudes on all modern-day discussions of either creativity or management.

There is no doubt about the revolutionary impact of the computer. We have been told about its revolutionary character for at least thirty years. Further, we have not been told prophesies—that the revolution was *about* to arrive. Rather, we have been told, for each of these thirty years, that the revolution was here *now* (i.e., then). And amazingly, the assertions have been true. Throughout its entire history, the computer has obliged us by being revolutionary.

In matters social and political, to be a revolutionary for thirty years is either to have promoted a failed revolution or to be living off the dreams of ancient glories. But this is not true of technologies, at least not of sufficiently revolutionary [*sic*] technologies. One is reminded of the property of exponential curves that they are translation invariant. Relatively speaking, they always have the same flattening slope looking back and the same explosive slope looking forward, no matter when one decides to look. Thus, a continuing exponential will generate a continuing revolution. That the whole scene continues to move to a more dramatic scale (indeed, an exponentially more dramatic scale) is something one is expected to adapt to. Thus, the current computer revolution, often referred to as the coming of the cheap microcomputer, looks to us a much bigger revolution than the revolutions of a decade ago. What we must remember is that the current revolutionary phase will look equally small a decade hence, and the future equally explosive. And yet again the story will repeat the decade next after. It is simply not possible to have any rational basis for what the changes will feel like two decades down the road.

What is the fundamental nature of the computer that is capable of generating such a continuing revolution? One is always tempted to start with the blind men and the elephant. The story is familiar, no doubt. One blind man touched the elephant's side and declared the beast to be like a wall. Another touched the elephant's leg and declared the beast to be like the trunk of a tree. And so on through the elephant's trunk (like a snake), tail (like a rope), and ear (like a blanket). Just so, there are all these different views of the computer. It is like a statistical clerk, a number cruncher, a game player, a text processor, and an image processor—to name only the first few that come to mind. Whatever your contact is, the computer looks like a different beast. But in all cases it looks mighty useful, at least once you get used to it (Arden 1980).

However, suppose it was the fashion of blind men to the biologists. Then each of them would have scratched away a small bit of cellular material from wherever he happened to be. Each, from his laboratory, would have emerged with the same bit of DNA. Each would have recognized that he had encountered the same animal. Furthermore, depending on how far we want to push our story into the future of revolutionary advances in biology, each would have described the same whole elephant.

Just so, we now know how to state the central character of the computer. The computer is a "symbol manipulation system" (Newell and Simon 1976). The symbols it can manipulate are not just meaningless tokens, but can designate or refer to all manner of things, just as can the symbols we humans use. This lets us see why the computer can be so many things to so many blind men. Whatever task domain is of concern—census data, numerical weather models, chess, whatever—representations can be created in the computer and the symbols in those representations can be given appropriate meaning by suitable systems of programs. Thus, just as with DNA, common mechanisms exist in the computer that account for its elephantine scope when viewed from the outside. From the user's point of view the situation can be put in nutshell: Wherever there is information to be processed, there the computer can provide help.

We know of nothing inherent in the computer that puts ultimate limits this prescription. There are, however, two kinds of real limits. First, there are limits on the power, memory, bandwidth, reliability, size, and power consumption of the computer, limits that are both relative (e.g., instructions executed per second per dollar) and absolute (what can be obtained at any price). In a stable technology such practical limits become as binding as theoretical limits. All of these practical limits on computers are receding at a prodigious rate, so that what is out of bounds this year may well be in bounds within half a decade. However, at any moment these resource limits are exceedingly real and constrain what can be done or even planned.

The second limit is in our understanding of how to construct processes that provide the requisite help. In our story above we had to admit that sharp limits existed in the ability of biologists to extract from the DNA of the elephant its gross characteristics, as felt by the blind crowd gathered round. Indeed, the geneticist's current abilities are so limited as to almost nix the story. Just so, we have only a slight ability to shape the computer to the information processing we desire. Actually, we are somewhat better off than the biologists, despite the growing promise of gene splicing. If the task domain is sufficiently narrow and if the demand for intelligent processing is sufficiently modest, then application systems can almost always be successfully created. Thus have we arrived at the present amazing spectrum and volume of using computers. Again, as with the limits from resources, the limits to our understanding are receding at a rapid rate, especially as more and more of society's efforts go into expanding what the computer can do. Still, at any moment, the limits to what we can instruct the computer to do are exceedingly real.

CREATIVE MANAGEMENT AND THE COMPUTER

It is certainly the common wisdom of our current age that creative management involves the computer. Having set out views of both creativity and the computer, we are in a position to follow this lead. According to the view of the computer just developed any information processing function is fair game, providing we keep one eye on the momentary limits of resources and understanding. Let us then consider some examples of current proposals to use the computer in ways that enhance management.

Perhaps the term "management" should not be taken completely for granted. I use it as I think was meant in the title of the conference, to stand for all of the leadership functions in formal, task-oriented organizations. However, a narrower sense of "manager" also exists, as someone who works within a fixed human organizational frame to implement a given overall plan to attain given organizational goals. With this more limited sense, it is then necessary to distinguish also an "executive" as someone who develops overall plans to attain given organizational goals, and an "entrepreneur" as someone who creates new organizational goals. Management here means all of these.

Decision Support Systems

One view of the computer is that it can help decision makers make decisions. An entire field has grown up around the design of so-called decision aids (Bonczek, Holsapple and Whinston 1981). This work is of particular interest here, since it has been generated by the management science community itself and thus represents, in some implicit way, its own image of how to make the computer useful to management itself. The idea underlying decision support systems is that one can help the manager structure his decision task, providing a framework for decomposing a decision into components and assembling information about the components so as to produce a better overall assessment of the alternatives. As in any field of endeavor, a diversity of specific techniques have been developed which are partly complementary, partly competitive. We need not go into these here; the area should be relatively familiar to management scientists.

The question for us is whether this use of the computer to support decision making helps in producing creative management? I think it cannot. From what we have seen, creativity does not reside in decisions. It resides in the generation of new combinations, the recognition in these combinations of the possibilities for some larger goal, and, in that recognition, landing you in some part of the world where others have not been. In short, by the time it is a question of decision—of choosing between a set of formulated alternative actions—then the creativity is long past.

There is of course the downstream expanse of problem solving that must follow upon a creative recognition, without which the event will be stillborn. Decision making is a central activity in this activity, and decision support systems have a proper role to play here. However, rather than being the essence of getting creative management, this problem solving is more like the essence of not losing it once you have it.

There is no argument here about whether decision support systems might contribute to more effective management, only that they have no contribution to make to creative or innovative management.

Expert Systems

The word is out that artificial intelligence can finally be applied. At least that is the word from the national press, the venture capitalists and, indeed, from many scientists involved. It is the nature of our capitalistic society to always mix all three estates together, whenever science produces anything of genuine economic interest. This makes it impossible to separate the rational expectations from the wishes. My own view is that the expections have some basis in fact.

There are several subareas of artificial intelligence that make up the frontier of this gathering wave of application, for instance, adding vision capabilities to industrial robots and providing natural language front-ends for large data bases. But perhaps the major area is what has come to be called "expert systems"—computer programs that, in a sort of pun, provide expert-level behavior on tasks normally performed by expert consultants.

The central technical idea is that programs can be built that contain large bodies of expert knowledge that can be brought to bear to provide advice on a task. Such programs differ from the normal use of computers in not doing very much computation on each bit of knowledge that they evoke. The programs do not problem solve so much as they simply know. Such programs also differ from data base systems (which can also contain large amounts of knowledge) in that it is the program that evokes the knowledge, not the user. This can be seen in one characteristic form of expert systems which is a large collection of "if-then" rules: If (1) the stain of the organisms is gramnegative, and (2) the morphology of the organism is rod, and (3) the patient is a compromised host, then there is suggestive evidence (with credibility 0.6) that the identity of the organism is pseudomonas. Whenever the information of the if-part occurs in the system's current knowledge of the situation, the new information in the then-part adds to the current knowledge. Data base systems, in contrast, are passive collections of knowledge, where the user must extract each item of information by means of a user-formulated query in some query language.

Much of the development of expert systems has occurred in the area of medical diagnosis (the example rule above was taken from MYCIN, an early pioneering effort (Shortliffe 1976)). But within the last five years examples have shown up in other areas, such as the geology of oil formations (Duda, Gaschnig and Hart 1979), and sales and manufacturing (McDermott 1982a; McDermott 1982b). It is such broadening that has generated much of the excitement. Consider an expert system called R1, which configures VAX computers from the initial sales request (McDermott 1982a). This system is especially of interest since it has been in routine use by Digital Equipment Corporation for over two years to process all incoming orders for VAX computers. R1 takes as input the data provided by the salesman about the major components of a system that has just been sold to a customer. It then fills out the order with all the other components (power supplies, cables, cabinets, and the like) to specify a complete computer system, and determines what components go where in what cabinets. This is a typical expert system: What is needed is intimate knowledge of all of the details of VAX computer systems with the implications of each component for which other components it requires, is incompatible with, and so forth. Further, it is R1 itself that must determine which aspects are relevant. But no extensive calculations are required on each item of relevant information that is retrieved. In R1 the knowledge is embodied in about 2,000 if-then rules and it takes about 1,000 rule applications to configure a typical order.

Here then is a second example of frontier computer application. It also is aimed in part at helping management. Even more than decision support systems, it embodies artificial intelligence ideas. Indeed, these expert systems are some of the best examples of intelligent systems, performing at the level of human experts in (very narrow) professional areas. Does this use of the computer help in creative management? Might it be able to help as the scope and availability of such system increase? Again, I think it cannot. And again, this answer comes from our analysis of what creativity requires. If you are a manager, having a consultant standing by your side may be useful and it may indicate good judgment on your part. It is not a central component to your being a creative and innovative manager. Expert systems, in their current guise, play a consultant role. And they are usually less than corresponding human consultants, although occasionally, as in the case of R1 above, they are definitely worth their cost because of thoroughness, reliability, absence of turnover, and so forth. This would seem to settle the matter. This particular use of computers, however helpful to management and business generally, does not appear to help in obtaining creative and innovative management.

The Computer as Resource

We seem to be heading toward a conclusion. The computer provides tools, but these tools don't seem to help anyone (here, the manager) be creative. This seems to fly in the face of some conventional wisdom that, in this day and age, using the computer in new and frontier ways is clearly innovative. Can this apparent confusion be cleared up?

The resolution is straightforward—and probably already apparent to the perceptive reader. *Discovering* how to use the computer in new ways can be creative. But once the new way is installed and proven out, then it becomes part of the technology of management. Then it is no longer innovative to use it—only prudent. Think of the telephone. Is it creative to use the telephone? Hardly, though it is central to all affairs of business. But it once was, for a brief instant, until its worth became evident to the entire business world.

Just so with the computer. It is a technological resource like any other. A new deployment of the computer can be highly creative, just like any technological resource. However, the computer does have one characteristic that makes it special, although not quite unique. Because the computer is not a fixed technology, it offers a continuous stream of possibilities for innovation. So it is with the installation of decision aids. Their initial installation can be a creative act. So it is with the installation of expert systems. But it is the recognition of the new use of the computer (and how it can actually work out successfully) that is the step of creative management, not the use itself.

A TEST CASE FOR THE PROPOSITION

When I had finally reached this resting place in my analysis of the relationship between creativity, management and the computer, I realized that my statement at the beginning about not being involved in any management science research was false. Not a little false, but completely untrue. I am in fact currently involved in such research. I just never think of it that way. Even more interesting, this research provides a nice test case for the proposition that we have arrived at above.

We are engaged in a project called ZOG, and have been since the mid-1970s (Newell, McCracken; Robertson and Akseyn 1982; Robertson, McCracken and Newell 1980). It is a combination of a user-computer interface and a management information system. It is because our initial interest was in the interface, and I always think of it that way, that its relevance to the present case slipped by me for so long. Parenthetically, this is testimony to the recognitional character of human cognition, showing that the potentiality for producing interesting connections carries with it of necessity the potentiality for failing to produce appropriate connections.

I do not need to describe the system itself in any detail. It is an attempt to build a system around extensive menu-selection into a very large network of information displays (or frames), keeping the selection of new frames always to be instantaneous. The application I will describe below is currently at about 70,000 frames and growing. ZOG may be thought of in part as a browsing data base, in which the frames not only provide the content, but also numerous indexes. From each frame one typically can directly access ten to fifteen other frames. However, there is more to ZOG than just the ability to browse—that is, to access information by association rather than by query language. Available at every frame is a structured editor, with which one can interactively modify frames and create new frames associated to the current frame. Also, every selection and every arrival at a frame can evoke the execution of an associated pro-

cedure (written in Pascal). These attached procedures may themselves crawl around the network as well as perform arbitrary other
computations. For instance, there are procedures for formatting sub-
nets of frames into a reasonable document and printing it out. Thus,
the system operates as a general management information and decision support system.[1]

Three years ago, Captain Richard Martin, USN, skipper of the
nuclear carrier USS *Carl Vinson*, found the ZOG project at CMU.
The USS *Carl Vinson* was about to come down the ways, and Captain Martin was her initial commanding officer, in charge of shep-
herding her through outfitting, commissioning, and initial cruise.
ZOG was at that point just a research effort, although we had been
using experimental versions for some time. Captain Martin convinced
us to put an experimental version of ZOG on the USS *Carl Vinson*,
using a distributed set of powerful personal computers (the Three
Rivers PERQ) on a high speed local area network around the ship.
There would be about thirty PERQs, essentially one for each department of the ship (the first-level suborganization).

The captain wanted to use the ZOG system to provide support for
the top-level management of the ship. A modern nuclear carrier has
a complement of about 6,000 souls and thus is a small city in terms
of its administration. We settled for two central management functions. The first was the SORM (the Standard Operations and Regulations Manual). This is the basic document of organizational procedures that undergirds the ship's operation. The SORM was to be
created as an electronic document (that is, a ZOGnet), and it was also
to contain extensive information about billets and responsibilities
with extensive cross-referencing. Moreover, it was to be constructed
from scratch as an extensively rationalized network of procedures, so
as to provide a much more thorough basis for operation than is typical of such manuals. The second component was the high-level Planning and Evaluation (P&E) function. The ship operates with a hierarchy of plans for one day, six days, thirty days and six months. All
these were to be ZOGnets, created and updated online and used
either online or from printed hardcopy. In this scheme there is a
close tie between the SORM and the planning, although such a link
does not exist under the normal mode of operation, where the
SORM is a typewritten multivolume written document. Many parts
of the SORM, if appropriately proceduralized, constitute generic
plans for actual operations. They can be accessed, copied and instan-

tiated to provide the initial data structure out of which to build a real plan. Multiple plans must be merged together, and they must be adapted to the specific situation. Conversely, plans that are repeatedly performed and perfected constitute an excellent source for incorporation into the SORM, so as to capture additional elements of practice for future reference and use.

As of this writing, the PERQs and the local area network (Ethernet) have been installed on the ship, the ZOG system is working, there is a functioning ZOGnet of some 70,000 frames, and the ship has just begun its initial cruise. As might be expected in a system of the general capabilities of ZOG and the distributed personal-computer system, the functions being performed have already expanded. The training and maintenance manual for the large weapons elevators is now a ZOGnet and links to a laser videodisc, so that pictures and film clips are available in coordination with the net. A small experimental expert system for the launch and recovery of aircraft has been created, which uses ZOG as its input and output interface. Since full operation of the ZOG system is just getting underway, it is still premature to judge if the system will be a success and what shape a mature system will take.[2]

Is this creative and innovative management? It certainly seems so to me. And, though I am hardly a neutral observer, being involved with the project, it seems hard to disagree with the judgment. Wherein does the creativity reside? The computer system is surely an innovation. It takes the Navy right to the frontier of advanced data processing systems. It accomplishes some of the key management functions of the ship in novel ways. It opens the way for a new attempt at rationalizing the management operation, perhaps with sufficient flexibility that it can work in practice. And more, no doubt.

But the real creative act seems to be Captain Martin's original conception—his vision that he wanted to revamp the management structure of the ship, that he could do this with a modern distributed personal-computer system, and that in ZOG there was a system of sufficient promise and sufficient maturity to justify commitment. But it goes much deeper, to his belief that he could work directly with researchers to obtain his system, to his seeking out ONR research contracts to explore, to his setting up a joint effort between the ship and researchers to design the management system—in short, to his entrepreneuring the whole thing.

If the project succeeds (and that still requires the confluence of many technical, organizational, and bureaucratic forces), such systems will become standard aboard ships. Then their use will no longer be creative or innovative. In fact, given the massive development and deployment of networked personal-computer systems, it is almost legitimate to believe that such systems will ultimately end up in the Navy—Captain Martin, ZOG or no. Thus, to come to the point, the creativity does not reside in the computer or in any inherent creativity it might encompass. The creativity resides in the manager (here a conjoining of all three of the specific functions of entrepreneur, executive, and manager). The computer (and the ZOG research team) were simply resources for him to exploit.

For purposes of a discussion of creative and innovative management this test-case example serves well. It is at the appropriate organizational level, compared to my title-juggling and algorithm-discovery examples, which seem a bit microscopic. Yet one might ask how it illustrates the details of the more individual view sketched out in the beginning—the background preparation of the appropriate goal, the generation of irrelevant possibilities, and the recognition of one of these fleeting possibilities as it flows by. The straightforward, honest answer is that I do not know. I do not know how the Captain first came by his vision. But there is a tad more to the story than that. For I do know that this was not the first time the Captain had attempted this strategy. Back in the early 1970s, Captain Martin had taken the assignment of setting up the initial F14 Wing on the West Coast. At that time he went to Dr. Marvin Denicoff at ONR, requested the names of relevant ONR research efforts. In fact, some organizational researchers at the University of California at Berkeley became involved in that effort. Thus, we know that the creative idea that was played out in connection with ZOG had been foreshadowed as a complete strategy a decade earlier. Indeed, Marvin Denicoff was again the main point of contact at ONR. This certainly does not bring us any closer to the moment when Captain Martin first saw this strategy as a good idea. Just the opposite; that moment is now clearly lost in the past. It does, however, serve to remind us that the unique things that go on in peoples heads in unique circumstances can have a macroscopic impact on the course of large scale organizations. The occurrence of creative acts may contribute more than their share of such impacts.

CONCLUSION

We have arrived at a conclusion, and a conservative one at that. It is the acts that *change* our systems that are creative, not the subsequent behavior of the changed system. Just so, it is not the computer system itself that is creative, but the act of discovering how it is to be used in a novel way. The computer figures in many creative happenings, because it is a source of so much power that can be adapted in so many different ways.

The Conference on Creative and Innovative Management was the occasion of much discussion of educational possibilities—of how to educate creative managers. What does the story told here have to say about that? If you educate MBAs (say) in the newest computer technology, such as distributed interactive systems, that is undoubtedly a good thing. You thereby certainly educate them in the agents of innovative management techniques. But, equally certainly, you do not thereby educate them to be innovative managers. To achieve the latter we are faced with the much harder task of trying to discern what will make those moments of recognition occur, not only more frequently but with a higher chance of productive results.

The picture we have drawn of the nature of creativity should not make us sanguine about our ability to educate for creativity. It is true that from this picture some things can be said. But these do not sound much different from the common wisdom. The recognitional capability is part of all cognition. It is not a mechanism that is evoked only in the case of the creative act. It must certainly pay to have a memory full of a diversity of things. This is what has sometimes been called the "garbage can" theory of creativity—that to be creative you want to stuff your mind with junk-knowledge of all kinds. But it is only conjecture that deliberate efforts to do this will help, more than the classical advice to be widely read and to seek much experience. The irrelevance of the moment of initial recognition suggests that it pays to be a little loose, psychologically speaking. You have to let yourself be open to possibilities. But again, this advice is the stock-in-trade of the how-to-do-it books on problem solving, with such notions as "block busting" (Adams 1974) and "lateral thinking" (DeBono 1968). There are no ways of helping this that have any known empirical validity. Finally, common sense and a deep faith in the apprenticeship method of learning tells us that to

become creative one should practice being creative. If I had to educate for creativity, this is certainly what I would do. But I do not
have any faith that it would scale—that learning to be creative in
little things would make students creative in larger management
situations.

One last remark. The computer has apparently been put in its
place as "merely" a resource. Does the argument developed here
finally say that the computer cannot help someone be creative? Not
quite. In fact, the touchstone for dealing with the computer was that
anywhere there was information processing to be done, there the
computer could be of assistance. Being creative is certainly a form of
information processing. Therefore, it should be possible to get the
computer to help in that processing. What was denied was that various forms of information processing, such as helping to make decisions or providing consulting, would aid in being creative, however
much their discovery and initial establishment was creative.

We can easily see the issues and the requirements for the computer
to help be creative by returning once more to our characterization.
The computer can certainly provide new situations—that is, produce
the irrelevant combinatorics. Indeed, that is the part of the whole
process that seems mechanical. However, in the essential factor of
irrelevancy it differs not at all from other things: the chimpanzee or
the stepping through the possible points (C, D and E) in a diagram
under the tutelage of some other goal. It certainly does no good to
exploit the power of the computer to generate ten million new things
rather than three or four, since the bottleneck is getting them considered, not just generated.

What about the recognition? The computer can certainly at some
point provide the creative recognition. What is required is very large
memories full of very large amounts of knowledge, with very good
associated access—the if-then memories of expert systems writ large.
When that occurs the computer will be able to retrieve connections
to the juxtaposition of irrelevant elements that are surprisingly related to its background tasks. But by those very acts, it will be the
computer who has become the creative agent. And the manager who
employs such systems will have become an impresario. Just so as it
is today with those who employ the creative among us.

NOTES TO CHAPTER 7

1. I should note that the idea of such a system is not entirely original with us. We had developed such a system in the early 1970s (Newell, Simon, Hayes and Gregg 1972), but had discarded it as premature, given the supporting technology. Later we discovered PROMIS (Schultz and Davis 1979), a medical information system, which fully developed the idea and this led to our own renewed interest.

2. When the talk was originally given as the banquet address at the October 1982 Conference, a few crucial months still existed before the ship would leave port, closing the window of opportunity to install the system aboard the ship. It is with some pleasure, then, that I note that the fully functioning system is on board.

REFERENCES

Adams, J. L. 1974. *Conceptual Blockbusting*. San Francisco, Calif.: Freeman.

Arden, B. W., ed. 1980. *What can be Automated? The Computer Science and Engineering Research Study (COSERS)*. Cambridge, Mass.: MIT Press.

Arieti, S. 1976. *Creativity: The magic synthesis*. New York: Basic Books.

Bonczek, R. H.; C. W. Holsapple; and A. B. Whinston. 1981. *Foundations of Decision Support Systems*. New York: Academic Press.

DeBono, E. 1968, *New Think*. New York: Basic Books.

Duda, R.; J. Gaschnig; and P. Hart. 1979. "Model design in the prospector consultant system for mineral exploration." In *Expert Systems in the Microelectronic Age*, edited by D. Michie. Edinburgh: Edinburgh University Press.

Gardner, H. 1982. *Art, Mind, and Brain: A cognitive approach to creativity*. New York: Basic Books.

Hadamard, J. 1945. *Psychology of Invention in the Mathematical Field*. Princeton, N.J.: Princeton University Press.

Kant, E., and A. Newell. 1983. "Problem solving techniques for the design of algorithms." *Information Processing and Management*.

Koestler, A. 1964. *The Act of Creation*. New York: McMillan.

Kubie, L. S. 1958. *Neurotic Distortion of the Creative Process*. Lawrence, Kansas: University of Kansas Press.

McDermott, J. 1982a. "R1: A rule based configurer of computer systems." *Artificial Intelligence* 19: 39–88.

McDermott, J. 1982b. "XSEL: A computer salesperson's assistant." *Machine Intelligence* 10, edited by J. E. Hayes; D. Michie; and H–Y Pau, New York: Wiley.

Newell, A., and H.A. Simon. 1976. "Computer science as empirical inquiry: Symbols and search." *Communications of the ACM. 19*(3): 113–126.

Newell, A.; D. McCracken; G. Robertson; and R. Akseyn. 1982. "ZOG and the USS CARL VINSON." In *Computer Science Research Review.* Computer Science Department, Carnegie-Mellon University.

Newell, A.; H.A. Simon; J.R. Hayes; and L. Gregg. 1972. *Report on a Workshop in New Techniques in Cognitive Research* (Tech. Rep.). Computer Science Department, Carnegie-Mellon University.

Perkins, D.N. 1981. *The Mind's Best Work.* Cambridge, Mass.: Harvard University Press.

Polya, G. 1965. *Mathematical Discovery* (2 vols.). New York: Wiley.

Robertson, G.; D. McCracken; and A. Newell. 1980, "The ZOG approach to man-machine communication." *International Journal of Man-Machine Studies 14* : 461–488.

Schultz, J.R., and L. Davis. 1979. The technology of PROMIS." *Proceedings of the IEEE 67* : 1237–1244.

Shortliffe, E.H. 1976. *Computer-based Medical Consultations: MYCIN.* New York: American Elsevier.

Stein, M.I., and S.J. Heinze, eds. 1960. *Creativity and the Individual.* New York: The Free Press at Glenco.

Taylor, C., and F. Barron, eds. 1964. *Scientific Creativity: Its recognition and development.* New York: Wiley.

Waterman, D.A., and F. Hayes-Roth, eds. 1978. *Pattern Directed Inference Systems.* New York: Academic Press.

BUREAUCRACY, CREATIVITY, AND THE NEED FOR NEW ORGANIZATIONAL FORMS AND RELATIONS

Jared Hazelton

Professor Holtzman has provided us with a useful road map detailing the terrain of the application of humanistic psychology to the field of organization in management. In so doing, I should note, he has definitely avoided the pitfalls, dead-ends, and other hazards with which that terrain is strewn. The result is a somewhat benign view of psychology as applied to managerial creativity. They are marvelous tools if only they are applied correctly.

Although they do not exhaust the potentials in Professor Holtzman's paper, I would like to talk about three things: (1) the definition and description of managerial creativity in group and individual experience and the role of management as a promoter of organizational creativity, (2) the darker side of humanistic psychology as used in managerial and organization contexts, and (3) bureaucracy and other organization forms in their bearing on innovation.

First let me turn to the definition of managerial creativity. Although we reserve the term "creativity" for the origination of very valuable inventions or novelties of concept and discovery, any adaptive change by an individual or a group has an element of creativity in it. It is new, valuable, and risky. Creativity thus exists on a continuum. Empirical conditions for individual creativity suggest a sort of golden mean. In order to make individuals creative, they have got to have some freedom (but not too much), high internal commitment to task (but not too high a commitment), a high proportion of intrinsic rewards (but some extrinsic rewards as well), and some competition (but not cutthroat, winner-take-all kinds of competition).

Turning next to the effect of group experiences on individual creativity we may observe that groups provide protection for the individual. They provide for sharing of responsibility, and they reduce risk and provide support—all of which tends to promote creativity. They can provide great diversity and richness of inputs that can be important in stimulating creativity. One of the most valuable things about creativity within a group is that you can get experts in a group. When they are experts from different fields, it is then all right to ask "dumb" questions. Often, however, it is the dumb questions that promote or stimulate the expert to be creative. This, indeed, is what Professor Newell is talking about when he refers to "going outside" and obtaining a "Eureka," a new idea.

Group experience can also provide rewards in the form of growing esteem and an arena for benign competition. We all know from experience and have observed situations in which competition between groups in trying to achieve goals has worked well to promote creativity. As a case in point, we have seen this in weapons development. Of course, on the other side of the coin, we can also say that groups can be an enforcer of conformity. When in existence for too long, they may begin to establish their own norms and require a degree of conformance that will begin to check the creative process.

To return to managerial creativity, the following three concepts of managerial creativity may be of interest even if they do not exhaust the universe of possibilities. The first of these is the manager as innovator. Dean Kozmetsky talked about the role of the creative manager in developing issues, generating solutions, selecting initiatives, using initiatives, and monitoring innovation as part of the creative input to innovation. Professor Newell used the example of "ZOGGING" the aircraft carrier, U.S.S. *Carl Vinson*, in which the captain was doing this as part of being a creative manager. That is, he was being creative himself.

A second concept of creative management deals with the manager as a facilitator of the creativity of others. Organizations are comprised of individuals having varying capacities to be creative. The role of the manager might then be viewed as a facilitator of creativity of those within his organization. In that role, he perhaps plays the role of a mediator well, mediating the needs of individuals to express their creativity versus the needs of the organization to meet its goals.

Dr. Holtzman speaks of the conflict between the organization's need for more effective and efficient use of resources and the individual's need for personal growth and development. But something more is involved in a dynamic development such as Professor Newell noted when he observed that once you got ZOG on board the aircraft carrier you probably opened up new potentials for creativity on the part of subordinates on that carrier who now had access to this system. Moreover, the role of the manager in how these opportunities might be exploited is also placed in prominence when those working under him observe, as is natural, that they are working for a man who is obviously willing to take risks and in the process of being creative. I would expect that such a man would value that trait in others and take other means to encourage its development.

A third concept about creative management is one in which the manager is a promoter of organizational creativity. Creativity can be defined, as I already noted, as simply the capacity to change and adapt. In the past, by and large, innovation in our society came about by the creation of new organizations and the death of old ones. One of the reasons why I am not as disturbed as others about the present "big merger movement" is that it may play a role in stimulating and changing the economy. We do need to have constant renewal of the economy, and one way to accomplish that is through a merger process. It does not always work that way, of course, and I am not saying that the process is totally benign. Having a company taken over by a much larger conglomerate may not be very creative, and it may even be stifling or destructive. On the other hand, if one thinks of new management coming into a corporation that has become stagnant over time and thus has become a target for merger, this could then involve a process of creativity, or of stimulating creativity, by organizational change.

The second thing I would like to talk about is the darker side of humanistic psychology. Modern bureaucratic organizations are framed around a powerful organizational stereotype, well outlined by Max Weber in the form of "The Monocratic Concept of Organizations."[1] This stereotype has two aspects. One is structure, another is ideology. This structure is characterized by hierarchy, specialization, and authority, and an argument can be made that it produces a distinctive psychological climate involving authority, power, and status. This concept of organization also leads to an ideology that might be termed "the rules of the game." This ideology involves many of the things that Professor Holtzman referred to in terms of high achievers, organizational loyalty, rational behavior, deference to authority, and reduction of ambiguity.

Organizations socialize through their authority systems, rational procedures, and limited objectives. An organization's socializing influence is generally worked out through the interpersonal relations of individuals within it. Personality and many forms of human behavior are the result of one's perception of oneself in relation to others, and organizations provide a highly structured context within which that perception occurs. The gains from such organizations are well known: material well-being, industrial efficiency, and so forth. The losses are subtle: problems of individual autonomy, integrity, and self-realization, displacement of value from the intrinsic value of the quality of the work to its by-products such as income, security, prestige, leisure, the problems of alienation, and so forth.

Organizations are more than devices for producing goods and services. They have normative consequences that are critical. They are versatile agencies for the control of human behavior that can employ subtle psychological sanctions that work to produce desired responses and inculcate consistent patterns of behavior. They push us in the direction that Weber referred to as the "iron cage of history."

What role does humanistic psychology play in all this? In the early 1940s when this work began to emerge, it was clear that the humanistic concern was with the individual's capacity for self-actualization being constrained by situational factors. If you change the situational factors, you achieve the humanistic result. Jacques Ellul foresaw the result of humanistic psychology as applied to organizations. In a brilliant chapter he wrote called "Human Techniques"[2] he correctly foresaw that much of the new behavioral research would eventually be adapted to serve as rational tools for managers. The result is that management practices have been sanitized along humanistic lines, thereby adding a previously missing dimension, namely, to management's legitimacy a demonstrable intention of benevolence toward those who are being managed.

Humanistic managers might argue that there is no cause for alarm since all personnel problems can be solved by techniques of humane management, job enrichment, quality of work life programs, decentralized and participatory decision making, and so forth. However, the dangers of such thinking have been pointed out by Robert Nisbet in the *Twilight of Authority*,[3] and others. There is a Janus-like character to organizations. On one hand they encourage individual autonomy by inculcating skills and values necessary for self-realization, but, on the other hand, they demand conformity with the organization's needs and the means used to achieve those needs. Thus, the role of humanistic psychology might alternatively be viewed as far from being benign. Simply put, it provides a legitimacy, augmented by niceness, which helps to "pad the bars of the iron cage."

William G. Scott and David Hart, professors at the University of Washington Business School, have written a book called *Organizational America: Can Individual Freedom Survive?*[4] In this book they see humanistic psychology as providing universal techniques to modern organizations or managerial systems to obtain obedience to managerial instructions, to integrate individuals into groups to achieve systems goals efficiently in mutually reinforcing relationships with advancing technology. Thus, at least to some people, humanistic psychology has been applied in organizations only to make them more tolerable, but not necessarily better.

The third point that I would like to deal with is bureaucracy in innovation. It seems to me that there may be a basic, inevitable, and perhaps irreducible conflict between bureaucracy and creativity. In *Bureaucracy and Innovation,*[5] for example, Victor Thompson points out that creativity involves things that are antithetical to organizational stability. Creativity involves risk and uncertainty and may engender conflict as a consequence of its attendant changes. This also promotes dissatisfaction and other things, too, that are not conducive to the stability of an organization in achieving its goals. Organizations today produce multiple outputs: production values, employee satisfactions, client/customer satisfactions, profit, community services, survival, and innovation. These are all output characteristics, and there may be trade-offs among them. I think it is at least a possibility that production efficiency and innovation are not necessarily compatible and that what leads to one may thwart the other. In schools, for example, it has been shown that making students more satisfied does not necessarily make them higher achievers. Thus, again, the role of humanistic psychology in making organizations more humane may not lead to greater creativity.

On the other hand, Professor Holtzman also discusses the impact of culture, and it seems clear that the United States is presently undergoing a basic change in cultural values. Modern survey research work indicates that our thoughts about family, and even about every important concept of our life, has changed dramatically over the last twenty or thirty years. Our culture is changing, and perhaps it is going to bring about changes in professional organizations. I am amused by the statement that, in the past, what we had was an uptight culture and a dynamic economy and what we have now is a dynamic culture and an uptight economy. I think this may actually describe the situation. However, we also are in a society with expanding information capabilities and a society that suffers from information scarcity. We have an excess of ends over means—that is, we know what we want to do, but we do not really have enough information to get it done. In the society of today, we may have the reverse problem—an excess of means over ends; that is, we have an awful lot of things we can do but we have difficulty getting agreement on what those ends ought to be.

We might take some hope from the fact that organizations may also be changing. As the nature of work has changed, as the nature of the economy has changed, as more and more of our economy has gotten into services and away from basic manufacturing, as the work force has changed, and as the development of professionals in organizations has emerged, we may begin to have a "professional" organization as an alternative to the traditional model of bureaucracy. In such organizations pluralistic and collegial kinds of relations may replace the strictures of monocratic and hierarchical organizations. We may have specialization of people rather than tasks. We may also have a situation in which workers, as professionals, will assume responsibility for defining the problem as well as for solving it. This may also produce greater creativity. But if it is going to produce greater creativity, it seems to me we are going to have to face up to the fact that in the end managerial creativity is also going to have to evolve. As George Kozmetsky observed, this will involve much broader concepts of decision theory and decision making, and it is going to involve a much more direct approach to the handling of values within organizations and to the distribution of power. If we can come to grips with these kinds of challenges, we might be able to promote managerial creativity and also point it in correct directions.

NOTES

1. See p. 15 in Victor A., Thompson *Bureaucracy and Innovation* (University of Alabama Press, 1976).
2. Chapter 5 in Jacques Ellul, *The Technological Society*, translated by J. Wilkinson (New York: Knopf, 1964).
3. Robert A. Nisbet, *Twilight of Authority* (New York: Oxford University Press, 1977).
4. W.G. Scott and David Hart, *Organizational America: Can Individual Freedom Survive?* (Boston: Houghton Mifflin, 1980).
5. Victor Thompson, *Bureaucracy and Innovation* (University of Alabama Press, 1976).

GEORGE KOZMETSKY: VITA

While this book was being readied for printing, we were surprised and pleased to receive from the University of Texas the following announcement that the entire multibuilding complex used for business instruction and research is to be named The George Kozmetsky Center for Business Education. We include this announcement here for two reasons. First, it provides a convenient summary of George Kozmetsky's professional career and allows us to update it to this point. Second, it serves as a brief and informative introduction to the detailed vita that follows it.

A. Charnes

August, 1983   W.W. Cooper

Dr. George Kozmetsky served as dean of the University of Texas College of Business Administration and Graduate School of Business from 1966 to 1982. He continues to be director of UT's IC^2 Institute and holder of the endowed J. Marion West Chair in Constructive Capitalism. He also has the rank of professor in the Departments of Management and Computer Sciences.

For the UT System Board of Regents, he serves as executive associate for economic affairs, conceiving and developing long-range plans and studies regarding the development and management of the economic resources of the System. Among his research interests are the study of capitalism, commercialization of defense technology, and asset management. Under Dr. Kozmetsky's leadership as business dean, UT's undergraduate business program was ranked as high as fifth in the nation; the graduate business program, seventh.

In his honor, a building complex for use in UT Austin business instruction has been named the George Kozmetsky Center for Business Education. The complex includes the new University Teaching Center (under construction), Business-Economics Building/Business-Economics Office Building and Graduate School of Business Building. In addition, private gifts have endowed the George Kozmetsky Centennial Chair in the Graduate School of Business.

ACADEMIC BACKGROUND:

BA, University of Washington, 1938
MBA, Harvard University, 1947
DCS, Harvard University, 1957

PROFESSIONAL EMPLOYMENT:

September 1966–Present
Executive Associate for Economic Affairs, UT System
Professor of Management, UT Austin
Professor of Computer Sciences, UT Austin (1970)
J.M. West Chair for Constructive Capitalism (1977)
Director, Institute for Constructive Capitalism (1977)

September 1966–August 1982
Dean, College of Business Administration, UT Austin
Dean, Graduate School of Business, UT Austin

September 1967–August 1972
Adjunct Professor of Bioengineering, UT Medical School at San Antonio

September 1970–June 1972
Consultant, The Conference Board, New York

1960–1966
Executive Vice-President, and Co-Founder, Teledyne, Inc.

1959-1960

> Corporate Vice-President and Assistant General Manager, Electronic Equipments Divison, Litton Industries, Beverly Hills, California

1954-1959

> Director, Computers and Controls Division, Litton Industries, Beverly Hills, California

1952-1954

> Assistant Controller and Member, Technical Staff, Advanced Electronics Laboratory, Hughes Aircraft Company, Culver City, California

1950-1952

> Assistant Professor, Carnegie Institute of Technology Graduate School of Industrial Administration

1947-1950

> Instructor, Harvard Business School

BUSINESS AFFILIATIONS:

> Director, Amdahl Corporation
> Director, Datapoint Corporation
> Director, Heizer Corporation
> Director, La Quinta Motor Inns, Inc.
> Director, MCO Holdings
> Director, Simplicity Pattern Co., Inc.
> Director, Teledyne, Inc.
> Director, Wrather Corporation
> Trustee, Federated Development Company

OTHER AFFILIATIONS:

> Director, Adlai Stevenson Institute for International Affairs (1968-1970)
> Member, Case Institute of Technology Advisory Board (1971-1974)
> Member, Hampshire College Advisory Council (1969-1975)
> Member, Claremont University Center Board of Fellows (1976-1981)

PUBLIC SERVICE AND GOVERNMENT ASSIGNMENTS:

Member, U.S. Air Force Scientific Advisory Board

Member, Presidential Advisory Committee on the National Data Center (1965–1966)

Member, Texas Legislative Committee on Wages, Employment and Related Economic Problems, (1968–1969)

Member, Texas Legislative Interim Study Committee on Oceanography, (1969–1970)

Member, Scientific and Management Advisory Committee, U.S. Army Computer Systems Demand, (1972–1973)

Member, Texas Council on Marine-Related Affairs, (1972–1973)

Consultant, National Science Foundation, Experimental R&D Incentives Program, (1972–1975)

Member, Management Advisory Panel, National Aeronautics and Space Administration, (1968–1970)

Member, U.S. National Commission on Supplies and Shortages (1975–1976)

Member, Governor's Task Force for Aerospace and Defense (1982–present)

PROFESSIONAL AND LEARNED SOCIETIES MEMBERSHIPS:

The Institute of Management Sciences	1954–present
Offices held: Chairman of the Board	
President	
Vice-President	
Secretary-Treasurer	
National Association of Cost Accountants	1946–1954
American Marketing Association	1954–1960
Academy of Political Science	1957–1960
American Astronautical Society	
Association for the Advancement of Medical Instrumentation	1967–present
The British Interplanetary Society (Fellow)	1968–present
World Future Society	1969–present
American Institute of Certified Public Accountants	1968–present
American Society for Oceanography	1971–present

PROFESSIONAL SPECIALTIES:

Systems analysis, organization theory, quantitative methods, information technology and study of capitalism

HONORS, AWARDS AND RECOGNITIONS:

Baker Scholar (Harvard)
1967 Leatherbee Lecturer, Harvard Business School
Visiting Scholar, George Washington University, 1968
Walker-Ames Professor, University of Washington, 1970
CBA Foundation Award for Distinguished Scholastic
    Contribution, UT, 1976
J. Marion West Chair for Constructive Capitalism, UT, 1977

CURRENT RESEARCH:

Management of Technology
Mathematical Programming
Information Technology and Its Impacts
Business Ethics, Morals and Value Systems
Energy
Portfolio Selection and Management

UNIVERSITY OF TEXAS FACULTY COMMITTEE SERVICE:

University: Member, Administrative Council (Deans Council)
             Member, University Council
             Member, Graduate Assembly
             Chairman, Advisory Board, Center for Energy Studies
             Chairman, University Energy Research Group
             Member, Council on Energy Resources Executive
                 Committee

College: Chairman, CBA Coordinating Committee
             Member, Business Research Committee

SELECTED PUBLICATIONS:

Books

Making it Together: A Survival Manual for the Executive Family, co-author with Ronya Kozmetsky, New York: The Free Press, a division of MacMillan Publishing Co., Inc., 1981.

Funds Management and Managerial Research, co-author with Isabella C. M. Cunningham, Austin, TX: Graduate School of Business, The University of Texas at Austin, 1979.

Industry Views of the Role of the Federal Government in Industrial Innovation, co-author with Kenneth E. Knight and Helen R. Baca, Austin, TX: Graduate School of Business, The University of Texas at Austin, 1979.

Spurring Synthetic Fuel Production. Simulated Government-Industry Negotiations on Six Proposed Incentives. Final Report of Phase II of the FEA/NSF Incentives Preference Project. (Project Co-Director and Chief Negotiator for the Industry Team.) Published jointly by Don Sowle Associates, Inc., Arlington, VA, and the Graduate School of Business, The University of Texas at Austin, February 1975.

Information Technology: Initiatives for Today—Decisions That Cannot Wait, co-author with Timothy W. Ruefli, New York: The Conference Board, 1972.

Electronic Computers and Management Control, co-author with Paul Kircher, New York: McGraw-Hill, 1956.

Centralization vs. Decentralization in Organizing the Controller's Department, co-author with Herbert A. Simon, H. A. Guetzkow and G. Tyndall, New York: American Book-Stratford Press, Inc., 1954.

Financial Reports of Labor Unions. New York: The Andover Press, Ltd., 1950.

Articles

"Reflections of a Twenty-First Century Manager," *Bell Magazine*, v. 48, no. 2 (March/April 1969): 27–32. Reprinted in *Graduate Comment*, Wayne State University, v. 12, no. 2 (1969) and in *The Futurist*, v. 3, no. 3 (June 1969), pp. 74–75.

"The Role of Information Systems in Management." In *Management Information Systems: Progress and Perspectives*, C. H. Kriebel, R. L. Van Horn and J. T. Heames (eds.), (Pittsburgh: Graduate School of Industrial Administration, Carnegie-Mellon University, 1971): 43–60.

"Newer Concepts of Management, Profits, Profitability," co-author with Timothy Ruefli. In *Information Technology: Some Critical Implications for Decision Makers* New York: The Conference Board, 1972.

"Technological Transfer." In *A Look at Business in 1990: A Summary of the White House Conference on the Industrial World Ahead*, Washington, D.C., (1972): 172–176.

"Information Requirements for Urban Systems: A View into the Possible Future," co-author with A. Charnes and T. Ruefli. *Management Science* 19, no. 4 (December 1972): 7–20.

"Measuring, Monitoring and Modeling Quality of Life," co-author with A. Charnes and W.W. Cooper, *Management Science*, 19, no.10 (June 1973): 172–188.

"Municipal Management Policy and Programs Development." In *Goals for the Texas Municipal League* (Austin, TX: Texas Municipal League, September 1983): 173–191.

"TIMS in Perspective 1954, 1964, 1974, 1984?" co-author with A. Charnes and W.W. Cooper. *Interfaces*, 4, no. 2 (February 1974): 11–20.

"Education for Management: A Framework, Implementation and Assessment." In *New Directions and Developments for Management*, edited by J.D. Hammond, College of Business Administration, The Pennsylvania State University, 1974.

"Organizing Higher Education for Effective Management: An Expanding Role for Business Officers," co-author with Reuben R. McDaniel, Jr., excerpted in *Business Officer*, The National Association of College and University Business Officers, 8, no. 4 (October 1974): 6.

"The Management of Large-Scale Systems." In *Management Systems: Conceptual Considerations* by Peter P. Schoderbek, Asterios G. Kefalas and Charles G. Schoderbek (eds.), (Dallas: Business Publications, Inc., 1975): 265–301.

"Schools of Accountancy: A Liberal Perspective," co-author with Reuben R. McDaniel, Jr. American Academy of Collegiate Schools of Business *Bulletin* 13, no. 23 (Winter 1977): 11–15.

"Impacts of an Auto Weight Limitation on Energy Resources and the Economy," co-author with P.L. Yu and C. Wrather, published in *Policy Sciences* 9 (1978): 97–120.

"National Energy Plan and Investment Analyses," co-author with E.B. Konecci, in *Preliminary Assessment of the President's National Energy Plan, May 11, 1977*, The University of Texas at Austin: 69–120.

"Evaluation of the Conversion of U.S. Industry and the National Energy Plan," co-author with E.B. Konecci, H. McMains, et al. Working paper, The Institute for Constructive Capitalism, Graduate School of Business, The University of Texas at Austin, 1978. Also in The Congressional Record 124 (May 11, 1978).

"The Economics of Energy, Trade and Interdependence," Policy Series No. 1, The Institute for Constructive Capitalism, The University of Texas at Austin, 1978.

"Foreign Operations of Multinational Oil Companies," Policy Series No. 8, The Institute for Constructive Capitalism, The University of Texas at Austin, 1979.

"Evaluation of Macro-Systems: Models and Case Analysis," In *How Big and Still Beautiful? Macro-Engineering Revisited*, Frank P. Davidson, C. Lawrence Meador and Robert Salkeld, eds. (Boulder, CO: Westview Press, 1980).

"Perceptions of Media Bias Toward Business," with I. C. M. Cunningham and R. A. Peterson, *Journalism Quarterly* 59, no. 3 (Autumn 1982): 461-464.

"Perspectives on the Human Potential in Technological Change." In *Work Organizations and Technological Change*, ed. by Gerhardt Mensch and Richard J. Niehaus (New York: Plenum Press, 1982): 3-16.

"Perceptions of Major Problems Facing Small Business," with Gerald Albaum and Robert A. Peterson, *Texas Business Review* 57, no. 4 (July/August 1983): 177-179.

Published Presentations

"How Much Revolution Does American Business Need?" Address to the Commonwealth Club of California, San Francisco. Published in The Conference Board *Record* 8, no. 3 (March 1971): 17-20; reprinted in *SCHISM* 2, no. 2 (Summer 1971): 5-8.

"The New Technology Challenge to Advertising Education." In *Challenge of Change to Advertising Education*, Proceedings of the 1976 American Academy of Advertising, C. Dennis Schick (ed.): 20-23.

"Capital Needs for Economic Growth in the Southwest: The Coming Decade," co-author with Hossein Askari. In *Proceedings*, Southwest American Assembly, 1977.

ABOUT THE RGK FOUNDATION

The RGK Foundation was established in 1966 to provide support for medical and educational research. Major emphasis has been placed on the research of connective tissue diseases, particularly scleroderma. The Foundation also supports workshops and conferences at educational institutions through which the role of business in American society is examined. Such conferences have been cosponsored with the IC^2 Institute at the University of Texas at Austin and the Keystone Center for Continuing Education in Colorado.

The RGK Foundation Building, which opened in October 1981, has a research library and provides research space for scholars in residence. The building's extensive conference facilities have been used for national and international conferences including the International Conference on Scleroderma and the Symposium on Current American Economic Policy. Conferences at the RGK Foundation are designed not only to enhance information exchange on particular topics but also to maintain an interlinkage among business, academia, community, and government.

INDEX

ABOUT THE EDITORS

Abraham **Charnes** is the University Professor across the University of Texas System as well as John P. Harbin Centennial Professor and director of the Center for Cybernetic Studies at the University of Texas at Austin. Professor Charnes received a Ph. D. in Mathematics/Physics from the University of Illinois and formerly was University Professor and Walter P. Murphy Chair in Applied Mathematics at Northwestern University and Professor of Mathematics and of Industrial Management and Transportation at Purdue University. He founded and directed the Management Sciences Research Group (Purdue) and the Systems Research Group (Northwestern). He is a founding member and past president of The Institute of Management Sciences. Fellow of the Operations Research Society of America, the Econometric Society, and the American Association for the Advancement of Science, Professor Charnes was co-recipient of the John von Neumann Theory Medal of The Institute of Management Sciences and the Operations Research Society of America in 1982. He was a finalist for the Nobel Prize in Economics in 1975 and received the U.S. Navy Medal for Distinguished Public Service in 1977. He is author or co-author of more than 350 published research papers and seven books including *An Introduction to Linear Programming* (with W.W. Cooper and A. Henderson), *Management Models and Industrial Applications of Linear Programming* (with W.W. Cooper), and *Studies in Budgeting* (with R.F. Byrne, W.W. Cooper, O.A. Davis and

D. Guilford). He has been industrial consultant to over 200 firms for thirty-odd years including, at present, General Motors, the U.S. Navy Office of Military Personnel, Softech, Inc., and Market Research Corporation of America.

William W. Cooper is the Foster Parker Professor of Finance, Management and Accounting in the Graduate School of Business of The University of Texas at Austin and holder of the Nadya Kozmetsky Scott Centennial Fellowship in the IC^2 Institute. He received an A.B. (economics) from the University of Chicago in 1938, and was awarded an honorary D.Sc. by Ohio State University in 1970 as well as an honorary M.A. by Harvard University in 1976 and an honorary D.Sc. by Carnegie-Mellon University in 1982. Professor Cooper was co-recipient (with A. Charnes and R.J. Duffin) of the John von Neumann Theory Medal jointly awarded by The Institute of Management Sciences and Operations Research Society of America in 1982 and has also been co-recipient of an American Institute of Accountants award for the most valuable article on an accounting topic as well as three McKinsey Foundation awards for the most valuable article of the year on a management topic. He has served as a consultant to more than 200 private corporations and government agencies including, at present, the U.S. Navy Office of Military Personnel, the U.S. General Accounting Office, Softech, Inc. and Market Research Corporation of America.

LIST OF CONTRIBUTORS

Claude le Bon is the Dean of the Faculty of Administrative Sciences, Laval University.

Jack L. Borsting is the Dean of the Graduate School of Business, University of Miami, and former comptroller for the U.S. Department of Defense.

Neil C. Churchill is the Distinguished Professor of Accounting and Director of the Caruth Institute of Owner-Managed Business at the Edward L. Cox School of Business, Southern Methodist University.

Bertrand Collomb is the Corporate Vice President of LaFarge Coppée.

Otto A. Davis is the William W. Cooper University Professor of Economics and Public Policy at Carnegie-Mellon University and former dean of Carnegie-Mellon's School of Urban and Public Affairs.

Karl Olof Faxén is Chief Economist and Director of Research at the Swedish Employers' Federation.

Lester Fettig is an independent consultant and former staff director of the U.S. Senate Subcommittee on Federal Spending Practices.

Jared Hazelton is director of the Texas Research League.

Wayne Holtzman is Professor of Psychology and President of the Hogg Foundation for Mental Health at the University of Texas at Austin.

Michael J.L. Kirby is the Senator from Nova Scotia in the Canadian Senate and was formerly the Senior Corporate Vice President of Canadian National and also the former cabinet secretary for Federal–Provincial Relations under Prime Minister Trudeau.

George Kozmetsky is Director of the IC^2 Institute and the Marion West Chair for Constructive Capitalism.

Robert Kuhn is Senior Fellow in Creative and Innovative Management at the IC^2 Institute and Senior Editor of Texas Business Magazine.

David L. Linowes is the Boeschenstein Professor of Political Economy and Public Policy at the College of Liberal Arts and Sciences, University of Illinois at Urbana–Champaign.

Bertil Naslund teaches at the Stockholm School of Business and New York University.

Allen Newell is the University Professor of Computer Science at Carnegie-Mellon University.

J. P. Ponssard is Professor of Management at the Centre de Recherche en Gestion at L'Ecole Polytechnique in Paris.

Maurice Saias is Professor of Business Administration at the Institut d'Administration des Enterprises at the Universitie d'Aix–Marseilles.

Elmer Staats is President of the Harry S. Truman Scholarship Foundation and former Comptroller General of the United States.

Sten Thore is a Senior Fellow at the IC^2 Institute and teaches at the University of Texas at Austin.